# Selecting, Developing and Retaining Women Executives

# Selecting, Developing and Retaining Women Executives

## A Corporate Strategy for the Eighties

## Helen J. McLane

 **VAN NOSTRAND REINHOLD COMPANY**
NEW YORK   CINCINNATI   ATLANTA   DALLAS   SAN FRANCISCO
LONDON   TORONTO   MELBOURNE

Van Nostrand Reinhold Company Regional Offices:
New York   Cincinnati   Atlanta   Dallas   San Francisco

Van Nostrand Reinhold Company International Offices:
London   Toronto   Melbourne

Published by Van Nostrand Reinhold Company
135 West 50th Street, New York, N.Y. 10020

Published simultaneously in Canada by Van Nostrand Reinhold Ltd.

15 14 13 12 11 10 9 8 7 6 5 4 3 2 1


**Library of Congress Cataloging in Publication Data**

McLane, Helen J
    Selecting, developing  and retaining women
executives.

    Bibliography: p.
    Includes index
    1.  Women executives.  2.  Employee selection.
3.  Executives, Training of.  4.  Affirmative action
programs.  I.  Title.
HF5500.2.M223      658.4'07'11      79-21876
ISBN 0-442-20165-6

TB  3/31/81

To meritocrats, both male and female

There is a tide in the affairs of women
which, taken at the flood, leads —
God knows where . . .

Lord Byron
*Don Juan,* Canto VI, Part II

# *Preface*

The world of work is undergoing a transformation. Although women are assuming new roles at all levels, females moving into the middle and upper echelons of management are destined to exert the greatest influence on the future of American business.

America's largest companies have already made dramatic progress in selecting, developing and retaining women executives, especially over the last ten years, but many more organizations are certain to take similar action in the decades to come. This book is designed to facilitate the process, to the benefit of both organizations and individuals.

HELEN J. McLANE

# Acknowledgments

This book would not have been possible without the involvement of men and women in corporations and consultancies from coast to coast. Singly or on occasion in groups, they shared with me their viewpoints and experiences regarding the successful integration of women into management in tape-recorded interviews ranging up to five hours in duration. With the exception of two telephonic conversations, all of these meetings were face-to-face. My heartfelt thanks to these organizations and individuals:

AMERICAN AIRLINES, INC.
Delores Wallace, Director of Selection and Affirmative Action

AMERICAN EXPRESS COMPANY
Judith A. Green, Vice President, Corporate Division, Headquarters Personnel Administration
Sandra W. Meyer, President, American Express Communications Division

AMERICAN TELEPHONE AND TELEGRAPH COMPANY
Gene E. Kofke, Director, Human Resources Planning

ATLANTIC RICHFIELD COMPANY
Owen T. Carter, Director, Personnel Resources

AVCO CORPORATION
Dr. Dorothy Simon, Vice President and Director of Corporate Research

AVON PRODUCTS, INC.
J. Alvin Wakefield, Vice President, Personnel Services Worldwide

BOOZ, ALLEN & HAMILTON INC.
Sandra Kresch, Vice President

CBS INC.
J. William Grimes, Senior Vice President, Personnel
Nancy C. Widmann, Vice President, Recruitment and Placement
Marilyn Walsh, Vice President and Director of Taxes

CITIBANK, N.A.
Janet L. Robinson, Vice President

THE CONFERENCE BOARD
Ruth G. Shaeffer, Senior Research Associate

CONTINENTAL ILLINOIS NATIONAL BANK AND TRUST COM-
PANY OF CHICAGO
Eugene R. Croisant, Senior Vice President
Owen C. Johnson, Jr., Vice President, Personnel Division

DIGITAL EQUIPMENT CORPORATION
Winston Hindle, Jr., Vice President, Corporate Operations

DUNHAM & MARCUS
Ana Jones, Associate Partner

THE EQUITABLE LIFE ASSURANCE SOCIETY OF THE UNITED
STATES
Coy G. Eklund, President and Chief Executive Officer
Nancy H. Green, Director of Executive Staff Communication
Carol Van Sickle, Director, Career Planning and Placement Division,
Corporate Human Resources

EXXON COMPANY, U.S.A., DIVISION OF EXXON CORPORATION
Joy Blake, Coordinator, University Relations
Mary Cook, Employee Relations Staff Specialist
Jerry Farley, Compensation Manager
Henry Lartigue, Employee Relations Manager
Paul Sparks, Coordinator, Personnel Research
Jan Stockstill, Manager, Employee Relations, Baytown Refinery

FIRST PENNSYLVANIA BANK, N.A., SUBSIDIARY OF FIRST
PENNSYLVANIA CORPORATION
Robert Kirkpatrick, Vice President
Evelyn Fennell, Assistant Vice President

FORD MOTOR COMPANY
Emily DeMattia, Personnel Planning Manager-Women

GAF CORPORATION
Juliette M. Moran, Executive Vice President and Director

GANNETT CO., INC.
Madelyn Jennings, Vice President, Human Resources

GENERAL ELECTRIC COMPANY
Marion S. Kellogg, Vice President, Corporate Consulting Services
Dr. Leonard C. Maier, Jr., Senior Vice President, Corporate Relations
Ray Stumberger, Manager, Corporate Executive Manpower Operations

GOULD INC.
Dr. Eric W. Vetter, Senior Vice President, Human Resources

INTERNATIONAL BUSINESS MACHINES CORPORATION
B. J. Faller, Program Manager, Planning and Women's Programs

INTERNATIONAL PAPER COMPANY
George Humphreys, Director of Equal Employment Opportunity

LEVI STRAUSS & CO., INC.
James W. Cameron, Corporate Vice President, Personnel

R. H. MACY & CO., INC.
Warren H. Simmons, Jr., Senior Vice President, Personnel and Industrial Relations

MCKINSEY & COMPANY, INC.
Dr. David Hertz, Director
Linda Fayne Levinson, Principal

MOBIL CORPORATION
Patsy J. Boglioli, Manager, Equal Employment and Affirmative Action
Marilyn Broad, Manager, Finance-Employee Relations Department

Dr. Eileen Morley, Consultant

NATIONAL BROADCASTING COMPANY, INC., SUBSIDIARY OF R.C.A. CORPORATION
Roberta V. Romberg, Vice President, Personnel Administration

NORTON SIMON, INC.
Philip J. Davis, Vice President, Personnel

ORGANIZATION RESOURCES COUNSELORS, INC.
William G. Shepherd, EEO Interaction Coordinator and Senior Staff Member

J. C. PENNEY COMPANY, INC.
J. Alan Ofner, Divisional Vice President, Corporate Personnel Planning

PHILIP MORRIS, INC.
Dr. Louise Stanek, Director, Training, Development and College Relations
William K. Transue, Staff Vice President, Personnel

POTLATCH CORPORATION
Irwin W. Krantz, Vice President, Employee Relations

THE QUAKER OATS COMPANY, INC.
Paul R. Pearce, Vice President/Personnel, U.S. Grocery Products
Robert N. Thurston, Executive Vice President-International Grocery Products and Director

R.C.A. CORPORATION
Francis L. McClure, Vice President, Personnel Operations
Patrick Farbro, Director, Industrial Relations Policy and Research

ROHRER, HIBLER & REPLOGLE, INC.
Dr. Bill T. Meyer, President
Dr. Allen S. Penman, Chairman of the Board
Dr. Beth B. Smith, Consulting Psychologist

SEARS, ROEBUCK AND CO.
Ray J. Graham, Director of Equal Opportunity
Sandra C. Hagerty, Manager, Women's Affirmative Action

SECURITY PACIFIC NATIONAL BANK, SUBSIDIARY OF SECURITY PACIFIC CORPORATION
Kathleen C. Hayes, Vice President and Equal Employment Opportunity Officer

STANDARD BRANDS, INCORPORATED
T. Allen Swann, Jr., Director of Employee Relations, Planters Division

TIMES MIRROR COMPANY, INC.
George C. Kuekes, Corporate Personnel Director
Suzanne B. Platt, Personnel Programs Administrator
Charles R. Redmond, Vice President and Assistant to the President

TOWERS, PERRIN, FORSTER & CROSBY
Samuel T. Beacham, Vice President
Gary McClung, Principal
Catherine M. Meek, Principal

UNITED AIR LINES, INC., SUBSIDIARY OF UAL, INC.
William B. Verplank, Director of Human Resources

I also wish to express appreciation to members of the board of directors of Heidrick and Struggles, Inc. for their support, to my secretary, Joan Michaels, for her assistance on this project and to my sister, Mary L. McLane. It was she who conceived the idea and contributed her time and talent in helping to bring it to fruition.

# Contents

## 1. Why Women Executives? 1

Impetus of sizable settlements . . . History of equal opportunity legislation . . . Scarcity of women at senior levels . . . Pressure from government . . . Pressure from women . . . Status of women today . . . Major reasons for women's movement into management: greater opportunity, higher motivation, greater educational attainment, more useful curriculum, later marriage, pregnancy by choice, rising divorce rate, growing acceptance of the working woman, desire for higher living standards, increase in household technology . . . What the future holds.

## 2. Effective Affirmative Action 14

Impact of legislation on contractors . . . Approaches to compliance . . . Requirements for success: commitment by the CEO, selection of appropriate AA head, communication of AA guidelines, role of line management . . . Circumstances affecting the program: amount of structure, industry group, promotion-from-within policy, rate of growth, performance consciousness, number of women employees, timing of program's inception . . . Manner of filling jobs . . . Procedure when employee fails . . . Incentives for managers . . . Evaluating results in recruitment, development, and retention . . . Dealing with anxieties . . . Attitudinal surveys . . . Communication with the public . . . Nonemployment aspects of affirmative action.

## 3. Awareness Training for Management and Women 36

Arguments in favor of training . . . Arguments of those opposing training . . . Considerations in determining advisability . . . Contents of train-

ing for management . . . Myths concerning women . . . Use of question-
naires and role playing in training . . . Problem of male unease . . .
Contents of training for women . . . Need for follow-up to training . . .
The possibility of joint training . . . Use of individual counseling . . .
Selecting trainers and subject matter . . . In-company vs. off-premises
site.

## 4. Where to Position Women Executives                                   58

How to eliminate "women's jobs" . . . Areas of concern: job analysis,
job evaluation, job posting, recruiting sources, evaluation of prospects,
training, placement . . . Reasons for infrequency of women at top: few
female engineers, women in professional roles, investment in training,
supposed unpopularity of women as supervisors . . . Time required to
move up . . . Assuring successful integration: bonds with co-workers,
match for job requirements, challenging position, clear performance
measures, necessary support provided . . . Positioning the first women
in management: level, function, location.

## 5. Looking Inside                                                        81

Size of female population, requirements of organization affect success of
promotion from within . . . Advantages and disadvantages of looking
inside . . . Possible pitfalls in the process . . . Identifying "promotables":
performance appraisals, assessment, psychological evaluation, temporary
assignments, internships . . . Job enrichment . . . Selecting with care . . .
Providing proper support . . . Overcoming resistance . . . Training . . .
The General Foods program . . . Better success rate with promotion.

## 6. Looking Outside                                                       99

Reasons for going outside . . . Standards applied to female candidates . . .
Factors determining success of the effort . . . Targeting specific jobs vs.
considering women for any vacancy . . . Where to search: level, industry,
function, location . . . Choosing the method: staff recruiter or outside
consultant . . . Selecting a consultant: general or specialty firm, male or
female recruiter . . . Preparing specifications . . . Developing a timetable . . . Establishing target and off-limits organizations . . . Telephon-

ing sources and prospects . . . Difficulties in developing female candidates . . . Face-to-face meetings . . . Degree confirmation and referencing . . . Importance of maintaining standards . . . Need for prompt meetings with management . . . Thanking those who have helped . . . Disadvantages of advertising . . . Desirability of candidates of both sexes.

## 7. Selecting Women Executives 115

Interviewer's preparation . . . How to treat female job prospects . . . The interview form—directed, nondirected, or a compromise . . . Accomplishing goals within time constraints . . . Need to avoid assumptions . . . Setting the stage for a pleasant conversation . . . Avoiding bias in interviewing . . . The question of note taking . . . The "learning phase": listening, not talking; avoiding display of surprise or displeasure; desirability of pauses; disclosure of negatives . . . Special concerns of women . . . The problem of oversensitivity . . . The "telling phase": describing the pluses and minuses of the position and environment . . . Evaluating the personal attributes for a "fit" . . . Reviewing career in relation to difficulties encountered and overcome . . . Avoiding subjective impressions.

## 8. Attracting Women Executives 130

Importance of annual report and other publications . . . Advertising . . . Supporting women's organizations . . . Providing role models . . . Avoiding discrimination charges . . . Quality of recruiting effort . . . Interface with school groups . . . Scholarships, internships, co-op programs . . . Record of success in recruiting, developing, retaining women . . . Formulating the offer . . . The concerns of women.

## 9. Developing Women Executives 142

Exclusion of women from some programs . . . Legal and business reasons for including women . . . Need for instruction and reward of managers . . . Meeting each individual's unique needs . . . Communicating a variety of opportunities . . . No assurances but personal growth . . . Superior's sensitivity required . . . Establishing evaluation by contribution . . . Avoiding overprotection . . . Combating the trait theory . . . Counseling women on noncombative style . . . Offering opportunities:

rotation between line and staff, cross-functional transfer, movement between headquarters and field, temporary assignments, task forces, committees, junior board . . . Coaching by superiors and co-workers . . . Preparing and presenting reports . . . Detached service . . . Association liaison . . . Membership in professional organizations . . . Company training courses . . . Outside training courses . . . College classes . . . "Women only" classes vs. mixed sex . . . Performance appraisal as a development tool . . . Male hesitancy to appraise women . . . Advantage of management-by-objectives appraisal . . . Need for feedback . . . Career planning . . . Assessment . . . Mentoring and sponsorship . . . Reluctance of males to serve . . . Intracompany women's groups.

## 10. Retaining Women Executives  161

Greater intercompany mobility of women . . . What women want from work . . . Need for top management support . . . Backing of immediate superior . . . Desirability of nonsex similarity . . . Overcoming co-worker prejudice . . . Minimizing sex in on-the-job treatment . . . Importance of language . . . Equal access to developmental opportunities . . . Desirability of objective appraisal . . . The matter of money . . . Sex-linked differences in benefits . . . New legislation on pregnancy . . . Work for new mothers . . . Paternity leave . . . Day care facilities . . . Alternate work schedules: flexitime, permanent part-time, shared jobs . . . Cafeteria benefits . . . Problems of relocation . . . When woman and employer part company.

## 11. Listening to Women Executives  183

On the role of women today . . . The executive woman's self-image . . . Combining career and marriage . . . Women executives view other women . . . On resistance to executive women . . . On preparing the environment . . . On interviewing women . . . On bringing women in from outside . . . On attracting women to opportunities . . . On assimilating women into management . . . On developing women . . . On retaining women . . . On distinctions between male and female executives . . . On the role of women tomorrow.

## 12. The Effects of Equal Opportunity  204

Larger talent pool . . . Elimination of artificial barrier encourages the able . . . Higher priority for personnel function, with improved programs for all . . . Advantage to moving more rapidly than others . . . Resistance from adversely affected parties . . . Advantages for both sexes of integrated management . . . Pluses and minuses of legislation . . . Impact of two-career families on companies . . . Influence of equal opportunity on economy . . . Time required to achieve equal opportunity in management.

# Selecting, Developing and Retaining Women Executives

# 1
# Why Women Executives?

American corporations are destined to place more women in middle and upper management and professional positions, those paying $30,000 or more. Government and a societal revolution are providing the pressure for this process. A growing number of sizable settlements has stimulated the attention paid to equal opportunity legislation and to affirmative action programs by top management, personnel departments, and legal counsel. Besides the landmark AT&T consent decree, which involved the upgrading of 50,000 women and 6600 minorities and payment of more than $55 million, the passing years have witnessed numerous settlements costing a million dollars or more. A recent agreement between General Electric and the Equal Employment Opportunity Commission (EEOC) calls for the expenditure of $32.4 million over five years to benefit females and minority males.

When The Conference Board surveyed 265 major companies, it found that "66 percent had been subject to a sex discrimination investigation by a state or local government agency; 64 percent had been subject to such an investigation by the federal Equal Employment Opportunity Commission; 33 percent indicated a state or federal lawsuit alleging sex discrimination had been filed against the company, while 37 percent noted they had signed a conciliation or consent agreement or had had a court decree dealing with sex discrimination entered against the company."[1]

## HISTORY OF EQUAL OPPORTUNITY

Equal opportunity without regard to sex has been the law of the land since 1964. Title VII of the Equal Rights Act specifically prohibits discrimination in employment policies and practices. And the Supreme

1

Court has decreed that the *results* of an employer's policies or practices, not his *intentions,* determine whether personnel practices are discriminatory.

To be sure, the number of women in the ranks of management has risen very slowly since antibias measures were adopted. It was not until 1972, when the Department of Labor's Revised Order #4 required government contractors to institute goals and timetables for employment of women, and the EEOC was empowered to file suit if conciliation could not be reached, that the pace of change quickened. Certainly, the corporate world paid heed to the 1973 settlement between the EEOC and AT&T. (In surveying companies The Conference Board found that "awareness of large back pay awards in class-action suits" ranked high among factors contributing to the overall success of corporate efforts to improve job opportunities for women.)[2]

As the AT&T consent decree expired in 1979, women held 28.5 percent of all management jobs in the Bell System, compared to 22.4 percent in 1973.[3] However, it was not until September 1979 that the nation's largest employer of women named one of its nearly 385,000 women employees to a corporate vice presidency. And the second largest employer of females in the country—Sears Roebuck—has no vice presidents among nearly 244,000 women employees.

A recent survey by Heidrick and Struggles[4] identified only 485 women officers among America's 1300 largest companies. Typically, the respondents were corporate secretaries or assistant corporate secretaries who had begun their careers in clerical positions, and made under $40,000. Popular estimates hold that currently only 5 percent of middle management and 1 percent of upper management are female. Actually, the number of women who have reached the top echelon of business remains infinitesimal. Of 4133 chairmen, presidents and vice presidents designated during 1978 and announced in the "Who's News" column of *The Wall Street Journal,* only 29 or 7/10 of 1 percent were women. Females at this level are nearly as exceptional today as they were 50 years ago.

These conditions are not surprising, since only in the past several years have women been admitted to corporate training programs. Traditionally, women hired for executive posts have been limited to narrow specialties outside the mainstream of the business. Management has been viewed as requiring "masculine" attributes, and few women have been perceived or have even desired to be regarded as "unfeminine."

Further, most women have worked only "temporarily," when such activity did not interfere with homemaking or motherhood. Regardless of talent, females have lacked the motivation and opportunity to sustain careers. Not only timing but location of work have restricted their employment opportunities. Research has shown that working wives and their husbands have been, on average, about equally well educated and employed at equally prestigious jobs. Yet the wives worked many fewer hours per year, had much less work experience, and earned far less than their husbands.[5]

Now, however, growing numbers of women will be entering the executive suite by government pressure, if not company choice. Until recently the Equal Employment Opportunity Commission had been hampered by frequent changes in its leadership and a mounting backlog totaling some 130,000 complaints. But the agency apparently has gained a competent and dedicated head in Eleanor Holmes Norton, former chairman of New York's Commission on Human Rights. Also, the President has instituted a reorganization of antidiscrimination authority: The EEOC and Labor Department have assumed more of the powers formerly disbursed among 18 agencies and departments, simplifying enforcement of nearly 40 statutes and regulations involving job discrimination.

In the past, EEOC has had 150 or so corporations in court at any one time, with 10 to 20 times that many consenting out of court. Norton has pledged a sizable and quick step-up in class action suits, noting, "We'll be looking at the largest companies because that's where the payoff is."[6] Corporate liability in class action suits embraces all applicants who were discriminated against, plus the so-called futility class, or those who did not apply due to an expected rejection. The financial exposure is substantial. EEOC will concentrate on companies that have lagged behind others in their industries in employment and promotion of women and minorities.

Part of the pressure for greater opportunity for women in the work place today derives from women themselves. Less than 20 years ago, females constituted only about a third of all employed persons. Today, 42 million women represent 41 percent of the labor force. More than 61 percent of women in the prime age group (25–54) are working.[7] Women have become a far greater proportion of a substantially larger number of workers, a development that the chairman of The National Commission for Employment Policy, Eli Ginzberg, considered "the single most outstanding phenomenon of our century." He warned, "Its long-term implications are absolutely unchartable."[8]

Among women working today are young females far more assertive than their mothers or older sisters. This new breed intends to pursue careers. The continuity as well as duration of female employment will more closely approximate that of males as women spend most of their adult lives at work regardless of marital status.

While it has always been possible for the exceptionally able woman to achieve, feminists will not be satisfied until the average woman attains the same measure of success as the typical man. In major cities throughout the country—Boston, New York, Chicago, and San Francisco, among others—can be found groups of activists agitating for stricter enforcement of equal opportunity law. Nationwide, these advocates are reported to have won 8 percent of their cases in court and another 8 percent on appeal. Their impact has been far greater than their numbers or financial support would seem to permit. As one example, Chicago's Women Employed has forced settlements with several major companies in the Windy City. WE has also brought about a Treasury Department investigation of alleged discrimination at one of the city's largest banks.

Women continue to outnumber men in the population, and their majority will grow over the next generation. The trend toward more women workers seems unlikely to abate; the participation rate already approximates a recent Department of Labor projection for 1990.[9] A more recent opinion by a Bureau of Labor Statistics economist holds that "female labor force participation rates are . . . to grow at rather strong rates during the 1980's. . . . Women are expected to be increasingly employed in all sectors of the economy."[10]

## WORKING WOMEN TODAY

Despite their growing numbers, working women by and large remain limited to so-called women's ghettos in the labor market. The most prevalent occupations of working women include secretary, sales clerk, bookkeeper, cashier, and typist. Seventy-nine percent of all clerical workers are women, and by far the largest proportion of female additions to the work force in recent years has been to clerical positions.

Their lack of intralabor force mobility serves both to heighten the jobless rate of women workers and to depress their compensation. Today, females typically earn only 60 percent as much as their male co-workers.[11] The disparity between average wages of men and women has continued to increase since passage of the Equal Pay Act of 1963. Indeed, the differential is greater now than it was a quarter century ago. Women tend to be concentrated in jobs where education is not as well rewarded. Female college graduates earn less on average than males with only high school educations. When occupational status and lifetime work experience are coupled with education, women still earn just 62 percent of what men do.

However, the tide may be turning. The desire for more meaningful work and greater rewards is shared by women in the business world who deem themselves underpaid and underutilized, and by those who are entering business because of limited opportunities elsewhere. In the former category are ex-secretaries now employed in blue-collar jobs for higher pay or in white-collar positions with equal or lower compensation but higher status and greater hope for promotion. Today's secretarial shortage will not be severe by tomorrow's standards. A recent poll by the National Commission on Working Women found that 60 percent of 19,000 secretaries surveyed nationwide think they are in a "dead-end" job and want a chance for advancement. Those expressing the most dissatisfaction were college educated.[12]

In the latter group are ex-teachers. Over the years the teaching profession has managed to absorb nearly half of America's female college graduates. Today, in the face of declining nursery and elementary school enrollments, perhaps only one of ten degreed women will be joining the public school system. More educated women than ever will be seeking positions in business without secretarial skills and with no intention of developing them.

True, the higher retirement age, a trend to centralization in business, and the slowing growth rate of our economy seem to offer less room at the top. But the nation's continuing shortage of superior managerial talent augers well for women who aspire to upward mobility, providing they qualify by talent and commitment. Not brawn but brains are important today. Our postindustrial economy grows increasingly complex and challenging for decision-makers. At the same time, recruiters are agreed that fewer and fewer of the younger members in the traditional management talent pool are willing to sacrifice "quality of life" considerations for the time-tested carrots of power, prestige, and pay. Trained and motivated women could fill this developing void.

## REASONS FOR FEMALE EXECUTIVES

Certainly a far greater number of women candidates for executive positions exists today than was true even a few years ago. There appear to be at least ten major reasons for this development:

*Greater opportunity.* College enrollment among blacks has doubled within the last decade alone. But there was little incentive for minorities to attend college in the days when a "career" as a Pullman porter awaited the new graduate. Similarly, there was little reason for women to educate themselves for a career and to aspire to advance in business when "Can you type?" was the most important question asked of them. While role models are still few in number, women recognize today that organizations are not only willing but anxious to place females in management positions.

*Higher motivation.* Less than 20 years ago, it was rare to discover a career-oriented woman. Her employment was something to apologize for, rather than a source of pride and personal satisfaction. She could be "feminine" or she could achieve; to do both was an impossibility. If she was unmarried, the assumption was that she worked because she had failed to attract a spouse. Before she was hired for any position other than those accepted as high in turnover, her employer would inquire whether she was engaged or likely to become betrothed in the foreseeable future. Despite her disclaimers, she would be considered a bad risk until she approached 40. At that point it was felt she had no choice but to be serious about her career.

If the woman was married and childless, the popular view held that she worked to fill that void. There were suspicions that she might become pregnant, however, or that she would turn to adoption and retire from the labor force. Even if she denied any interest in motherhood, she was likely to be queried on how her husband felt about her working. If the woman was a mother, she was regarded as shackled to a financial failure and/or uncaring as a parent. The would-be employer asked her how she could possibly meet the demands of a job, a husband, and children without letting one or more of her responsibilities suffer.

Whatever a woman's marital status, she might be denying employment to a man with a family to support. And even if she needed a paycheck to support a husband and/or children, her employer felt guilt in contributing to the supposed instability of her marriage and the delinquency of her children.

Shaped by societal expectations, women did not have careers—they had jobs. But in 1963, questioning homemaker Betty Friedan declared in *The Feminine Mystique* that there was "something very wrong" with the way American women were trying to live their lives. "Who knows what women can be when they are finally free to become themselves?" she asked. Her views gained currency, abetted by the organized women's movement which regrouped after a lapse of several decades.

No longer was destiny to be shaped by biology alone. In their consciousness-raising sessions, women determined that it was not only possible but proper for them to have goals of their own, as well as to support those of others. A revolution of rising expectations was under way. In 1967 six of every ten adult women agreed with the statement, "A woman's place is in the home." Within ten years those supporting this concept fell to a minority of one in four.

Traditionally, society has regarded women as participating in the labor force because of economic considerations. However, in the early seventies the National Opinion Research Corporation conducted interviews nationwide. White women working full time were given a list of five job characteristics and asked to select the one preferred: high income, job security, short hours, chances for promotion, and important, meaningful work. Sixty percent chose "important, meaningful work," while just 15.5 percent opted for "high income." The proportion of married women (63 percent) placing importance of work first exceeded that of single women (53.2 percent).[13]

Indeed, a recent survey shows that the majority of women would choose to go on working even if they received the same amount of money for staying at home! The reason may be revealed by a long-term California study which interviewed a group of females as children in 1921 and again in 1977 when their average age was 67. "Whether a woman was married, widowed, divorced, or single, there was a strong link between happiness and working for pay," Dr. Eleanor W. Willemsen reported to the American Association for the Advancement of Science. The women who worked full time for pay at least half of their adult lives had a greater degree of satisfaction with their lives than women who did not work.[14]

Since 1976, the number of two-income families has surpassed the number with only one breadwinner. Today 24 million wives (48 percent of all married women) are in the labor force. Nearly as many suburban as city-dwelling women work. The pressure upon homemakers to be employed for pay is nearly as great as that upon their mothers to devote their lives exclusively to homemaking. Over the past few years, well-to-do women have been returning to the labor force at a much faster rate than other wives.[15] Sociologist Valerie K. Oppenheimer has pointed out, "When women look upon work as a possible lifetime activity, one of their major adult roles, they'll want a career—not a job." With each passing year, more members of the female labor force are sharing the aspirations for career success that have traditionally characterized the male manager.

*Greater educational attainment.* American women were not permitted to obtain higher education until 199 years after the first college had opened its doors. Society has expected husbands to work and wives to provide household services and child care. Traditionally, women have been far more likely to end their college careers prior to graduation due to family considerations. If the disparity between numbers of women and men obtaining baccalaureate degrees has been substantial, the difference between the number of each sex obtaining an advanced degree has been overwhelming. And as the master's in business administration evolved into the sorting device for executive positions which the bachelor's had been a generation earlier, women appeared to be less well equipped for business careers than ever.

In the last several years, however, a significant turnaround has taken place. Now, women represent 50 percent of those enrolled in colleges and universities and actually outnumber males by 200,000 at the undergraduate level. This proportion is finally analogous to the representation of women in the total population. And in the professional schools most important to success in business—management and law—female enrollment has climbed to as high as 25 to 35 percent. The Harvard Business School, which did not admit women until 1963, now has an enrollment which is 25 percent female. In the last ten years the number of working women with college degrees has doubled.[16] Sixty-five percent of female college graduates are in the labor force, compared to 52 percent of women with high school diplomas.

Historically, the more highly educated a woman was, the more likely she was to work. Educated wives are more eager to enjoy the mental stimulation of the marketplace rather than limiting themselves to the home, regardless of how significant their monetary contribution may be. Of course, thanks to their training, the college graduates generally obtain better jobs. Two-thirds of the degree holders are employed in professional-technical positions, compared to just 6 percent of the women high school graduates; and the college women earn more than twice as much as women at the lowest end of the educational scale.

*More useful curriculum.* Men rising to the top in business typically have had a liberal arts or technical undergraduate degree, coupled with a master's in business administration or a JD.[17] Over the years, women directed by family and school counseling have favored such undergraduate majors as education, sociology, art history, or language and have not pursued advanced degrees. Now, however, due to less stereotyping of education and of jobs into "male" and "female" categories, women feel free to pursue studies far more appropriate to a career in business. Mathematics and science are gaining in popularity among coeds, to the detriment of more traditional and less practical pursuits. Some are even selecting engineering: the General Motors Institute enrolled no women until 1965; now 28 percent of the student body is female.

*Later marriage.* Contributing to the advance in education of women has been an unmistakable trend toward later marriage. About 48 percent of females 20–24 remain single these days, in contrast to just 36 percent in 1970.[18] While the "MRS. degree" formerly preceded or at least followed closely behind the bachelor's, today's typical college-educated woman defers marriage.

Once a woman has embarked upon a career, she is more likely to return to work at some time after marriage, or to maintain continuity in employment despite her taking of a spouse or even bearing children. When women first entered the labor force, they worked only until their wedding. Later, the trend to return after childbearing came into vogue. Now, the presence of children of any age is becoming less and less of a deterrent. Since 1974 the labor force participation rate of mothers has exceeded that of women overall.[19] A recent poll found that a majority of women think working mothers are at least equal in parenting to non-working moms.[20]

Indeed, the most remarkable change in the composition of America's female labor force has been the burgeoning number of mothers with school-age children. This participation appears to be relatively unaffected by husbands' income level. Mothers of children under 18 are as likely to be working as are married women without such youngsters.[21] About 40 percent of mothers with children under age six are holding jobs despite the paucity of nonfamilial child care facilities.[22] Furthermore, the Urban Institute has predicted that 55 percent of all married women with children under age six will be in the labor force by 1990.

*Pregnancy by choice.* No less important in the career development of women has been the ability to decide whether to have children, and if so, when to have them and how many to bear. The span between marriage and arrival of the first child is longer now than a few years ago. Availability of the pill and abortion on demand, as well as acceptance of zero population growth, have permitted women a freedom not previously possible. Women today also complete childbearing earlier, despite a later start, and are able to embark upon a much longer span of uninterrupted employment. The proportion of working wives does not drop sharply until age 60 is reached. With the higher retirement age recently approved and the 76-year life expectancy for women exceeding that of men by nearly a decade, even this figure may rise.

The nation's fertility rate has dropped from a peak of 3.8 in 1957 to 1.8 now. And, according to the Rand Corporation, low levels of fertility are here to stay.[23] The director of the Office of Population Research at Princeton agrees; he has suggested that America may have to implement a financial incentive to encourage childbearing.[24] Certainly, unless child care becomes more readily available, women with management aspirations may have no option but to remain childless.

*Rising divorce rate.* Divorce, once a mark of disgrace for a woman, if not for a man, is commonplace today under liberalized law. No longer is dissolution of matrimony a cause for raised eyebrows, since it happens in one of three unions. Enhanced opportunities for employment of women have perhaps contributed to the demise of many marriages which in earlier days would have survived from economic necessity if not affection. The new trend in divorce settlements is "rehabilitative alimony," whereby the man pays his ex-wife a monthly allowance for a limited time, perhaps two years. This permits the woman to take training to prepare herself for better employment opportunities.[25]

Single women—whether never wed, separated, or divorced—are more likely to hold jobs than are married women. The number of households headed by women (7.2 million) has increased by more than a third since 1970 and has more than doubled in one generation. The total constitutes 13 percent of all families.

*Rising acceptance of the working woman.* In the early days of business, even secretaries were male. Gradually, as the need for labor expanded, women entered the work force to assume the less interesting, lower compensated positions not favored by men. Both they and their employers saw their participation as a temporary, rather than long-term commitment. In the work place, women accepted as proper the same supporting roles they filled at home. The pejorative "woman's job" described a position no male would elect to assume because of its low status, low pay, and dead-end outlook. Half of all women workers have been hired into just 21 occupations, while the same proportion of males has been spread over three times as many fields.

Since equal employment legislation and the heightened aspirations of women, however, both female employees and their organizations have had reason to break down the characteristic polarization of the work place into segregated-by-sex occupations. Contributing to the success of the change has been the assumption of more powerful positions by younger managers, who by and large are more accepting of women in nontraditional roles. A recent poll showed that Americans believe marriages in which both spouses work, both do housework, and both engage in child care prove a "more satisfactory way of life" than the traditional split-responsibility unions. Acceptance of the "liberated" alliance gained rapidly as age of interviewees declined.[26] Little wonder that nearly half of all two-income families fall in the under 35-year age group.

*Desire for higher living standard.* Over the past decade the number of affluent families has advanced at twice the rate of growth in families overall. Today, nearly half of total family income is earned by families with two working spouses. Typically, the wife's contribution reaches almost 40 percent when she is employed full time and year-round. Working wives are found in increasing proportion through rising family income levels; only at the $50,000-and-over mark does their percentage decline. "Of all homes in the broad $15,000–$50,000 earning bracket, some 55 percent contain a working wife," pointed out Fabian Linden of The Conference Board.[27]

Not only our long-standing inflation, but the desire for more luxuries than one job could as quickly make possible has led to the two-career family. Many couples in their twenties and thirties have a combined income of $50,000 or more. The result is assumption of an upper-income life style which otherwise might not be reached until much later in life, if ever. Women "have become the mainstay of the middle-class economy. The number of men who could support their families at a reasonable standard of living by their own earnings is few," noted Eli Ginzberg.[28]

*Increase in household technology.* "I think housework is the reason most women go to the office," a household hints columnist commented.[29] For every woman who is employed, and in particular for the wife and mother, the rapid advances in household technology have been key. Despite male lip service to the concept of shared housework, studies have demonstrated without deviation that when both husband and wife are employed, the woman remains responsible for homemaking tasks with very little help from her spouse. The wife spends 40 hours a week on such chores, while the husband spends only 4.[30] Fortunately, frozen foods, self-cleaning ovens, and other aids undreamed of by their grandmothers, or even mothers, make today's working women free of much of the food preparation and cleaning drudgery of yesterday.

## WHAT THE FUTURE HOLDS

Despite both legal requirements and the greater number of women in the work force, relatively few women can be termed executives. While a few companies have been successful in naming women to the middle and even upper echelons of management, the vast majority of organizations encounter sizable difficulties in endeavoring to do so. Some companies claim that women executives are impossible to find. ("Tell me the truth," one client commanded of me recently. "Are there *really* women executives out there? If there are any, *I* haven't seen them.") Other organizations contend that the demand so far exceeds supply, that any woman promoted into or recruited from the outside for an executive position is bound to be attracted away within a relatively short time.

Even more firms assert that the entry of women into management is inevitably accompanied by a severe backlash problem. White males allege "reverse discrimination" when women and minorities are given priority or what is at least taken as favored treatment. Organizations remain sensitive to charges of reverse discrimination, despite the Weber decision of the Supreme Court.

Admittedly, moving women into management is not an easy task. Improperly conceived or executed, the naming of females to posts in the executive cadre may not only be disruptive to the organization over the short term but cause severe and long-lasting difficulties.

The ultimate question is, "Who *needs* women in management?" Many businessmen have yet to be convinced that overlooking women as candidates for the executive suite causes hardship for the country, company, or themselves. However, the law exists and will be enforced, finally, at every firm. When futurist Herman Kahn was asked not long ago to estimate the length of time that would be required for women to account for 25 percent of Fortune 500 chief executives, he opined, "about two thousand years. But make it 10 percent, and I'll say within twenty years."[31] Only a minority of women officers are this optimistic, however. Seven out out 10 think more than two decades will be required, and 2.8 percent are pessimistic enough to think that females will *never* occupy 50 chief-executive slots at major industrial companies.[32]

The well-managed corporation has no wish to be among the last to accept societal trends. Indeed it will make every effort to attract the best women for the company just as it seeks out the best men. Properly armed with knowledge gleaned from the experience of others, management can meet its affirmative action goals and actually strengthen its management team with women to the advantage of the organization, the women executives who have been promoted or newly hired, and the company's other employees as well.

## REFERENCES

1. Shaeffer, Ruth G. and Edith F. Lynton, *Corporate Experiences in Improving Women's Job Opportunities,* New York: The Conference Board, 1979, p. 77.
2. Ibid., p. 21.
3. "AT&T Has Complied with Antibias Decree, U.S. Attorneys Say," *Wall Street Journal,* 18 January 1979.
4. Heidrick and Struggles, Inc., *Profile of a Woman Officer,* Chicago, 1979, p. 3.
5. Treiman, Donald J. and Kermit Terrell, "Sex and the Process of Status Attainment: A Comparison of Working Women and Men," *American Sociological Review* **40**(2):174 (April 1975).

6. Reinhold, Robert, "U.S. to Monitor Hiring Practices of Big Concerns," *New York Times*, 5 January 1978.

7. U.S. Department of Labor, Bureau of Labor Statistics, *Employment in Perspective: Working Women*, Report 547, Third Quarter, 1978.

8. Briggs, Jean A., "How You Going to Get 'em Back in the Kitchen? (You Aren't.)," *Forbes*, 15 November 1977, p. 177.

9. U.S. Department of Labor, Bureau of Labor Statistics, *U.S. Working Women: A Databook*, Bulletin 1977.

10. Saunders, Norman C., "The U.S. Economy to 1990: Two Projections for Growth," *Monthly Labor Review* No. 101, pp. 36–46 (December 1978).

11. U.S. Department of Labor, Bureau of Labor Statistics, *Employment in Perspective: Working Women*, Report 547, Third Quarter, 1978.

12. "Secretaries Want Better Job," *Chicago Tribune*, 23 April 1979.

13. Weaver, Charles, N., "What Women Want in a Job," *Personnel Administrator* No. 22, p. 66 (June 1977).

14. Kotulak, Ronald, "Working Women Are Happier," *Chicago Tribune*, 9 January 1979.

15. Ignatius, David, "The Rich Get Richer as Well-to-do Wives Enter the Labor Force," *Wall Street Journal*, 8 September 1978.

16. Carmichael, Carole A., "The Working Woman: Her Income Becomes a 'Must'," *Chicago Tribune*, 5 September 1977.

17. Heidrick and Struggles, Inc., *Profile of a Chief Executive Officer*, Chicago, 1977, p. 8.

18. "More Americans Delay Tying Marriage Knots," *Wall Street Journal*, 27 June 1979.

19. U.S. Department of Labor, Women's Bureau, Employment Standards Administration, *Working Mothers and Their Children*, Report 720-065/6711 3·1, 1977.

20. Meislin, Richard J., "Poll Finds More Liberal Beliefs on Marriage and Sex Roles, Especially Among the Young," *New York Times*, 27 November 1977.

21. Rawlings, Stephen, *Perspective on American Husbands and Wives*, Washington, D.C.: U.S. Dept. of Commerce, 1978, p. 23.

22. Gottschalk, Earl C., Jr., "Day Care is Booming, But Experts Are Split Over its Effect on Kids," *Wall Street Journal*, 15 September 1978.

23. Butz, William P. and Michael P. Ward, *The Emergence of Countercyclical U.S. Fertility*, Santa Monica: Rand Corporation, 1977.

24. Snider, Arthur J., "Oh, Baby! U.S. May Pay to Ensure Birthrate," *Chicago Sun-Times*, 5 April 1978.

25. "A Modern Compromise: Short-Term Alimony," *Business Week*, 25 September 1978, p. 171.

26. Meislin, Richard J., "Poll Finds More Liberal Beliefs on Marriage and Sex Roles, Expecially Among the Young," *New York Times*, 27 November 1977.

27. Linden, Fabian, "Woman, Worker," *Across the Board* 14(3):25 (March 1977).

28. Briggs, Jean A., "How You Going to Get 'em Back in the Kitchen? (You Aren't.)," *Forbes*, 15 November 1977, p. 177.

29. Heloise, quoted in Leta W. Clark, *Women, Women, Women: Quips, Quotes and Commentary*, New York: Drake Publishers, 1977, p. 29.

30. Morgan, James N., Ismail A. Sirageldin and Nancy Baerwaldt, *Productive Americans*, Ann Arbor: University of Michigan, 1977, pp. 102–4.

31. Robertson, Wyndham, "The Top Women in Big Business," *Fortune*, 17 July 1978, p. 59.

32. Heidrick and Struggles, Inc., *Profile of a Woman Officer*, Chicago, 1979, p. 5.

# 2

# *Effective Affirmative Action*

Sex discrimination in employment is now illegal in any organization with 15 or more employees, and organizations with 100 or more on their staffs are subject to filing an annual report with the Equal Employment Opportunity Commission (EEOC). The law prohibiting sex discrimination in employment applies to recruiting, selection, job placement, training, promotion, benefits, discipline and discharge.

Every corporation holding a government contract for as little as $10,000 is subject to federal surveillance of its personnel practices. Each supplier of goods or services with a prime or subcontract exceeding $50,000 is expected to maintain a written affirmative action plan. And affirmative action calls for more than passive nondiscrimination. It requires employers to take specific actions and make special efforts to recruit, employ, and promote qualified women and minority group members.

Affirmative action (AA) does *not* mean quotas, but numerical goals which the company is expected to attempt, in good faith, to meet. AA does *not* mean hiring unqualified individuals or any who are not needed, considering only women and minorities for openings, or appraising women and minorities by different performance standards than white men. But affirmative action *does* mean a significant change in corporate personnel practices.

## IMPACT OF AFFIRMATIVE ACTION

Chief personnel officers of sizable companies—those with the largest contracts as well as the greatest visibility to both the public and regulators—overwhelmingly cite government regulations, and particu-

14

larly equal employment opportunity (EEO), as their primary concern.[1] But different industries and various companies have been subject to varying degrees of pressure. Those organizations which have been the target of government charges find that what might have been thought of previously as a social issue is now an economic one. And no choice of action remains if their court cases are lost.

For other corporations, which thus far have been found in compliance with the law, or which due to size or type of business have yet to bear close scrutiny, alternatives remain. Such firms can choose to do as little as possible as late as possible, or move more rapidly than external forces demand. The course of action is likely to be based on whether equal opportunity is viewed as a passing fad or a new dimension of doing business. Personal views of decision-makers regarding EEO, while they may be strong, probably won't influence the decision. Some acknowledge EEO as the most appropriate utilization of the human resource, although decrying the short-term cost and disruption it creates. But others, as a recent Conference Board study pointed out, "argue that if the government forces all major employers to 'take their share' of minority group members and women in executive jobs, the result is likely to be mediocrity."[2]

In any event, it is unlikely that the truly astonishing advances made by women in business over the past decade would have occurred this quickly, if ever, without the force of law. After all, American men built the world's greatest economy with scant involvement of women at the decision-making level. Why, male executives might argue, should seemingly unnecessary changes be made now? Admittedly, the number of women qualified by education and experience for the middle and upper echelons of management remains small. Further, many women not only themselves lack any managerial aspirations, but consider this an inappropriate sphere for the entire feminine gender! Only time will tell whether equal opportunity will diminish in importance, but many of the largest organizations in the country by this point are convinced the issue will not fade.

Following passage of the Civil Rights Act in 1964, major companies concentrated their attention on minorities. It was not until the early seventies that most of these firms developed affirmative action plans to hire and advance women executives. At least one, National Bank of Commerce of San Antonio, went to court rather than furnish an affirmative action plan. The bank's attorney said AA could be a violation of the Civil Rights Act, which calls for equal employment opportunity.[3]

In some organizations the effort to hire and promote women has been half-hearted, sporadic and aimed solely at satisfying legal requirements.

"Making the numbers" under such circumstances becomes an end in itself. Tradition remains uppermost at these companies, but it is joined by tokenism. For other companies, the aim has been to move beyond short-term government compliance, from a reactive stance to one designed to meet the best interests of the organization over the long run.

"I remember when the subject of sex equality in industry first arose," recalled a consultant. "The male executives guffawed. They don't any more. They take it very, very seriously. They are trying to do their best, being practical people who are aware that if you don't obey the law, you get into trouble. But there are still very real obstacles to overcome."

Commented a key official of a Midwest company, "Top management people are paid enough to set aside their personal feelings and to be primarily concerned with the good of the company and the shareholders. If they explore the laws of the land and the pressures from society at large, they'll conclude it's inevitable that the company must develop a program that will produce numbers of women in management. Once you accept the inevitability issue, you can move on to the availability question. And it's a little ridiculous with 53 per cent of 220 million Americans being female to say you can't find the few women who can meet the same qualifications we white men have been meeting all these years. Put aside the question, 'Why are we fooling around with this?' and apply your energy to how best to do it!"

In leading companies, boards of directors and senior managers have accepted the requirement for equal employment opportunity as another business objective to be met. They believe affirmative action must be built into the regular processes of the business; to the extent that AA remains tangential or extraordinary, they feel certain it will never be accepted. At times, the progress of these firms has seemed painfully slow compared with the more rapid percentage gains in female representation elsewhere, or the more highly placed women cited by some companies. However, the research, planning, and considered actions which have characterized programs to achieve real equal opportunity will minimize future difficulties from any source, public or private. Even more importantly, these companies will have the competitive advantage of selecting and retaining the most able talent to be found in the pool, regardless of sex.

"Improving the status of women takes time. You can't do it overnight," emphasized the chief personnel officer of a major New York-based company. "I think the companies which get into trouble are those that say, 'Okay, this is just like any other business problem—we can correct it fast because it's a numerical problem.' But it's much more than that. You can put women into jobs, but the women aren't going to succeed unless they get training and support. If they fail, you'll be looking for more women for the same jobs. And what will you have accomplished?''

Echoing this sentiment, an EEO specialist in the oil industry declared, ''When companies think it can happen overnight, they end up hiring unqualified people. That's what creates backlash, when the white males believe they don't stand a chance, and the women believe they're moving because they're women and not because they're good.''

## KEY CONSIDERATIONS FOR AN EFFECTIVE PROGRAM

What are the key considerations in an effective affirmative action program for bringing women into middle and upper management?

*Commitment by the chief executive officer.* First and foremost, commitment on the part of the chief executive officer (CEO) is needed. His responsibility is not merely to launch the program, but to remain involved to assure that desired results are obtained. The corporate leader must demonstrate, by word and action, not a grudging compliance with legal requirements but an unequivocal endorsement of personnel policies blind to all considerations but merit. He will lay to rest once and for all the belief that there are ''men's jobs'' and ''women's jobs'' in the organization; instead, he will make plain that each employee is to be judged on performance and will be considered for whatever position he or she qualifies on the basis of talent and interest. He will hold his organization accountable for making this policy a reality.

A Midwest personnel executive emphasized that his top management's involvement is essential. ''When I make suggestions on affirmative action to line managers and they say, 'No way,' all I need to do is ask, 'Would you be willing to tell that to the chairman? Would you like to sit down with him?' You can take a tough line when you know the support is there.''

In his initial address as chief executive of Equitable Life Assurance in 1975, Coy Eklund addressed the desirability of advancing women within the organization. The following month he hosted a summit conference of women from throughout the company. A few months after that, an advisory panel of women was formed which has since met on a regular basis with the chief executive. Affirmative action goals were established and built into the executive appraisal process. While the company traditionally had had one female officer, now there are nearly 30; four women serve on Equitable's board of directors.

The reasons for the chief executive's commitment will vary from person to person. Some may endorse the concept on moral grounds alone, or believe that good management calls for color- and sex-blind utilization of talent. However, virtually all accept that the time for action has come. There is value in demonstrating leadership and not being among the laggards on an issue which seems destined to survive. By responding more promptly many CEOs will have better access to a largely untapped resource. Further, they know that waiting too long may subject their companies to unwelcome pressures and reduce their options. It behooves the chief executive officer, in any event, to support EEO both in public and private. And since an example is the very best sermon, he should consider naming a woman as one of his direct reports—perhaps the highly visible and enviable "assistant to" slot or any other staff or line position for which a woman with appropriate experience can be found.

The CEO needs to understand the problems that will be encountered in moving women into management and developing them. It's possible for management to get desired input from women employees by establishing a women's advisory council, as Equitable did, or as CBS formed in the early part of the seventies. CBS's 12-member council, elected by all women at the company, is composed of three representatives of each of the company's four businesses. Monthly meetings take place with senior management at which the representation of women at every job level is reviewed, and council members present concerns from an agenda submitted to management in advance. CBS is proud of its progress, especially since it is not a government contractor and therefore is not required to have an affirmative action plan. Nevertheless, more than a quarter of all exempt employees are now females.

*Identification of the problem.* At the inception of the program, the chief executive may name a task force to examine where in the company discrimination exists. A consultant specializing in affirmative action matters might be retained to assist in the review. Ideally, the task force would comprise both sexes. Having determined the problem areas, the group would be better able to suggest corrective programs and policies.

Mobil Oil Corporation formed a task force in 1970 which studied, for more than a year, the position of women in the work force generally and at Mobil in particular. Myths concerning women—such as their higher rate of absenteeism and lower level of performance—were examined and exploded. The task force recommended to the board of directors increasing the representation of women in the company's management, particularly at higher levels. Since that time, the company has conducted a program that goes beyond legal requirements in moving women into and within management.

Questions a task force might address would include these: Are women found at all levels of the company, from the board of directors through entry level management and professional positions? How many women officers are there? Are females in line responsibilities as well as in staff jobs? Are women in all of the company's geographic locations? Are they found in all functional areas? How do the salaries paid men and women compare?

Are women as frequently transferred to enhance their development as are their male counterparts? Are women selected for training courses within the company, and are they sent to courses conducted on the outside? Do women serve on important task forces and committees, and are they invited to attend high level meetings? What targets should be set for women at varying levels, over one year, five year, and longer time frames? What women currently employed are promotable, and what training do they need to develop to their fullest? Must the company go outside for women, and if so, how many and with what backgrounds?

"Answers to these questions require a special census," emphasizes a key manager in a billion dollar company based in the Midwest. "The EEO-1 report, which divides the work force into nine very broad job categories, is inadequate. You've got to subdivide the first three categories—officials and managers, professionals, and technicians—into smaller cuts. And forget titles, look at earnings; if you have a woman who's called a vice president and she's earning what a first-line male supervisor is, you're only playing games. In many companies today there are very few or absolutely no women making more than $35,000!"

*Selection of the AA head.* Having made evident his personal commitment and having pinpointed problem areas, the chief executive officer must identify an individual to spearhead the ongoing affirmative action program.

As an outgrowth of many factors, including the imposition of government into the personnel decision-making process and the changing value system of tbe work force, the personnel function has gained significantly greater stature at progressive business organizations in recent years. Frequently, the chief personnel officer reports directly to the CEO who himself is closely involved in personnel matters. Thus, in most companies, the head of personnel directs the equal employment opportunity effort.[4] In contrast, other companies position EEO specialists outside the personnel function. Reporting directly to the CEO or another member of executive management, such EEO specialists audit personnel's performance as staff support for line management in matters relating to EEO.

The individual selected to run the program day-to-day will depend upon the nature of the problems the company has to overcome in moving women into and up through management. "When mistakes are made in selection," a consultant pointed out to me, "it's because management hasn't really thought through what is needed in the way of experience and personal characteristics to get the job done in that particular setting."

It's more important that the equal opportunity head have ready access to the top and that the CEO's commitment to the program be known, than it is for the position to report directly to the chief executive. As one EEO officer in the East put it, "It's not the level of the reporting relationship but the level of the CEO's interest that spells success or failure for the program."

Clearly, to succeed in directing affirmative action for women, the program head must command the respect of senior management and be personally committed to the success of the program. The individual must also be able to establish credibility with women both in and out of the company, as well as those of either sex, in and out of government, who are devoted to the cause of equal employment for females.

A female EEO officer advises, "The person selected must have a sense of justice, a feel for what's right, reasonable interpersonal skills, and pleasant persistence to see that good personnel practices are in place for *everybody.* My success is not in the placement or promotion of women—that will come if I can relate to male management. They don't feel guarded with me. I've convinced them I'm interested in what's right for the organization. I go out of my way to assure them that I'll support their canning a woman who isn't hacking it. I couldn't feel differently; keeping such a person on would be bad for the whole program."

Is it preferable, even mandatory that the person selected be a female? Not so, said most of those with whom I spoke while surveying companies coast to coast. A number pointed out that organizations had been prone to favor women in establishing such programs, but sometimes made a bad choice. In certain cases the woman was an advocate whose viewpoint was irreconcilable with that of management. In other instances she was a woman who had succeeded before the days of EEO, who actually resented adoption of the program she had been called upon to promote. Even more frequently, the woman was chosen without regard for her management capabilities. "Too many minorities or women are picked who don't know anything about affirmative action," stressed one consultant. "They become glorified clerks doing the statistical analysis, which is only a miniscule part of the job. It should be somebody who knows the industry, the company, and all of the human resource functional areas as well as affirmative action."

Regardless of sex or color, a competent manager and fair individual who truly believes in *equal* opportunity has the best prospect for success as head of EEO, providing he or she has the authority and resources to get the job done and fits the style of the company. "I succeeded a woman," reported the white male head of EEO at a large capital goods company. "Her effectiveness had plateaued (and that's a polite way of putting it) because she could not develop the necessary relationship with the manufacturing managers, who basically are male chauvinists. It wasn't a lack of competence on her part."

At another company the vice president of human resources explained, "We hired an individual to head EEO who should have been very good at the job. It turned out he wasn't. He had a peculiar way of dealing with people; he overstated his power, never bothered to find out what the other guy's problems were. It hurt him, and it hurt our program. Somehow or other he tended to equate himself with the chairman of the board, rather than the inhouse consultant he was supposed to be."

The equal opportunity post initially was looked upon by most companies as an easy one; today it is regarded as demanding, usually entailing:

1. Establishing goals and timetables with line management.
2. Assisting line management in the collection and analysis of data.
3. Monitoring progress and reporting to executive management, or even the board of directors, on a regular basis.
4. Identifying problem areas and counseling line management regarding them.
5. Serving as the liaison with federal, state, and local regulatory agencies.
6. Serving as the liaison with women's groups inside the company and with national and local women's organizations in company locations.
7. Working with appropriate departments to disseminate affirmative action information to employees and external audiences.
8. Informing line management of new EEO laws and regulations.
9. Acting as the liaison with corporate EEO heads in other organizations, particularly those sharing the company's locations or those within the company's industry.

What about experience? Should the head of EEO be from inside the organization or outside? If either, an attorney or not? If from inside, an individual out of operations or someone from personnel? If from outside, an ex-regulator from a local, state, or national enforcement agency?

Here again, competency and sensitivity are more important considerations. However, if the company typically promotes from within, an employee transferred into this post will gain easier acceptance. An ex-regulator, while closely conversant with the workings of the bureaucratic mind, may find the corporate heart hard to win over. The EEO head at a major Eastern company confessed that many months were consumed following the individual's arrival from an agency in winning the trust of the EEO staff. Meanwhile, vital information was withheld from the department head, who was still considered "the other side" by subordinates! "I couldn't blame them—my name used to be on the bottom of complaints against companies just like ours," the ex-regulator admitted.

Because of the importance of the EEO post in the thinking of some companies, it is often looked upon as a developmental opportunity for high potential individuals, who may spend a relatively short span of time in the post between other positions in or out of personnel.

One senior executive suggested the best choice was an individual out of marketing. "Those people usually have persuasion skills and can sell the program properly. Managers don't like to be told what to do. A marketer can position AA so it's helpful to the line people in the conduct of their operations. That's much more palatable than simply stating, 'Do this or you'll hear from the law department!' At the same time you've got to understand the regulator's mentality. An awful lot of people did not appreciate, for example, that in the EEOC's view Title VII was civil rights legislation and not labor legislation. Individuals who lack that understanding cannot respond in a way which is helpful to the company."

EEO considerations impact every aspect of an organization's interface with present and prospective employees. All personnel policies and practices must be reviewed for bias.

*Communication of AA guidelines.* Initially, equal opportunity guidelines should be communicated to every level of the organization and at every location. A message from the CEO in writing is acceptable, but a filmed communication, such as the one utilized by Chairman Raleigh Warner to reach all employees at Mobil, is preferable. Mr. Warner stated the company's intention and his own personal backing of moving women into management, not only because this was the right thing to do but because it was good business.

The CEO can transmit the EEO message personally to his direct reports or all key members of management, and they to their reports, on down to first-line supervisors. Arthur C. Woods, then CEO of Sears, Roebuck & Company, in 1973 called a meeting at headquarters for the company's 250 top executives, the first conclave of this size in 23 years. All those present were white and male. The subject was affirmative action, and the only time sales and profits were mentioned was to emphasize that AA goals would be established just as in the financial area.

Whether in person, on film, or in writing, it is vital that the chief executive officer be the bearer of the message, for apathy or even active opposition may be the reaction both within the organization and among those outside who influence employees. Individuals working for the company need to know not only what "equal opportunity" means, who will be affected, when and how, but that the matter is a priority concern.

Affirmative action plans should be formulated with the character of the company in mind. Ultimately, the program's success will depend on the organizational climate; it must be accepting and supportive of qualified women, or the best intentioned efforts will fail.

From the outset, the affirmative action program should be the responsibility of line management, with support from personnel specialists in recruiting, developing, and retaining women. It is the day-to-day decisions of line management that determine whether equal opportunity will exist within the organization.

A major Midwestern company conducted its program during the first three years as a personnel department activity. Progress was minimal. The CEO then placed responsibility squarely on line managers, down to the first supervisory level. Everyone had goals for the recruitment, development, and promotion of women just as he had always had goals pertaining to his functional assignment. Those who did not meet their objectives in affirmative action received smaller bonuses. "We now have 45 women department managers, compared with one when the program started," explained an EEO executive. "But placing the responsibility on line management was the turning point. Up until then we were just a cheering section, shaking our pom-poms in their faces with little effect."

Managers must participate in the establishment of their goals; these should not be imposed by a senior executive or an EEO staff member. The goals should be specific: how many women in management, where and within what time frame. Goals should take into account the difficulties to be encountered and should be realistic yet challenging enough to attain satisfactory progress. They should be treated as budgeted nonfinancial objectives, indicating they are integral to the short- and long-term planning and review process. The demand that they be realized will enhance management's stature in the eyes of both male and female employees and minimize controversy with compliance authorities.

The message of management to the line should be unmistakable: The program is viewed as beneficial to the financial results of the organization. Goals for hiring and promoting women have been established on a reasonable basis; there will be no relaxation of standards, merely an elimination of artificially imposed barriers to individual achievement. There will continue to be opportunities for personal growth for *all* employees, in accordance with their performance.

The superior and above average males and females in the management ranks are unlikely to feel threatened by the prospect of additional contenders for positions at the middle and upper echelons. Those least receptive are destined to be marginal managers worried that they have plateaued out, or that they could be made more susceptible to dismissal should company results deteriorate. It is these marginal managers who will assume that women get most of the promotions, whether qualified for them or not. Their feelings of anxiety will be reinforced by family members who are made aware of the circumstances.

However, adverse sentiment will be minimized if employees recognize that affirmative action is a priority established by the CEO himself. The company must concentrate on changing behavior, not attitudes. The work place does not fix employee values, and only the employee's compliance with policy should be the concern of the organization.

## CIRCUMSTANCES AFFECTING THE PROGRAM

The manner in which affirmative action is communicated should be in keeping with the style of the company. If there is strong control at the top, orders should be issued as they are customarily with the same expectation of obedience. If the environment is paternalistic, management should anticipate the usual employee deference. More democratic environments will offer subordinates some degree of participation in formulating the appropriate program.

The company's efforts should take into account the kind of business in which the organization is engaged. Technical companies, where a large part of the management group possesses scientific or engineering degrees, will find it more difficult to add women to the middle and upper echelons of management since a shortage exists of women with appropriate training. On the other hand, consumer companies with large marketing forces can be far more flexible on educational and even experiential requirements. Manufacturing companies are likely to have geographically dispersed installations, often in small communities, to which it is more difficult to attract women. Service companies, in contrast, may be located in major metropolitan centers in which women can be found or to which they can be moved relatively easily.

If the company nearly always promotes from within, the addition of women to the management ranks will be a much lengthier process than in an organization with more rapid turnover at the upper levels. Companies in mature industries are unlikely to have as many positions to fill as are those in dynamic businesses. If the company is performance conscious, and there is a close tie between contribution and reward, introducing women will be much less difficult than in an environment where seniority, social relationships, or other considerations are of great significance.

"The reason we've been successful in introducing women into management is our emphasis on results," declares the personnel head of a rapidly growing company in America's heartland. "I don't think there's any great intellectual or emotional encouragement to pushing women forward. There may even be some psychological resistance. You know, male managers will say, 'Why, they couldn't do *that* job!' But our executives are very conscious of the fact that an able subordinate is invaluable. They know what the cost is to them when somebody can't deliver. They want good people on their team! If a woman proves herself, the manager isn't going to be hung up about her sex."

Antagonism to equal opportunity will be least in an organization which is enjoying increased employment. Digital Equipment Corporation, which added 30,000 jobs in just five years to quadruple in size, has been able to offer employees of every race and both sexes ample opportunity for advancement, and resistance to the progress of minorities and women has been minimal. A capital intensive company may not be able to add women rapidly even when the company is prospering; a West Coast firm doubled its volume without increasing employment. On the other hand a labor intensive corporation with equal growth in sales could have afforded significantly more opportunities.

CBS has increased the percentage of its female exempt employees by nearly ten percentage points in less than a decade, but the company has grown dramatically during this span, and males too have had many opportunities to advance. While Atlantic Richfield has been relatively static in terms of total employment, a high rate of retirements has permitted movement in the management ranks for promotable individuals of both sexes. In contrast, American Telephone & Telegraph Company operated under a consent degree to meet numerical goals and timetables for women in all job classifications at the very period when overall employment was shrinking. (Nevertheless, the company was able to achieve most of its goals.)

The vice president of human resources at a large service organization admits that "we have more talent in our management group than we're going to be able to utilize. We've created a syndrome that says anybody who wants to can get ahead, and it just isn't true. And it's even less true as you try to get some female and minority representation. But we think we need to let our management group know the truth. We're better off to tell them than try to kid them along and hope they won't figure out what's happening. Then they lose all confidence in the company. Some may decide to pursue a career elsewhere, and they may be the best people. But I think you're better off to lose than to keep them, stifle them, and frustrate them. Their performance will decline."

Another consideration influencing the affirmative action program is the number of women already in the organization's work force, and in particular the type and level of positions occupied by them. If the corporation has been exposed to women succeeding on their merits in nontraditional roles, or even if the company has had a large number of women on its staff, there will be far less resistance to the prospect of additional females in various functions and at different levels. Had AT&T not had women historically representing a third of its management ranks, its program to move females into higher ranking and better paying positions could not have proceeded as rapidly as it did. Banks, insurance companies, airlines, and retailing companies are others with the advantage of a ready pool of women.

Finally, the course of affirmative action will be related to the timing of its inception. If the company has instituted the program under very specific pressure from the government, the need for haste may bring about results that are not always in the best interest of the organization.

When a company undertakes affirmative action, the manner in which the jobs are filled must be addressed immediately. The goal of the organization will be not merely to hire and promote women, but well-qualified individuals. Staff support must inventory female resources by education, skills, experience, and performance rating. Management potential of women employees may be judged by assessment, a more reliable process than the typical supervisory appraisal.

Top management must emphasize that sex will operate neither to the advantage nor detriment of any employee. Enforcement of this dictum will alleviate fears of both men and women. Men will not be as concerned that unqualified women will be favored. Women employees who, for whatever reason, do not wish to assume increased responsibility will recognize they'll be free of pressure to do so. And women who expect to gain advancement simply because they are women will be discouraged from this sense of entitlement.

Certain companies are hesitant to bring women into management, ostensively because of the legal ramifications. "If they fail to perform, how would we get rid of them?" is the attitude of these managements. However, companies with good personnel practices have no hesitation in terminating women. This problem is minimized by maintaining standards in selection and appraisal of performance. Nonetheless, there will be marginal women under an affirmative action program, just as there are excellent and average female employees. "Employees are very aware of who's good and who isn't," emphasized the chief personnel officer of an Eastern seaboard company. "Taking action against those who aren't minimizes backlash. Then nobody's likely to say, 'She's there only because she's female.' "

Progressive discipline is not only the means of assuring adequate communication with affected employees and minimizing turnover costs; it also makes unlikely a successful complaint of sex discrimination. A verbal warning should be followed by a written warning, a probationary period, and if all else fails, termination of the employee. The organization which follows this process and maintains proper documentation quickly establishes a reputation with regulators for acting appropriately.

Sometimes the organization is able to salvage the employee by identifying a cause other than the individual's perceived lack of talent and/or motivation. The problem may result from the particular job responsibilities with which the employee is confronted, or from a management climate which is not conducive to the employee's success. Recognizing this, personnel may attempt an alternate placement. Companies report that some individuals respond well to progressive discipline, while others prove successful in a different position in the corporate structure.

"Sure, we're concerned about the possibility of suits," confesses the director of EEO at a major manufacturing company. "Before an exempt minority or woman is fired, we review the situation. If it's illegal, we're not going to do it. And legal considerations aside, if the manager is acting from a sexist point of view in discharging a woman, it doesn't matter whether she can prove discrimination or not. She's not going to be let go, and if necessary we'll transfer her to see that she gets a fair shake." He added, "My aim is to get to the point where I don't have to review. We're not quite there yet."

The vice president heading personnel at a consumer products company declares, "Hiring females, hiring minorities forces you to put your house in order. You're measuring people by what they're actually doing, not on somebody's whim. You have standards and apply them across the board to everybody. When it comes to a firing, we know with the trend of the times we might get sued. But if we're determined we're right, we expect to win. We're not going to ride with a mistake even if the scales seem tilted against us!"

## INCENTIVES FOR MANAGERS

Numerous companies which initiated affirmative action programs at the beginning of the seventies failed to provide appropriate incentives to stimulate the desired response to budgeted nonfinancial objectives. While performance in this area was considered a factor in the appraisal process, the direct tie to compensation was nonexistent, or dependent upon the subjective evaluation of a superior who might consider affirmative action to be relatively unimportant. Hence, managers saw no need to comply; it was not worth their while to do so, despite top management directives. These organizations discovered that hoped-for change does not occur when ignoring policy brings the same rewards as aggressively supporting it. Since line management is beset by many demands, affirmative action must be treated as being just as important as any financial goal, such as sales, profit, or return on assets.

A large transportation company had not been making its goals until the CEO gave each manager a specific affirmative action objective with a weighted value in his or her performance evaluation. Within the first half of the next year, the 12-month objectives for females and minorities had been reached.

More and more organizations are specifying the impact of affirmative action goals on executive compensation, while many others are contemplating such action. Not only is good performance reflected in salary or bonus, but failure to achieve results means decreased salary or bonus or denial of promotion. In some instances the reward/punishment mechanism applies to selected senior operating managers only; in other cases the incentive is provided through the lowest level of the line organization.

Companies that limit the compensation tie to a few key individuals claim that this strategy is sufficient to get the job done. "When the head of an operating unit knows that this is a factor which directly influences his pocketbook, it subsequently becomes a factor that commands significant attention throughout his organization," notes a West Coast affirmative action officer. Further, the limitation of accountability avoids the problems which may arise if goals are set for the smallest units. A first level supervisor may not encourage promotable women to seek new opportunities because their departure from the unit could prove disadvantageous to his meeting his goals. Or, on the other hand, the organization may be so fluid that interunit mobility makes it impossible to hold the lowest level manager responsible. Under either set of circumstances, EEO management time will be expended unproductively in reviewing results with every supervisor.

With a properly devised incentive in place, the impact is immediate. The human resources staff of a major service organization frequently heard line management lament that qualified women were impossible to find. However, when the reward-punishment plan fell into place, managers began to call human resources personnel to express concern that their goals might not be met. "What are you going to do to help me, and when are you going to do it?" were the most frequent questions posed by the line organization.

The review process demands sufficiently detailed information to permit affirmative action personnel and/or senior management to pinpoint where the successes and failures are so that appropriate action can be taken. A senior personnel executive at an Eastern conglomerate declared, "We hedge our bet a little bit. We make our internal objectives a little bit tougher than we think our compliance agency would insist on. That gives us some flexibility. We don't want to pinpoint specific jobs for women and then get slapped with a reverse discrimination charge! Our lawyers have told us to be careful in this regard for several years now. We're walking a fine line. The government says we must do it (affirmative action); our CEO says we must do it, but we are intelligent in the way we approach it." Of course, the Supreme Court has yet to settle what constitutes reverse discrimination; Bakke didn't make the answer plain for business, but Weber was a clearer sign. "The main battlegrounds over the next few years seem likely to be union halls, corporate board rooms, university campuses and political forums, rather than the courts where the attention has been focused recently," declared the *Wall Street Journal* in the fall of 1979.[5]

In most organizations, affirmative action results are evaluated annually; in others, the review process is carried out twice yearly, quarterly, or even monthly. One of the country's largest industrial companies publishes results every month. The report shows five-year and one-year targets and the standing of each component in relation to objective. Operating management reviews results and finds out why lagging units are underperforming.

A bank which uses a similar system points out that peer pressure is an important motivator. "Sure, managers are being rewarded or punished for their affirmative action, but it's also important to them to look good to their peers. They don't want to be missing their targets, particularly when they're part of a small group below par," explained an officer.

In the most sophisticated programs, not only recruitment but development and retention of women are factors in the size of the monetary reward. In these well-developed programs, too, the manager is appraised not only in relation to his results, but with regard to difficulties encountered during the time span under consideration. A careful monitoring process can confirm those factors beyond the manager's control.

"When we started our program, all we were doing was getting numbers," emphasized the director of EEO at a large Eastern company. "We would give a manager a monetary reward for hiring, but at the end of the year he wouldn't have any more women than at the beginning! Now we have retention goals. That covers the quality issue. And next we're going to factor in promotion because that is essential if we're ever going to have women in top management."

Sears does not consider for promotion any manager "who either cannot or will not meet his affirmative action goals on the same basis as he meets his other major management responsibilities." IBM evaluates the EEO performance of each manager as part of its formal appraisal process, while American Express relates affirmative action progress to size of bonus paid to key people. At Atlantic Richfield Company a fifth of the merit pay increase of division managers is dependent upon affirmative action. In addition to numerical goals, Arco evaluates such factors as endorsement and discussion of EEO policy with subordinates, active and continuing participation in the development, review, and evaluation of EEO efforts of subordinates, and implementation of training and development activities for women and minorities.

Norton Simon ties a portion of the bonus paid to managers through department supervisor to EEO results. And International Paper pays approximately half of its incentive compensation award to managers on the basis of performance on budgeted nonfinancial objectives, including affirmative action. Other parts of BNFO include strategic planning, management and professional development, technology transfer, government affairs, and employee communication. In each of these areas, managers are judged first on the objectives themselves and second on performance against them.

With the closer involvement of today's boards of directors in corporate affairs, the entire roster of directors or a committee may examine, on a periodic basis, EEO data as well as other corporate social responsibility information. Most major companies now have at least one female director, who typically displays a particular interest in statistics regarding female employees. At a leading financial institution, a woman director annually meets face-to-face with several women from throughout the organization to get their views.

At Sears an affirmative action task force includes 12 company officers as members. The group provides policy and guidance to EEO efforts of the company and also serves to keep top management informed on progress, problems, and efforts to deal with difficulties. A public issues committee of the board also hears at least once yearly from the EEO department.

## COMMUNICATIONS ARE KEY

There will be anxieties regarding affirmative action, and the organization should provide a mechanism for dealing with them. Unfamiliarity with the law on the part of a line manager or even a receptionist can result in unfavorable publicity, a suit, or both. Complete and current information on equal employment opportunity is essential for employees at every level and at every location. Meetings and/or publications should be utilized to keep staff updated on changes in the law and their implications for the organization. Otherwise, employees may relate such developments as the Bakke decision to their own situation in a manner which could be harmful. Even pending legislation is important for the corporation to take into account so that cost of complying with future requirements is minimized.

Continental Illinois Bank employs a series of brief film clips highlighting a variety of work-related problems as a reminder of potentially discriminatory actions. Managers are cautioned, for example, not to assume that a woman being considered for a promotional opportunity requiring travel would not be free to make trips.

Internal communications gain credibility by devoting space or time to detractors as well as supporters of EEO. One of the country's largest organizations, which has open communications as a corporate objective, explains, "That means ventilating conflicting views. The worst thing we could do would be to tell the skeptics in our company, 'We will not listen; the door is closed. Go away and convert your concerns into sloppy work.' "

At another company, a variety of means is employed to achieve two-way communications not only on EEO but any matter of concern to management or employees. An open door policy encourages any individual to speak to any member of management, and each new employee is advised of the program. There is also a "private line" mechanism whereby an employee may submit his concern or criticism to the personnel department, which investigates and responds while respecting the anonymity of the employee. In addition, heads of all company facilities, as well as department heads at headquarters, meet regularly in small groups with subordinates. The informal conversation lasts as long as employees have questions to ask or comments to make. Thus, while the organization has sales of more than $1 billion, and employees number in the thousands, each person has an opportunity to be well informed.

An internal mechanism should be provided to review and evaluate complaints of discrimination by employees; this system minimizes employee recourse to outside agencies. In some companies the plan is simply the same open door policy which prevails when an employee feels strongly enough about any matter to carry it to his superior, superior's superior, or beyond. Sears finds this plan works well. The company estimates it is involved with roughly half a billion personnel decisions yearly affecting its 450,000 employees. The number of formal complaints, nonetheless, is very small, although the number of women and minorities in the organization has advanced in numbers and levels. Today more than a third of the firm's officials and managers are female, compared with a fifth 12 years before.

One consultant emphasizes that, "I personally believe a lot of EEO suits arise as a result of shabby treatment of an individual by a supervisor. It may be just insensitivity on the supervisor's part, but the employee has nowhere to turn inside. So he or she brings a charge." Among other avenues, United Air Lines encourages employees to write directly to the president, and many of them do so. Administrative channels investigate, and a reply comes from the president to the employee.

In some organizations, the affirmative action or personnel staff is charged with adjudication of discrimination complaints. Often, employee performance proves to be the problem; in other instances discrimination does exist, and the situation is remedied with the complainant being protected from retribution. In still more cases, however, the employee's dissatisfaction arises exclusively from insufficient communication on the part of the supervisor.

At a major Eastern company the head of EEO remains aloof from the complaint procedure. "Here, if you don't like the way you're treated, you go to your boss's boss or to personnel. I don't want to be the ombudsman for women to management. Once that happens, in my opinion they're dead. I want to be credible to both women and management as the person who sees that we have a working program. I can't do that carrying complaint baggage. Once I get involved in individual cases, my department is destroyed. How can we tell people to go to their boss's boss or personnel in some cases but if they're black, female, Chinese or native American, to come see me? That's very, very harmful.''

The chief personnel officer of a Midwest company explained, "We flirted a few years back with having a counselor to women. It turned out most women wanted no different treatment than the men; they wanted to talk to the same individuals when they went to personnel. It seemed demeaning to set them apart.''

One New York-based diversified company currently has no internal process for resolving dissatisfactions. The organization's personnel and law departments are considering the advisability of a new position, that of grievance officer, who would hear a complaint from any individual who feels discriminated against before that employee might turn to a government agency or initiate litigation. Over the years the company has lost only one case among 100 or so to which it has been a party in the discrimination area. "But there is a growing trend toward more employee suits," emphasizes the chief personnel officer. "The number of our potential problems is increasing." The figures support his contention: more than 200,000 complaints are filed each year with the federal government and its various agencies and with the states.

Another Eastern company maintains that it's very difficult to succeed in having the internal mechanism viewed as totally equitable, particularly in relation to considerations of race and sex. The organization is planning publicity on all sorts of problem-solving processes throughout the company in the hope of encouraging their use in preference to alternatives.

Increasingly, major companies are utilizing, on a regular basis, attitudinal surveys of all or a representative sample of employees of various levels, functions, and locations. Such studies are valuable in spotting problem areas. Men and women and all races are questioned concerning their views of their own treatment and the treatment of others in the areas of promotional opportunities, compensation and benefits. Typically, at least some white males feel that minorities and women receive an advantage, while certain blacks and females believe that their situation, though improving, is not as good as it should be.

"We're about to begin an organizational climate survey," reported the head of human resources for a West Coast organization. "Together with our procedure within the company for people to register complaints about perceived discrimination, and our turnover studies, we'll have a good fix on problems that may exist in certain parts of the company.''

A sizable manufacturer, which regularly asks salaried personnel how they feel about their opportunity within the organization, had never had negative feedback from white males. In the most recent study, both women and blacks proved unusually positive, enthused about the company's progress in providing equal opportunity, and confident of their prospects for the future. However, for the first time, more than 10 percent of the white male participants felt they had been denied promotion due to advancement of a woman or minority. Yet, the overwhelming majority of white male managers continued to feel the company needed to do more to reach true equality in employment under a program pursued aggressively for just five years.

Another company based in the Midwest reported, ''We've had white males leaving our company who said they didn't believe their chances were as good as they'd be somewhere else because of our affirmative action effort. We candidly admit that ours is a demanding program, but the loudest protests are from those who aren't as qualified.''

Citibank has had an attitudinal survey for the last six years. One feature is a feedback session, in which surveyed groups meet with a discussion group leader in an effort by management to learn the thinking behind their opinions. Appropriate personnel are notified of matters in their areas of responsibility for follow-up.

Over time, organizations argue, behavior can influence attitudes. After all, it becomes increasingly difficult to contend that women are too emotional to be managers when exceptions to this myth are close at hand and too numerous to explain. Finally, the futility of hostility to equal opportunity becomes apparent, and tensions are fewer.

The corporation's public image depends not only upon its accomplishments, but how well they are communicated. It is advantageous to the company with effective affirmative action to reflect its commitment and results in communications with the outside world, as the chief executive officers of Avon, American Express, Norton Simon, and Equitable have done in speeches before various audiences. Sears was the first corporation to publish figures in the annual report on minority and female representation at various levels and continues to do so. Since 1973, First Pennsylvania Corporation has published a *Social Scorecard* which reveals to the public not only the total number of minority and female employees, but number of blacks and women at management and officer levels, as well as minority purchasing, inner-city real estate and minority business lending activities, minority advertising, and contributions.

Norton Simon is another company whose affirmative action program extends beyond employment. A council of purchasing agents from operating companies meets quarterly to establish goals for buying goods and services from female-owned firms. The company also makes deposits in women's banks. Sears looks upon affirmative action as embracing four areas: equal employment opportunity; minority economic development (the company is one of only eight in the country to have its own Minority Enterprise Small Business Investment Corporation); corporation contributions (of which 70 percent is earmarked for disadvantaged Americans); and urban involvement (centering on such current issues as rejuvenation of the cities).

Most companies agree that much remains to be accomplished in maximizing return on investment in the human resource. However, many affirm that concerns over affirmative action requirements have led to a comprehensive review of long standing personnel policy and practices, resulting in better management processes for recruitment, employment and development of all employees, regardless of race or sex. In the view of these organizations, superior talent is and always will be in short supply. A corporate reputation for affording individuals the opportunity to gain recognition on their merits and to develop to their full potential will provide an increasingly important competitive advantage in attracting the best performers in the years to come.

## REFERENCES

1. Heidrick and Struggles, Inc., *Profile of a Chief Personnel Officer,* Chicago, 1977, p. 5.
2. Shaeffer, Ruth G., *Staffing Systems: Managerial and Professional Jobs,* New York: The Conference Board, 1972, p. 23.
3. "Some Companies Fight Tougher Federal Drive on Job Discrimination," *Wall Street Journal,* 2 February 1978.
4. Heidrick and Struggles, Inc., *Profile of a Chief Personnel Officer,* Chicago, 1977, pp. 4–5.
5. Falk, Carol H., "A Lid on Reverse Bias Suits?" *Wall Street Journal,* 1 October 1979.

# 3

# Awareness Training for Management and Women

Organizations are divided on whether to provide awareness training for management and/or women as part of an effective affirmative action program. All agree that every employee should be fully informed regarding the legal requirements of equal opportunity and affirmative action. Disagreement arises as to what other instruction is necessary or even desirable. Awareness training (otherwise known as consciousness raising, sensitivity or attitudinal modification training) claims both enthusiasts and detractors.

Those who favor awareness training emphasize that any company adopting affirmative action is leading not lagging society. No mere promulgation of the law will be sufficient to offset a lifetime of conditioning, proponents argue. The consistently different treatment that the sexes receive from birth causes many men and women to look upon the creation of a peer group of both sexes in management as inappropriate or even unworkable.

As the authors of *The Managerial Woman* point out, "Our value system has always emphasized male superiority, our laws have embodied it, and they are only now beginning to change. People, both men and women, have accepted it, and roles, relationships, and individual personalities have been structured by it."[1]

According to Victor R. Fuchs, vice president-research of the National Bureau of Economic Research, role differentiation "begins in childhood and eventually affects labor force attachment, choice of occupation, location and hours of work, post-school investment, and consumer and fellow-employee attitudes."[2]

Parental, school, and business counseling have directed females, regardless of their interests or abilities, to traditionally female fields. The concept of woman's proper role, whether at work or at home, has been that of dependent who is supporter and nurturer; in contrast, the male has been seen as achievement-oriented provider. The result has been segregated labor markets, for few men or women have cared or dared to depart from societal expectations.

"We've done no awareness training," explained the head of EEO at a capital goods company. "Sure, we've had instruction on the law, but our management feels we're just naturally smart enough to know how to make women an integral part of management. But we're not. Most of the men around here have no idea that they're displaying sexist attitudes every day of the week. They just don't know. Before we get too far, we've got to get at the gut of our problem; and that means facing up to the need for awareness training."

One major New York-based company started its awareness training with executive management. Except for the chief executive officer (CEO), these individuals felt no problem existed. The consultants hired by the firm—a man and woman—first surveyed attitudes of a representative sample of employees. They wrote a report in advance of meeting with top management which "dropped like a bombshell" in the words of the executive with whom I spoke. An awakened group attended the meeting, and "there was an interesting turnaround," I was told. "People said, 'I didn't think we had a problem, but now I know we do; and we're going to do something about it.'" The consultants subsequently met with other levels down to first line supervisor.

The companies supporting awareness training contend that corporate policy is not enough; everything possible must be done to establish the proper organizational climate if affirmative action is to succeed. Men must be sensitized to the special problems facing women in management and coached on what they can do to ease the assimilation process. In contrast, organizations which oppose training for men or women to modify attitudes regarding women in management feel that instruction will only serve to magnify whatever difficulties do exist. Implement policy without discussion, they maintain. Women will be accepted in management as soon as their abilities become apparent.

It is not advantageous to the success of the affirmative action program, they contend, to suggest to both sexes or either one that women are "different." This isn't true, they claim. The needs of women vary from individual to individual, just as the needs of men do. To suggest that "women" need assertiveness training, or to caution men that "women" never have career plans, is to perpetuate stereotyping. If courses are to be conducted, these critics propound, content should stress what the sexes have in common, rather than point up differences which will be interpreted as female deficiencies. In the view of these companies, the preferred route is to offer programs in various disciplines to both men and women who may need them. Thus, possible male backlash to any special treatment of women can be avoided.

Substantiating this view, a woman in business wrote a letter to the *Wall Street Journal* declaring, "The theory that women have unique 'perceptual differences' solely because of their sex and that programs must be created in order 'to cope with these differences' is insulting and ultimately fatal to the concept of equal opportunity. As long as women permit themselves to be 'special' and in need of 'special help,' they will be viewed as burdensome and expensive accoutrements to corporate entities dependent upon the competitive and able for survival. It is my privilege to know and work with a few good managers, and each of them, male or female, is able to set concrete goals, to define and time successful behavior, and to appreciate the challenge in appropriate risk taking."[3]

"Awareness training has very limited value," said a leading Midwest-based consultant with whom I talked. "What's really important is proper management training. When managers aren't effective in supervising women, it's because they're not very good managers, not because they're male chauvinist pigs."

A major financial institution handles awareness in its management development course. "As part of our officer and manager training, which is done on our premises by outside consultants, we cover sensitivity to women and minorities; but this is for everyone at that level. We don't believe in special courses by sex or race."

At a banking organization in another city, an executive explained, "We have a tuition refund program and work with one of the local colleges to assure courses appropriate to our employees' needs. When a career development course was first proposed to us, it was suggested for women and minorities only. Instead, we made it available to everyone. As it turned out, no white males signed up. We still think we were right not to restrict admission. It could have generated ill will among those excluded, as well as conveying second-class citizenship on those for whom it was offered."

A large services company in New York dropped its sex-segregated courses and has no intention of resuming them. "We got a new head of human resources a few years ago," explained a personnel executive.

"He believed that what we needed was a good employee relations program that dealt with all individuals as ones to be developed and moved in the corporate structure. He avoided separating women or any other group from the rest of the corporation. His point was to consider people as people. This coming year we're going to conduct two-day training for all of our line management, company-wide, not only on the legal side of EEO but on the practical side too. We'll deal with how to get the most out of the population. Actually, we've been a leader in affirmative action because we're a company that has always tried to make the most of people, not because we were out to do good, or even to comply with the law. There was suddenly a new pool of women available, and we were going to make the most of it."

Still another major company offers both "women only" and "men and women" programs. "Some women don't want to go to something remedial," pointed out the affirmative action officer. "Other women say, 'I really need it. If I go to a group where there are men, I won't open my mouth! I want to be in with other women.' "

## APPROPRIATENESS OF TRAINING

The advisability of awareness training depends upon two primary considerations: first, the circumstances at the particular organization; and second, the choice of the trainer and content of his or her courses. If the company is one in which no women have ever been present in the management ranks, training for men and women is likely to be much more useful than in a company where at least some women have reached higher levels. "When we started awareness training, a paternalistic attitude existed toward women in our company," pointed out an official of a petroleum organization. "Our managers knew what women wanted (or so they thought) and what women could or could not do."

If the organization is training minded and routinely makes available instruction on a wide variety of topics, addressing the entrance of women into management will be much more appropriate than in a company where training has never been conducted on any other subject.

"We're not a big training company; we're strictly meat and potatoes," said a key executive at a Midwest-based organization. "We do have an annual two-day EEO seminar, which is legalistic in nature. I don't know if ideally a company *would* have awareness training. We stage several management meetings by grade each year. Topics include how to assess potential, how to develop people, how to give a performance review.

Thanks to our affirmative action program, most of these meetings are well attended by women. So you have men *and* women discussing these topics; not development for women vs. development for men, but managers talking about subordinates.''

If the company is extremely results oriented, and performance in every management slot is measured by objective standards, training is much less likely to be needed than in an organization which rewards seniority and political acumen.

''All of our operating groups are very lean,'' pointed out the vice president of a West Coast organization. ''Most people are making and selling and turning in profits. The tangible is more important than lofty goals, so elaborate staff-type programs are alien to the nature of each of our businesses. We provide a great environment for a woman who's really ready to compete head-on with everyone else. But we aren't set up for someone who needs to be brought up to speed.''

If the organization is sufficiently sophisticated in the human resources area to address routinely the individual needs of its employees in order to optimize their contribution, men who require assistance in relating to women managers and women who need help in moving to or within management can obtain that counsel without class instruction.

Said the head of affirmative action at another West Coast firm, ''We've tried to avoid having any special in-house programs for either women or minorities. We basically have felt that we will take a broad career counseling and career development approach, and that tends to be individually oriented. We have, in an informal sense, encouraged mutual support groups among women and minorities. But we have not developed or presented programs tuned to what might be termed the unique needs of these groups. We do use some special outside programs. For example, we have sent several women to the Simmons College management program for women, which focuses on the special needs of women. Even that is a subject of debate within the company, as to whether they wouldn't be better served going to Stanford. There, many of the attendees are men, and they would be functioning in a real world environment.''

What should sensitivity training for managers include? It should contain: a reaffirmation of the organization's commitment to affirmative action; an examination of societal changes influencing the movement of women into and upward within management; a presentation of scientific findings on sex differences; examination of sex stereotyping regarding women at work; experiential learning via analysis of case studies or role playing; and suggestions on how to interface successfully with women as subordinates, peers, and superiors in management. Sessions should be conducted on an informal and relaxed basis, with differences of opinion aired. Time should be allowed for questions.

Said a senior executive at a major organization, "In our awareness sessions we attempt to get people to reexamine their thinking and ask themselves whether some of the sexual stereotypes to which they have clung for so long are right or wrong. We don't make them take a pledge that they'll change. We just say think about it. And it's voluntary attendance; you don't have to go." He paused and then added, "However, if you worked for me, and you'd been giving me a lot of static about all the women I want to bring into supervisory vacancies, I'd probably pressure you to attend."

A study conducted under an Equal Employment Opportunity Commission contract at ten companies[4] found that a third of the managers perceived women as less decisive than men, less aggressive, less committed to a career, less likely to use independent judgment, less interested in seeking responsibility, and less competitive. Almost a third thought that workers resented or disliked having female supervisors. Almost half thought that women had higher turnover rates and absentee rates than men.

One researcher had 300 male middle managers rate women in general, men in general, or successful middle managers on 92 descriptive terms. There was a significant resemblance between the mean ratings of men and managers, whereas there was no resemblance between women and managers.[5] She later replicated the study, asking 167 female middle managers for the same ratings. The women, too, perceived successful middle managers to have characteristics, attitudes and temperaments more commonly ascribed to men in general than to women in general.[6]

In all likelihood, not many managers will be aware in advance of awareness training that virtually all differences between men and women are caused by societal conditioning, rather than biology. Psychologists Maccoby and Jacklin[7] of Stanford examined 2000 sources on sex differences in intellectual ability, motivation, and social behavior. They concluded that the sexes do not differ in self-esteem, suggestibility, sociability or motivation to achieve, among other considerations. Indeed, just these few areas of real difference exist: men are superior at visual-spatial tasks; women possess higher verbal ability; and men are better at mathematics. However, while these are distinctions between the average male and average female, there is a wide range in each sex with considerable overlap between the two. Hence, it is not possible to predict the behavior of any individual from looking at the averages.

The managers should be urged to regard every woman as an individual, who may or may not reflect the average characteristics of her gender, just as every man is looked upon as a person in his own right. Decisions made on the basis of sex without considering the individual's education, experience, motivation, and personality are likely to be as wrong for women as they would be for men.

The Psychological Service of Pittsburgh[8] recently examined 46 women and 41 male managers from 13 companies, most divided into male/female pairs holding comparable jobs. The participants were scored on 36 items; only 3 distinguished between females and males as groups. The males scored higher on the "masculinity" measure and displayed a greater interest in mechanical things; actually, it was the women who scored higher on the measure of energy, drive, and urge to produce results. These, of course, are the characteristics which typify successful managers.

Concludes the study, "The results should not be taken to imply that there is no need for special efforts to help women succeed in management. Rather, it indicates that by the time a woman becomes successful as a manager, she is likely to resemble the successful male manager in many respects of ability, temperament, values, interests, and background. . . . The women managers resemble male managers more than they resemble other women. Conversely, with some exceptions, the male managers were more like the women managers in their test and questionnaire responses than they were like typical males."

Similar results were recorded by a group of four academicians, who administered a values test to 51 successful women in the Dallas-Fort Worth area. The Allport, Vernon, Lindzey Test was employed, which examines theoretical, economic, aesthetic, social, political and religious values. The researchers found that the 51 women "had a profile which differed markedly from the average female profile. In fact, their profile is much closer to that of the average male." The authors added that their research revealed "that successful women in organizations tend to have profiles similar to not only men in general but successful men in particular." Both the women and their successful male counterparts evidenced high economic and political scores; they were primarily oriented to what was useful and possessed a high power drive.[9]

Confirming that the characteristics of management are not sex-linked are the findings of Morrison and Sebald[10], who compared 29 executive women with comparable nonexecutive women. "The executive group was significantly higher in (a) the self-esteem component of need for achievement, (b) the need for power, and (c) mental ability."

## MYTHS ABOUT WOMEN

Despite such evidence, myths concerning women at work persist. Among those most prevalent are these:

- *Turnover of women is higher.* Women will quit to get married or if they're already married, they'll quit to have a family, the common perception holds. However, those who so contend are guilty of generalization. Attributes such as age and level are more important in determining tenure than is sex. A study of more than 5000 MBAs found the turnover rate to be the same for men and women.[11] Only two organizations with which I talked cited a higher quit rate among women managers, and executives at the organizations attributed the differential to females being recruited more actively by other companies.

- *Absence by women is higher.* Absence is more closely tied to level than to sex. A Public Health Service survey shows that women lose an average of 3.9 days due to injury or illness yearly while men lose 3.1 days.[12]

- *Women are immobile.* A study of women officers showed that only 14 percent were unwilling to move.[13] While most organizations indicated to me that women managers are more likely to be unwilling or unable to relocate geographically, they added that this is true of many men. The characteristic appears to be more influenced by age than sex, with young people being most reluctant due to two-career marriages and greater weight being given to life style vs. career progress. Of course, there is a higher proportion of women managers in the lower age ranges.

- *Women want jobs, not careers.* "When a male and a female are equal in other respects, the fact still remains that a male has a lifetime commitment to a career because of his economic responsibilities," said the president of a major company in a letter to the *Harvard Business Review.*[14]

    In fact, level is more important than sex in determining career orientation. Women in management appear to be driven by the same motivations as men. Recent studies of male and female officers have shown that the females consider challenge, scope of responsibility, opportunity for upward mobility, and compensation package most important, in that order. Their male counterparts cite scope of responsibility, challenge, compensation, and level of reporting relationship.[15] The similarity of results is all the more striking after comparing the two sexes' profiles: the women are less highly educated, have lower prestige positions, and earn considerably less than the men.

Three professors surveyed more than 5800 men and women in the labor force at various job levels, from unskilled to owners and managers, in a single state. The authors concluded that "men and women appear to be satisfied to the same degree with their work, and they tend to be dissatisfied with essentially the same things."[16] Furthermore, other researchers, after questioning a national sample on the importance of five different job attributes, concluded, "It is dangerous to automatically assume a pattern of sex differences in work attitudes. Indeed, the preference ordering of a file clerk may differ from that of an executive, but to assume differences between a male and female executive is unwarranted."[17]

- *Women can't balance work and family demands.* No evidence exists that the quality of life in families where the wife/mother works is lower than in those where the female is a full-time homemaker. Since nearly half of all U.S. wives are employed or seeking work, the presumption must be that they and other family members agree that the pluses outweigh the negatives. A recent Nielsen survey showed that 97 percent of working mothers liked their jobs, even though there were more demands on their time than there were for men who work. Only 15 percent said their husbands help at home, although 23 percent had help from their children.

- *Women are too emotional.* Males and females are both subject to mood changes on hormonal cycles. The differences are that the male cycle length is more variable, and there are external signs of the female cycle.[18]

- *Women can't get along with male or female co-workers.* There are very few differences between the sexes in social relation skills.[19] The relation problem, if one exists, may be due to others' lack of acceptance rather than to the women managers themselves. Generally speaking, both men and women who have worked with women in management are "more likely to be strongly favorable to the idea of women in management than are their colleagues lacking such experience, while those who say their views are based on 'their knowledge of human nature and how people react to management situations'—theory rather than experience—have a greater tendency to be strongly unfavorable in their overall evaluation of women managers."[20]

"Some sociologists hold that when groups of human beings meet, they normally pass through four successive stages of relationship," points out Allport in his classic, *The Nature of Prejudice*. "At first there is *sheer contact,* leading soon to *competition,* which in turn gives way to *accommodation,* and finally to *assimilation . . .* but this progression is far from being a universal law. . . . whether or not the law of peaceful progression will hold seems to depend on the *nature of the contact* that is established."[21] Understandably, most companies make certain that pioneering women are of unquestioned competence and character.

- *Women take jobs away from men.* The implications are that women don't have to work and that they are a detriment to the economy. Yet, two-thirds of all working women are economically independent. The size of our labor force is at an all-time high, with women representing more than four out of ten workers. "Today, the American economy could not possibly stand the withdrawal of any portion of the women from work because so much of the economy is geared to the income level that women make possible," notes Eli Ginzberg.[22]

- *Women have inappropriate education.* If success in management is dependent upon possession of an MBA, there are admittedly far fewer women with this credential. However, the nature of women's education is changing dramatically: in the last ten years the number of MBA degrees granted annually to women has risen tenfold from 630 to 6664.[23]

- *Women are less logical than men.* "I think many men are concerned with the physiological and psychological aspects of women, because this is something not many of us understand," declared a senior vice president of a giant corporation. "Certainly, unpredictability is something that all businesses abhor," he added. "It is difficult enough to make a forecast in today's dynamic environment without complications caused by any irrationality which men may feel women are prone to on occasion."[24]

According to Maccoby and Jacklin,[25] both sexes shift toward higher-level problem solving strategies from childhood to adulthood, but at the same rate and with equal success. No scientific evidence exists to suggest that women are less logical than men. When Samuel Johnson was asked which was more intelligent, man or woman, he responded by saying, "Which man and which woman?"

- *Women lack confidence.* Only at college age are women less confident than men. Sex difference in self-concept does not extend beyond college years.[26] However, many women undoubtedly lack confidence in what they and many men perceive to be the male world of management. One women officer told me the factor which had impeded her career the most was "always having to prove I can do a job before I'm accepted, whereas a man is assumed to be able." Another told me her biggest detriment was "fear of not being competent enough, which is brought about by men not approving of women in business." Such views by women have been all too prevalent. However, times are changing. After examining women at its assessment center, AT&T concluded:

1. Women and male managers do not differ in managerial ability.
2. Women managers, especially those with high potential, are highly career oriented and interested in advancement.
3. Women managers, especially those with high potential, compete well and seldom hesitate to take risks.
4. Women managers are leaders and socially active.
5. Women managers value success, feel they are successful, report past success, and expect to remain successful.

On the job, men often treat women one way and men another without even recognizing this is the case. In 1974 two professors surveyed 1500 subscribers to the *Harvard Business Review.*[27] (Only 5.3 percent of the sample was female.) The questionnaire had two versions, differing only in the sexes of the employees involved in the 11 vignettes which comprised the mailing. The professors found:

- Managers expect male employees to give top priority to their jobs when career demands and family obligations compete. They expect female employees to sacrifice their careers to family responsibilities.
- If personal conduct threatens an employee's job, managers make greater efforts to retain a valuable male employee than the equally qualified female.

- In selection, promotion and career-development decisions, managers are biased in favor of males.

Such a two-version questionnaire could be utilized in awareness training. Role playing has been employed by Quaker Oats Company to good effect. The company developed a skit which is used in equal opportunity workshops for supervisory personnel. The playlet centers on a male job applicant who interfaces with several women executives. They question his marital status, feelings regarding parenthood, and the degree of his career orientation. Yet, as one woman admits to another in his praise, "He's not the run-of-the-mill male candidate." Three thousand copies of the skit, which won enthusiastic reception at the company, have been sent around the world for use in business, education, and government. Copies remain available upon request and without charge.

Another major company in the East employs role playing to heighten insight of managers. In one recent session, a manager pretending to hire another attendee posing as a woman applicant said he would do his best to support the new employee on the job. "But I'm leaving you on your own as far as relations with the others are concerned," he said. "And I can tell you now they're going to resent your being here." After being hooted down by his classmates, the chastened manager explained he didn't realize how the remarks would be taken and felt that such honesty could only be beneficial. The fact that he made the error, and that it was corrected by his peers, undoubtedly had greater impact than if the instruction had been on a purely tutorial basis.

## PROBLEM OF MALE UNEASE

A substantial problem which many organizations fail to recognize is the feeling of unease experienced by men who must learn to develop new types of relationships with women. Males who have known women only as mothers, wives, and secretaries suffer discomfort in interfacing with them as peers, superiors, clients, customers, suppliers, and consultants. Such individuals need help in developing a posture acceptable both to them and to the women with whom they will be associating. Many men have been taught that women are less competent than they, so witnessing women succeeding at their jobs is understandably disturbing. At the same time the men may be overly fearful of the new competition offered by women, since the first females in nontraditional jobs are likely to be superior.

"Men who have worked under a certain set of expectations for say twenty-five years or more now find those expectations changing," noted a female officer at a New York-based organization. "It isn't resistance as much as the fact that they've grown up in a different environment. They are certainly polite; we don't get open hostility. It's just that fifty-five year old men are having more trouble coming to grips with the different image of women than thirty-five year old men who grew up in a different world."

Negative attitudes about women in management are not restricted to men; they are shared by women themselves. The feelings of men toward women as well as the feelings women have about themselves may point to the need for awareness training for women. If staged at all, such training should be offered to all females in the company but presented only to those who elect to participate. Instruction probably will be most helpful to long-service employees, usually in the secretarial or clerical ranks.

"I think I was probably one of the hardest people in the world to persuade of the advisability of awareness training for women," recounted a woman officer in the West. "I couldn't believe that forty-five year old women would *want* to be called girls, or that they'd turn down promotions to avoid making more than their husbands! The differences among women is not an age thing. We have women of sixty who are strong feminists, and others who at twenty-five are still playing Betty Boop."

Certain women will benefit from an examination of the rewards and costs of working in management, a realistic appraisal of the requirements for their promotability, and a review of the support which will be available should they attempt to qualify. They may or may not welcome promotion after this briefing, but in any event, they should be counseled that time will be required to bring about changes.

"Back in the fifties," recalled a senior executive at a New York-based giant, "a number of major organizations initiated what became known as charm schools—training programs for high potential young white males. These schools created unrealistic expectations; the graduates would say, 'I've finished the school; when are you going to make me a general manager?' The same thing can happen with today's programs for women, and it can cause a tremendous amount of resentment, not only among the women who attend a program but among all the others in the company."

An officer of another company, in consumer services, explained that his firm had hired consultants to present a program for women. "They were too theoretical and really not very practical in trying to counsel our employees. The program created the belief that women could move very quickly. And that simply isn't true, if you don't create jobs. Our philosophy has been to put women into positions that have been held by males traditionally, real jobs where there is a basis for measuring performance. It takes time to get them into the system properly.''

In general, women have been reared not to command and make things happen but to submit and let them happen. In all likelihood, the women will be concerned about losing their femininity if they advance, for to this point "man" and "management" have been virtually indistinguishable.

Women considering advancement know they'll face the same responsibilities as male managers in similar positions and need the same knowledge, skills, and attitudes to succeed. But females recognize they'll also have problems peculiar to their holding what have been traditionally "men's jobs." They will be concerned about lack of acceptance by both male and female co-workers, lack of encouragement at home and disapproval of others important to their self-image. In any event, they'll be worried about their ability to handle greater job responsibilities along with family obligations without having one or both suffer. They will probably underestimate their abilities and display a strong fear of failure. This is complicated by their recognition that they will be representing not only themselves in moving to a nontraditional role, but the entire female sex.

Awareness training for women should emphasize the differences between making decisions and following orders. The women should be assured that the choice is theirs, and if they elect not to advance, that development can take place in their present positions. Some organizations were so anxious to identify women for management slots in the early stages of affirmative action that they selected some who were not capable of meeting the challenge. Such mistakes were not only misfortunate for the individuals appointed but for all women then in the organization or destined to join it later.

"We discovered the hard way that you can undermine the confidence of women employees if you emphasize that 'up' is good, and that's all that's good," said an official at a financial services organization. "You can destroy their effectiveness in their present jobs, as well as eliminate any prospect of their advancing, if you in effect say, 'There's something wrong with you if you don't want to be a manager.' Give them a little time and don't push. Help them make their current jobs more rewarding as a starter, to their advantage and that of the organization. If they find their job satisfying, they're going to give it everything they've got. And if they're ready to move up right now, of course do everything possible to help them do just that."

A vice president in Chicago reiterated this point. "My secretary came away from a session she attended with very mixed emotions. The drift of the presentation was, 'Come on girls, let's get some ambition.' She told me, 'I always thought I had a very honorable occupation, and I felt I was making a major contribution. Now I feel guilt that I'm content; it makes me feel that maybe I'm a dummy out of step with the times.'"

International Multifoods developed its own videotape program in which executives gave their views of requirements for success in management. Prospective female managers "quickly learn that many managers got where they are because Multifoods is their top priority," points out Ronald C. Pilenzo, director of compensation and management development. "Sometimes, after listening to how our top managers got there, a person decides that the job she already has is a great job," he adds. "In that case we say, 'Congratulations, you've just learned something about yourself. After all, there are lots of people whose priorities are just not in business.'"[28]

## NEED FOR FOLLOW-UP

The worst thing an organization can do is provide awareness training for women, heighten their expectations, and then not follow up. Females should be assisted in setting realistic goals and accomplishing whatever is necessary to reach those goals. Of course, the same is true for men in the company's employ.

The head of human resources at a major consumer products company explained, "We've had a fairly high level of participation in various external seminar programs especially designed for women. Here at headquarters we've helped women gain some of the management tools they need. We've got a goal assessment program which helps women define what they're interested in and assists them in developing an action plan for growth. We've also got an outside counselor who comes in to consult privately with selected women and helps them work out any problems they have. At a certain point we looked at what we were doing and said, 'Why shouldn't we do this for everybody?' So we've expanded our efforts. Now we have general programs of interest to men *and* women and all races. These are for people who need just a certain kind of help in order to move up."

The head of personnel at a diversified consumer company explained, "We've had career planning seminars, career management seminars, middle management seminars, advanced management seminars—each of these targeted to deal with women at various stages of their careers at this company. They cover: What is a career? How does it differ from a job? Do you want a career? The seminars help our women identify what their strengths are and where their interests lie. The emphasis is on recognizing that women really have different needs and problems in a corporation which is still male-dominated.

He continued, "Over the past year we've had more than 100 women who wanted to attend one or more sessions whom we just couldn't accommodate even though in all we have over 100 different sessions for women every 12 months. Despite the number of training programs we have that relate to all employees, the women feel strongly that there should be separate sessions for them. We continue them because we feel women are correct when they say that they need to be with other females in talking about the elements of corporate life that are different for them."

Confirming this view, a female vice president told me, "My major criticism of women is that they're not risk-takers. They're comfortable. When they are looking at a new opportunity, they look upon it as an end in itself, and whom they're going to report to, even what floor they'll be on. Men think about what they'll learn, what kind of a stepping stone it's going to be, and how quickly they can move on. Women have to change their viewpoint or they're not going to move ahead. And this feeling applies to all ages, not just to older women."

One management consultant advised, "Women don't look at their own behavior and assume responsibility for the situation they may set up. I conducted some workshops for women who were executive assistants being promoted to management at a major company. It became obvious that they were using feminine wiles, being emotional, not thinking clearly, not making decisions, not following through and expected those things to be tolerated because they were women. They were not holding themselves accountable, and this point had to be brought home to them."

Most organizations emphasize that "hiding behind your skirts" or blaming your failure on your sex isn't acceptable. One major New York company has held women's awareness workshops, with separate sessions for lower level employees and for managers and professionals. "We make a point of trying to separate business issues and women's issues," an executive reported. "We wanted to avoid the negative mind-set of their seeing everything as a women's issue, of thinking every adverse happening resulted from being a woman. That was a danger, after we got out on the table what had and hadn't been done for women in years past."

"We've had three-day women's forums, as well as black and Hispanic forums," noted a manager at a major retailing concern. "These were to enable participants to identify their problems as well as their opportunities. What came out of these forums was a realization that many of the problems each of the groups has, the white males also have. A woman might discover, for example, that the boss doesn't talk to her, not because she's female, but because he's not a very good boss. He doesn't communicate with *anybody*. An outgrowth was establishment of informal, ongoing support groups for women who meet regularly to discuss their situations. We're repeating the program whenever we have sufficient new employees to make it worthwhile."

In some cases the organization may decide to stage awareness sessions at which both men and women are present. If this approach is adopted, skillful leaders are needed to avoid the possibility of emotions becoming destructive of mutual understanding. However, the technique is invaluable in demonstrating to men their misconceptions about women and vice versa.

One major consumer products company elected to stage a single attitudinal course at each facility. In one location, following the opening remarks by a representative from headquarters concerning the company's new program to afford improved opportunities for women, the plant manager responded. "You don't have to worry about us," he remarked from the audience. "Our girls are happy where they are." Anything he might have added was drowned out in the chorus of protest which arose from the many women present!

A sizable retailer brings together peer groups of mixed race and sex. A well-known consultant talks about the evolution of antibias legislation and shows several films as springboards to discussion. "A film might depict two job candidates with X credentials, one male and one female. We ask which would you choose," explained an AA officer. "Some heated interchanges take place. Some people will go away and attempt to change their views. Others will just say, 'That's a bunch of stuff.' But that's human nature, and you've got to make the attempt. Because affirmative action isn't just a book you keep numbers in; it's something that requires rational decisions."

A few companies are making available individual counseling to selected women in management and their immediate supervisors, either in addition to or instead of awareness training for large groups. The head of EEO at an Eastern seaboard company said, "Instead of getting everybody together and saying, 'You fellas have problems; you women have problems,' we're going to pick a handful of women who have demonstrated they're promotable and offer them a chance to meet with an outside consultant to discuss their goals, their development efforts. The consultant will also meet with their managers to see that they're attuned to the subordinate's aspirations and needs. After all, there's no point in working with the employee if her manager responds like a — —— rock.''

## CAREFUL SELECTION NEEDED

Even if the company is one where training appears to be the proper course, the result will be negative unless the trainers and subject matter are selected with care. Opportunism exists in attitudinal modification training, just as it does in other areas. Hence, any organization must be cautious in choosing a consultant, should in-house capability be lacking. The leaders must be not only able presenters, but individuals who are knowledgeable concerning the way in which corporations work. In addition they must be aware of the peculiar nature of the company at hand, and any deviations from the general character which exist in different levels, functions, or geographies. The subject matter should be appropriate to the specific needs of each audience.

"We used our own staff to present an awareness program for men," explained the personnel head of a New York-based company. "If we had it to do over, I'd use outside consultants because I think they can be more honest. But it's essential that top management get across, 'We're doing this to help you learn this part of your job just as we help you learn any other.' ''

A major Eastern bank was approached by women consultants who offered awareness training for management. The women were retained and alienated their audiences with a depiction of women as victims of oppression who were thus deserving of advantages. While their services were canceled after four sessions to different segments of the executive roster, the resistance to affirmative action throughout the entire institution had already stiffened appreciably. "It took the organization several years to recover fully from that experience," admits the affirmative action officer. "We haven't had any awareness sessions since then, and we have been very, very careful only to place women in positions for which they are qualified and never to give them special privileges."

A similar problem developed for a capital goods company which retained a woman consultant to interview women employees concerning their views and to formulate a report of the findings to management. "She let her zeal get the better of her. Her report was so strident that she failed to make any of her points," recounts the human resources vice president. "And if you can't get management to buy, it doesn't matter how true your facts are."

The right consultant may fail with the wrong audience. One company assumed that every female in the organization would be receptive to the presentation of two well-known female consultants who counsel women on the weaknesses which retard their progress in management. "The program had barely begun," recalls a personnel executive at the company, "when a woman several years out of business school came storming from the meeting room. 'Why in the world did you put *me* in there?' she asked. Of course, she was right. It just didn't apply to her."

The best way to identify a consultant is first to pinpoint the problem. Is training needed for management, for women, or for both? Is the training to be confined to certain levels or locations, or to be offered as broadly as possible? Having identified what is required, the organization should seek out recommendations from other companies which have undertaken programming. However, it's necessary to ascertain whether the climate in those other companies is similar. "I'd be very reluctant to recommend our consultants," points out the head of affirmative action in a major industrial company. "Sure, they were successful here, but how do I know the conditions would be the same elsewhere? I've talked with other clients of theirs who think they did a terrible job or who liked what they did in one department but not in another."

This sense of caution is well founded, as the experience of one of the country's largest financial services organizations attests. "We brought in top-drawer women consultants," explained a senior official. "We reviewed their format and tried to make some changes. But their attitude was, 'This is what you need whether you know it or not.' Well, our men who heard their presentation got mad; our women got mad also. The presentation just wasn't right for us. The next time we picked, we looked at half a dozen different consultants. We had had this bad experience, and frankly we chose our present consultants because we didn't think they would do any harm. And that's how it's worked out. In fact they've done a lot to increase the confidence of women without alienating the men."

As in the choice of an affirmative action head, it is far more important to employ a consultant who understands what is needed and is capable of implementing it than simply to find a woman. However, under otherwise equal circumstances, a female probably could gain greater credibility with both sexes in the awareness training area.

"As it happens, our consultant is a woman," advised the head of EEO at a New York company. "But that's not why I picked her. I interviewed a considerable number. I wanted somebody who had seen the inside of a big corporation before and not just somebody who'd worked at the EEOC for a year and a half. After all, we know more about the law than most of the government people we deal with. It costs us money if we don't! What we don't know is how to go beyond the legal requirements. I wanted somebody with common sense who could understand our problem and with whom we could maintain a good working relationship."

Some companies feel it's a plus to provide women with off-premises awareness training. In this way, male co-workers will not as easily gain the impression that the women are deficient in needed skills. One of the most ambitious awareness training efforts for women is the three-day residential seminar sponsored by the University of Minnesota College of Business Administration's Continuing Education Department. Focus is on development of the attendee's self-concept and managerial skills, in an effort to demonstrate that womanhood and achievement are not incompatible. Each woman has the opportunity to assert her leadership behavior and to work as a team member in solving business problems. Since many of the women are without female colleagues at work, their interaction with other women managers at the seminar lends assurance that their problems are not unique.

Other programs, shorter in duration but with the same objectives, are offered by many colleges and universities around the country. The American Management Associations offer three-day courses for executive secretaries and administrative assistants at cities around the United States and Canada. Subjects covered include time management, communications skills, and working with others as a team.

"Summing up, I'd say the report card is mixed on awareness training," declared a key executive at one of the country's largest employers. "Certainly the decision on whether to utilize this particular device requires a thorough front-end analysis. What is the company's problem? What is the environment like? Are there skill or knowledge deficiencies? I'm very skeptical of 'All women take this' or 'All bosses of women take that.' A company must get into awareness training carefully. Management must have expert help and not expect quick results. And they can forget trying to justify it on a cost/benefit basis. But then, in training and development, they really should be doing many things they can't be absolutely sure of."

He continued, "Unfortunately, awareness training is built on a median mind-set. Ideally, organizations should be counseling individuals or at the most pairs of people, but many companies can't afford to do that. If awareness training is badly done, it can do more harm than good. If you use a consultant, give informed consent. Know what's going to be done, and be sure you're able to handle the consequences.''

Said the vice president at another company, "Be selective. Don't do too many programs at once. Subjects can be muddled if too many are handled, and time away from the job is too valuable to waste. Select for participation people who can carry information back to their jobs and put it to work. You need credibility, and you need visibility. So present the right programs to the right people, if you do it at all.''

## REFERENCES

1. Hennig, Margaret and Anne Jardim, *The Managerial Woman*, Garden City, NY: Anchor Press/Doubleday, 1977, p. 58.
2. "Women's Earnings: Recent Trends and Long-Run Prospects," *Monthly Labor Review*, U.S. Dept. of Labor, 97(5):23 (May 1974).
3. Neal, Patricia, "Special Women," a letter to the *Wall Street Journal*, 17 April 1978.
4. Lyle, Jerolyn R., *Affirmative Action Programs for Women: A Survey of Innovative Programs*, Report submitted to the Office of Research, Equal Employment Opportunity Commission, under Contract 71-45, 1973.
5. Schein, Virginia Ellen, "The Relationship Between Sex Role Stereotypes and Requisite Management Characteristics," *Journal of Applied Psychology* 57(2):98 (1973).
6. Schein, Virginia Ellen, "Relationships Between Sex Role Stereotypes and Requisite Management Characteristics Among Female Managers," *Journal of Applied Psychology* 60(3):343 (1975).
7. Maccoby, Eleanor Emmons and Carol Nagy Jacklin, *The Psychology of Sex Differences*, Stanford, CA: Stanford University Press, 1974, p. 370.
8. Fitzpatrick, Robert and Mary E. Cole, *Some Characteristics of Female and Male Managers*, Pittsburgh, PA: Psychological Service of Pittsburgh, 1977, p. 30.
9. Hodgetts, Richard M. et al., " A Profile of the Successful Female," *Academy of Management Proceedings*, 38th annual meeting, San Francisco, August 1978, p. 373.
10. Morrison, R. F. and M. Sebald, "Personal Characteristics Differentiating Female Executive from Female Nonexecutive Personnel," *Journal of Applied Psychology* 59(5):658 (1974).
11. De Pasquale, John A. and Richard A. Lange, "Job-hopping and the MBA," *Harvard Business Review* 49(6):151 (November–December, 1971).
12. U.S. Dept. of Health, Education and Welfare, Public Health Service, *Vital and Health Statistics, Current Estimates from the Health Interview Survey*, 1977.
13. Heidrick and Struggles, Inc., *Profile of a Woman Officer*, Chicago, 1979, p. 4.
14. Van Gorkom, J. W., "Letters to the Editor," *Harvard Business Review* 52(3):148 (May–June 1974).
15. Heidrick and Struggles, Inc., *Profile of a Woman Officer*, Chicago, 1978, p. 2.
16. Keaveny, Timothy J., John H. Jackson, and John A. Fossum, "Are There Sex Differences in Job Satisfaction?" *Personnel Administrator* No. 23, p. 58 (March 1978).
17. Brief, Arthur P., Gerald L. Rose, and Ramon J. Aldag, "Sex Differences in Preferences for Job Attributes Revisited," *Journal of Applied Psychology*, 62:646 (1977).

18. Jacklin, Carol N. and Eleanor E. Maccoby, "Sex Differences and Their Implications for Management," *Bringing Women Into Management,* Francine E. Gordon and Myra H. Strober, eds., New York: McGraw-Hill, 1975, p. 35.
19. Ibid., p. 31.
20. Bowman, G. W., N. B. Worthy, and S. A. Greyser, "Are Women Executives People?" *Harvard Business Review* 43(4):166 (July–August 1965).
21. Allport, Gordon W., *The Nature of Prejudice,* Garden City, NY: Doubleday/Anchor, 1958, pp. 250–1.
22. Briggs, Jean A., "How You Going to Get 'em Back in the Kitchen? (You Aren't.)," *Forbes,* 15 November 1977, p. 183.
23. Telephone Conversation with Dr. Vance Grant, U.S. National Center for Education Statistics, Dept. of Health, Education and Welfare, 13 February 1979.
24. "Letters to the Editor," *Harvard Business Review* 52(3):149 (May–June 1974).
25. Maccoby, Eleanor Emmons and Carol Nagy Jacklin, *The Psychology of Sex Differences,* Stanford CA: Stanford University Press, 1974, p. 108.
26. Ibid., p. 162.
27. Rosen, Benson and Thomas H. Jerdee, "Sex Stereotyping in the Executive Suite," *Harvard Business Review* 52(2):47 (March–April 1974).
28. Bree, Marlin, "Women Welcome," *Corporate Report* 9(11):20 (November 1978).

# 4

# *Where to Position Women Executives*

"Where should women be positioned in the corporate structure? Why, anywhere," declared a senior officer of one of the nation's largest companies. "Anybody still thinking in terms of 'men's jobs' and 'women's jobs' is seriously out of date." There are others who hold a different view. "A woman's intuition marks a very distinct difference between men and women," a consultant in New York told me. "How can a woman find the type of work where she'll benefit from this? What are those women's jobs that men have had for many years? Women recruiters like yourself have a capacity to recognize women's jobs now occupied by men better than men do. Don't you think you know better than men how to recruit women? What jobs women can do better than men?"

It's not too surprising, in light of our highly segregated labor market, that some individuals considering how to open up more opportunities for women feel that the answer lies in identifying those "women's jobs" which up to this point have been mistakenly labeled "men's." They see nothing wrong with designating certain jobs as off limits to one sex or the other, provided sufficient consideration is exercised in making the judgments.

One of the most highly placed women in American business told me that the single greatest impediment to her career had been "society's concept of what is appropriate for a woman to do." Being such an unusual individual, she was able to overcome all obstacles. But countless thousands have tried and failed, or never even tried.

## HOW TO ELIMINATE "WOMEN'S JOBS"

To make optimal use of talent, any organization should place both men and women in those positions for which their individual abilities and interests best qualify them. Indeed, the law calls for virtually every job to be made available to both sexes.

Former "women's jobs" should be occupied by men, just as previous "men's jobs" should be held by women. Male file clerks and secretaries can contribute to the organization's acceptance of women in management roles, as can female truck drivers and mechanics. Men and women in similar positions should be given comparable responsibility and authority. Their performances should be judged by the same standards, and recognition and reward for both should be appropriate to their contribution. To think differently is to fall victim to sexual stereotyping.

"You know, it isn't just women who suffer from sex stereotyping," a bank officer told me. "We have male secretaries, and we're trying to get more. But there was terrible resistance at first on the part of male managers. They thought any man who'd do secretarial work was gay and would chase them around the desk all day! But now we have guys saying, 'He's the best secretary I've ever had. We need more in the bank!' And currently the complaints are coming from the female secretaries, who feel their turf is being encroached upon."

The story of what one organization has accomplished in putting women into a variety of jobs is spelled out in *Getting the Job Done: Women at ARCO* which portrays in pictures and text the wide variety of occupations in which Atlantic Richfield's women employees can be found. Those featured include a "roustabout" at Prudhoe Bay, Alaska; a refinery craftsman in North Carolina; a research chemist in Pennsylvania; a geophysicist in Houston; and the company's investment officer at corporate headquarters who has since been promoted to treasurer.

Yet, women comprise 79 percent of ARCO's clericals and only slightly more than 3 percent of officers and managers. "Most of our minority employees and women are bunched in the lower-level job categories," points out President Thornton Bradshaw. "And until we are able to have them move up and assume a proportionate place within each category, then we haven't achieved our goals." But the progress from just a few years ago, when virtually all women were confined to secretarial work, is striking.

## PROCEDURES TO FOLLOW

Companies cannot be successful at moving women into non-traditional jobs unless their personnel practices are helpful, rather than a hindrance. An organization in the East which asked consultants to survey its female population discovered that:

- Women felt they didn't know enough about the company, including what it did and how it operated. Some believed that this was the result of a deliberate policy on the part of management.
- Many of the women were unaware of the function of the personnel offices and the employee relations managers. They said they weren't aware of job openings or other opportunities available to them.
- They recognized that some white male managers felt uncomfortable with women and evidenced attitudes that were interpreted as sexist by the surveyed group. A number of women as a result felt isolated, frustrated, and unable to communicate with their supervisors.
- The women expressed concern about their growth at a company which appeared unconcerned about helping females, other than the politically astute or superstars.

Responding to these perceptions, management:

- Instituted awareness training for managers and supervisors.
- Reorganized and restaffed employee relations.
- Developed an employee sourcebook to communicate corporate systems, policies, resources, and procedures.
- Restructured educational and training programs and educational assistance programs.
- Initiated a formalized system for placement, promotion, and transfer, along with a career reference and counseling center. The system is linked with exempt internal placement procedures and the college recruiting system to provide a means by which nonexempt employees can enter exempt ranks.

To make certain that both men and women are properly positioned and appropriately rewarded, management of any organization must concern itself with the following areas:

*Job analysis.* The content of any job should be examined so that skills and personal characteristics needed for success can be pinpointed. Research has demonstrated that when job requirements are ambiguous, decision-makers fall back on sex-role stereotyping to evaluate males and females. However, they rely more on actual job requirements when these are clearly defined.[1] Specifications should be reviewed for unintended bias such as nonessential qualifications which would eliminate or disadvantage women. "MBA required" or "MBA preferred" has such an effect and should not be used unless it is possible to demonstrate the impact of this degree on effectiveness in the position.

The Supreme Court, in *Griggs vs. Duke Power Company,* held that women cannot be excluded from employment simply because they fail to meet selection criteria that are unrelated to job performance. The burden of proof is on the employer if his hiring and promotion practices exclude a disproportionate number of women. Yet management jobs are still held so overwhelmingly by males that both men and women tend to think that such jobs require "male" characteristics. Under this mind-set women would be disqualified, regardless of abilities, solely on the basis of their sex.

"It's very easy to fall into the 'qualified' trap," pointed out a personnel officer of a New York-based services organization. "We have to ask line management, 'What specifically are you looking for in an individual? Why does this man have it, and why does this woman not have it?' Such a conversation can border on the absurd. The manager will say, 'I don't know; it's just something about him.' And I'll respond, 'Can't you be a little more specific? Are you sure it isn't the three-piece vested suit?' By injecting a little humor maybe I can get that manager to recognize what he's doing."

Some companies have restructured jobs so that the abilities of the female talent pool inside and outside the company can be tapped more easily. On occasion this strategy has proven highly beneficial both to the organization and the individuals affected. However, one example that apparently does little more than help the employer "make the numbers" is naming a woman corporate secretary or assistant secretary. Until very recently the secretary post was held by an attorney who had other responsibilities as well. Now, many companies have separated this position and named a woman employee, usually a long-service clerical, to the job. Indeed, while the number of women corporate officers at major companies is increasing, and the variety of titles is growing, the preponderance remain corporate secretaries or assistant secretaries.[2]

*Job evaluation.* To avoid charges under antidiscrimination law, jobs should be evaluated to determine their value to the organization, using either a point system or factor analysis. In either case skill, effort, responsibility, and working conditions should be taken into account. Job evaluation rates the position, not the person or persons filling the post, and is designed to eliminate or to prevent inequalities between jobs that are substantially the same.

"We have gone through a total re-evaluation of every exempt job in the company over the last 18 months," reported a vice president at a

New York-headquartered firm. "We're installing the Hay system which analyzes and evaluates jobs on three factors: know-how, problem solving, and accountability. "Our descriptions on exempt positions deal with the level of know-how required to do the job; how it was obtained isn't considered. On some jobs an MD or JD is called for, but otherwise no college degrees are mentioned. Skills are what we're focusing on, not race or sex or even education. We've just finished writing such descriptions for 2000 jobs, a massive effort. We're saying to employees and prospective employees, 'We don't care who you are or where you came from or how you got your skill. We just want to know if you can do the job.' Next month we're starting on nonexempt jobs; and when we complete that, we believe we'll be 100 percent EEO-proof."

Recently the Equal Employment Opportunity Commission (EEOC) has raised the concept of equal pay for work of equal value. Since the median pay of full-time women workers is substantially below that of men, one way of eliminating the differential over time is to allow women to move into managerial jobs as their talents and motivation allow. This is the approach now being utilized by business. However, the EEOC's alternative would reappraise the worth of work now being performed by men and women.

Opponents of the EEOC proposal insist that attempting to counter the laws of supply and demand is ridiculous. They contend that the fault of the present system lies not with the remuneration established for various positions, but in barriers to placement based on irrelevant considerations such as sex. The EEOC, however, holds that current job-evaluation systems discriminate against "women's jobs." The agency has enlisted the aid of the National Academy of Sciences to determine whether a job-evaluation system could and should be developed that is "fair, objective, comprehensive, and bias-free." The NAS report is due at 1979 year-end.

The presumption therefore exists that any company with a marked difference between wages of men and women employees would be forced to change its job-evaluation procedures and increase the pay of its women. This possibility may encourage organizations to speed the movement of women into management.

*Job posting.* As many jobs as possible should be posted to permit self-nomination by interested individuals who otherwise might be excluded from consideration. This removes dependence upon personal knowledge, the immediate supervisor, or the grapevine as a source of information on availabilities.

At a New York-headquartered firm the vice president-human resources recalled that there had been no executive job posting until the early seventies. "Actually, it was our women's advisory council which led us to post levels 1 through 10. That's the bulk of our executives. This past January we went a step further. We agreed, once again at the instigation of the Council, to post levels 11, 12, and 13 as well. All of these jobs have to be posted for two weeks before they can be filled. That gives employees—both men and women—a chance to make their qualifications known to the hiring executive. That's a perfect example of something the women have initiated which has benefited all the people in the company."

Job posting discourages the advancement of favorites and allows employees to assume more responsibility for their own progress. Thus, the plan serves to heighten morale.

*Recruiting sources.* In addition to looking within, organizations should tap the proper external sources to increase the number of qualified women among prospects to be considered. Personnel specialists can be of great help to hiring managers in this regard. "I know of every management vacancy throughout the company," explained a staff member in corporate personnel at a major transportation company. "As soon as I see an opening in a job group where the representation of women is low, I point this fact out as well as making some referrals."

*Evaluation of prospects.* Companies screen individuals either by establishing definite pass/fail standards or by ranking members of the prospect pool on a comparative basis, eliminating all but a certain percentage who appear to be most appropriate. Either approach can discriminate illegally against women if not restricted to job-related characteristics. Now, many organizations include women among those performing the screening duties.

As one personnel executive pointed out to me, "Objective selection procedures have never been a problem for women; exclusion from consideration has been." Managerial jobs described as demanding and challenging as opposed to routine administrative positions are perceived to be less appropriate for females than for males.[3]

## SCREENING WOMEN FOR MANAGEMENT POSITIONS

A number of companies admitted to me that they seek wonder women in identifying candidates for pioneering roles. "After all, those women aren't representing themselves alone," explained one personnel vice president. "Their performance spells success or failure for the entire program. What's more, the hiring manager is taking a bigger risk with an untested commodity. He's really sticking his own neck out when he selects a woman."

Perhaps for these reasons, several individuals indicated to me that the quality of the average woman in management today is higher than that of the average man. "But there should be failures among women too," said an EEO officer at a retailing organization. "And that shouldn't retard advancement of females. After all, we didn't stop hiring or promoting white males because one or two of them failed somewhere along the line."

A variety of means is typically employed by companies to screen prospects. Generally, interviewing is used either alone or in combination with other procedures. Those conducting the interviews should not only be knowledgeable concerning antidiscrimination law, but should have received training to become effective at the interviewing process. A bias-free interviewer is not necessarily a good interviewer. Some companies use testing; if so, the law requires that tests be validated to demonstrate that they are predictors of success at the job at hand.

One major company has a history of testing that goes back more than four decades. In the early seventies the test was desexed. The business situations used to evaluate judgment were changed to include references to women as well as men. And questions were altered to take into account the different experiences of women. To determine leadership the company uses questions such as, "When growing up, I had ambitions to be. . . ." The multiple choices were expanded; as one example, "nurse" as well as "doctor" was included among career options.

"We're looking for the same characteristics in both men and women, although they may have been expressed in different ways," explained the staffer in charge of the program. He noted that the test has proven to be as good a predictor of success for females as for males, "and indeed, reveals leadership regardless of sex, race, or socioeconomic class."

The Office of Federal Contract Compliance holds that affirmative action does not require a lowering of job standards. Some companies believe this is possible, while others know from experience that it is. But there are those organizations which regard bringing increasing numbers of "less qualified" individuals into executive positions as an unfortunate, but necessary, cost of doing business with the government.[4] However, none of the companies with which I spoke felt their standards had been lowered in the hiring and promotion of women managers and professionals.

"We've never settled for less in hiring women or put them into jobs tailored for them and given them a new title," emphasized a vice president at one of the nation's most dynamic companies. "We don't have time to play games. We're very tightly run, and there's just no room for excess baggage.'' Confirming this view, an officer of a diversified New York-based concern said ''We haven't operated from the premise that we were going to make it easy or difficult for women. We've said, 'We'll give you the opportunity in part because you're a woman, but once you take the offer, you're going to have to make it.' ''

And women should be able to make it, as well as men. Research has shown repeatedly that individuals with a strong motivation to manage tend to move up faster and are more likely to perform effectively in managerial positions. One academician hypothesized that female managers tended to have a lower level of motivation to manage than male managers. However, he tested males and females at a major automobile manufacturing company and found no differences between white males and females.[5]

*Training.* The individual selected for the job should be given not only the usual orientation training but also any job-related training necessary to achieve a certain level of proficiency within a set time frame. Whatever gaps exist in the individual's skills should be addressed.

If training is to be left to the supervisor of the new or newly promoted employee, that manager must be aware of his responsibilities in this area, competent to carry them out and motivated to do so. If training is to be handled in a more formal manner, then women and men in similar positions must be offered the same opportunities.

*Placement.* The selected individual should be positioned in the organization where his or her abilities and interests enhance prospects for success. The immediate supervisor should also be motivated to abet that outcome. Whether he or she is a supporter of the concept of sex-neutral jobs, the supervisor is likely to furnish the desired cooperation as a matter of self-interest, providing rewards are structured properly.

''Our company is full of pragmatists,'' said an executive in a petroleum company. ''When managers see the handwriting on the wall and know their next job might depend on their record in EEO, they'll do it whether they believe in it or not. So we don't have to worry about 'supportive superiors'; the good game players will produce good results.''

Everything possible should be done to foster a woman's inclusion in the informal network of the organization, although ultimately only her competence, confidence, and recognition of its importance can gain her a proper place in the political structure. It will always be more difficult for her, but with considerable effort, she can forge the necessary alliances.

While there are many more women in the lower echelon of management today than was true even a few years ago, the number at the middle and upper echelons remains small. Indeed, Bureau of the Census statistics show that in 1977 only 1 percent of women officials and managers earned $25,000 or more. A story in a major magazine in 1978 regarding the nation's ten most highly placed women included only three who were not related to male executives in the same firms by either blood or marriage.[6]

"The characteristic feature of the country's female labor force has been and continues to be severe occupational segregation," The Conference Board found. "Unlike the men, most women workers are crowded into a relatively narrow range of lower paying, less desirable occupations. They are also heavily concentrated within certain industries that rely heavily on these occupations."[7] Despite the large number of women workers—42 million—three-fourths remain in five female occupations: secretary-stenographer, household worker, bookkeeper, elementary teacher, and waitress. There are, of course, a number of factors contributing to the paucity of women in management.

One reason is that women in engineering have been rare until the last several years. Even now, the number of women engineers is small; only 4631 women won engineering degrees in 1978, the latest year reported, and the Society of Women Engineers boasts only 2500 professional members nationwide. Yet, a number of the nation's largest companies hire very few nonengineers into the management ranks, and such individuals have little hope of advancing in the mainstream of the business.

Another factor is that in virtually all organizations women have been slotted into nonsupervisory, professional roles rather than into management positions which lead to the apex of the corporate pyramid. This has seemed more in keeping with "female" attributes of kindness, consideration, and helpfulness. How many women, after all, have *wanted* to be toughminded? At the lower executive level " . . . two entirely different progression paths begin," notes The Conference Board. "One is a technical/professional path that is likely to go up only to the lower middle-management level of the organization. The other is a more general managerial path leading all the way up to the top management level."[8]

Probably part of the reluctance to put women into the track to the top has been concern over investing in the training of individuals who might leave the work force for motherhood or who were perceived as being geographically immobile. Organizations have also known that nobody—not men, not women—wanted to be supervised by a woman. And women themselves have known that a position of leadership over men and women, or even women alone, was not in keeping with the accepted role of woman as supporter and nurturer.

"We have a woman in our treasurer's function who's very bright, very capable, and doing a good job," reported the vice president of a fast-growing technical company. "That's a specialized area that will dead-end her. She's not learning the money-making side of the business, but that's where she wants to be, even though we've offered her better opportunities."

Subordinates are likely to respond to a woman as an individual sometimes, but as much or more to the stereotype of a woman. While some subordinate dissatisfaction has developed from the apparent sexual incongruity of woman as manager, some also undoubtedly derives from the perception that women are lower in status within the organization and therefore less able to exert influence in behalf of those reporting to them.

A few years ago an electronics company named a woman to succeed the male vice president of purchasing, who had been promoted. Her title became director of materials. Shortly after, a number of her subordinates requested transfers. The consultant who was called in by an anxious management to deal with the problem discovered that the director of materials was both liked and respected. However, the employees had received a clear signal from management that the job and the department had been downgraded. Said one of the staff to the consultant, "We've all been moved down one slot, and that's where we'll stay."[9] Fortunately, most organizations are more sensitive than this and do not reinforce stereotypical thinking regarding the powerlessness and lack of prestige of female executives.

Another possible reason for the lower popularity of women supervisors was revealed by the author of a study of corporate affirmative action programs. He interviewed managers and clericals at various companies and declared, "The average female manager reports that she handles men no differently from women. In fact, the women clericals who stated that they preferred male bosses explained their preference by pointing out that male bosses expect *less* of them than women bosses do. This set of responses was reinforced by interviews with male managers who typically state that as bosses they handle women differently from men. Most male managers found that they *expected* women to be more emotional than men with respect to task-oriented demands at work, to take criticism more personally, and to sow seeds of intraoffice discord more frequently than men. Yet, they also did *not* find that these expectations were realized."[10]

A *Harvard Business Review* survey[11] showed that 61 percent of 1000 male and 47 percent of 900 women executives questioned in 1965 believed that the business community would never wholly accept women executives, and about a third of the men and women saw no opportunity for women in terms of top management. Acceptance of women in management has progressed considerably since then. Yet, in 1979, women officers at leading companies ranked business corporations last when asked the segment of our society affording women the greatest opportunity for advancement regardless of sex. The creative and performing arts were most frequently mentioned by the women, followed by health, education and social services and then federal, state and local government.[12]

Even today, a man's success as a leader is often ascribed to ability, while a woman's is attributed to extra effort, luck, or the fact that she is "exceptional." Indeed, a woman is fortunate to even gain acknowledgment as a leader. Two social scientists pointed out that "both men and women are socialized to accept a strongly held stereotype of women as possessing legitimate authority only to nurture. Therefore a woman is likely to have difficulty exercising authority in those areas which are seen as inappropriate to her sex role."[13]

Yet, as one personnel executive emphasized to me, "Men and women line managers will be needed to get the work of equal treatment done. The tendency to promote women into staff and specialty positions rather than true management jobs must be guarded against and prevented." He added that company surveys had demonstrated that there was no "problem" with male managers reporting to females. "If there's something wrong," he noted, "it has to do with some other facet of the superior/subordinate relationship. The data from research we've done, and the experience we've had as a company with women managers have helped immensely our organizational climate. There's been a general improvement in terms of equitable treatment for women and recognition of ability and performance regardless of sex."

"The women aren't in a position to be promoted to decision-making spots yet," declared the EEO officer of a heavy manufacturing company. "No woman has ever faced the problem of #3 machine being down and 1600 people being out of work and $5 million worth of orders not being filled because the machine's got to be fixed. You can't expect the manufacturing manager to put somebody from market research in as his deputy, and as a result, women tend to end up in three or four kinds of jobs."

A vice president-human resources at another company emphasized,

"When you give a profit center job to someone, you're really putting yourself on the line. Because women haven't been around long enough and therefore don't have close relationships with men, women tend not to get those jobs. But we're beginning to see some change. There's a woman VP-sales in one of our businesses now, and that's a key line responsibility. The man who named her knew that she'd sold and knew what it was like. He trusts her. And we'll be seeing more of that."

The higher ranking the position, the more important becomes "chemistry" in the selection and appraisal process or a judgment as to whether an individual's personal qualities jibe with the preferences of key associates. As a consequence, women have been underrepresented at the higher levels of organizational hierarchies even within those industries which are female intensive. The American Bankers Association, for example, reports that women make up 62 percent of the work force in the top 49 banks but hold only 26 percent of the managerial slots. Undoubtedly, since the greatest progress has been made in the largest organizations, these figures are more favorable than those representing that industry as a whole.

Further, Harvard professor Neil Churchill has emphasized that "many people are likely to become very frustrated and disappointed because they have unrealistic expectations about how far most major American corporations—and other kinds of major U.S. employers too—are going to be able to move toward EEO parity at higher job levels in the next ten to fifteen years." As substantiation, he utilizes a human resource flow analysis of a hypothetical company which requires more than 30 years before women constitute close to half the top management group. "The low attrition rate in the predominantly male middle- and top-management ranks exerts an enormous effect. . . . Unless a corporation is growing very rapidly or is experiencing very high top-level turnover, it has limited opportunities to effectuate change in the composition of its top management group."[14]

"Our effort has really been in two phases," explained an executive in a major retailing concern. "First was start-up, where the emphasis was on numbers. We were successful there; we're now more than half female. Now we're in the second phase which asks: Where are the women? Are they in decision-making positions? What is their earning capability? This is going to be a much more difficult task, and will cover a much longer time frame."

Certainly, women will never get to the top unless they are placed in positions which lead there and then are developed so they can vie on an equitable basis with male contenders.

## STEPS TO ASSURE A WOMAN'S SUCCESSFUL INTEGRATION

There are a number of steps an organization can take to help assure the successful integration of a woman in the management ranks. First, the organization should have determined, on the basis not only of her experience but her personal qualities, that the woman is a fit for the position for which she is being considered. Too often, in their eagerness to name a female to a particular post, companies pay little or no attention to whether the individual possesses appropriate attributes other than her sex.

"We have a young woman doing pricing work in one of our divisions who has said she'd like to go into manufacturing management," noted the vice president-human resources of a technical company in the Midwest. "It's very questionable as to whether her personality would lead to success in that area; it's hard to prejudge. If she were a man, you'd say no. But since it's a woman, you find yourself saying, 'Well, *maybe* it would work.' "

Several years ago I met, at her request, a woman from the academic world who was anxious to enter business. She assured me that she intended to take full advantage of her gender and would not object in the least to a token position. Despite her impressive educational credentials, I felt she could be described best as "flighty" and not a suitable candidate for any of our firm's assignments. Nevertheless, within a matter of months I read, to my surprise, a newspaper announcement of her appointment to a newly created position within one of the Fortune 500 companies. I was not so startled less than a year later when I learned that the position had been eliminated, and she was no longer with the organization.

To succeed in even the most meaningless job, a woman must be able to gain the respect—or at least the acceptance—of her co-workers. As sociologist Cynthia Fuchs Epstein points out,[15] it is helpful and possibly more crucial for a woman than a man to share statuses other than sex with her colleagues and clients. Whatever characterizes the group—race, religion, socioeconomic background, quality of education, rank of residential community—should also be true of the woman.

However, beyond this, the woman must match the requirements of the particular job. If a high degree of intelligence is needed, she should possess it. If a commitment of 60 hours weekly is demanded to get the job done, she should be willing and able to devote that much time. If the position calls for the ability to juggle many balls simultaneously or to appear to be nonthreatening, then these factors should be taken into account. Applying different criteria to the selection of women does not help solve the problem of a sex-segregated work force; such distinctions perpetuate it.

Usually, it is those companies which remain skeptical that women are ever as qualified as men which pay the least attention to this matching process. But even if an able woman is chosen, she cannot succeed unless she is allowed to do so. If management is convinced in advance that she will fail, the outcome will be determined by the expectation. Then the fact of the failure serves in the minds of management as substantiation that women simply aren't suited for executive jobs!

Second, besides the woman being a fit for the job, she should be placed in a substantive position with definite and meaningful responsibilities, and not a post that has been created for the occasion. The job should be sufficiently difficult for her to be challenged. As has been pointed out, an easy assignment "may eliminate the possibility of failure, but it also prevents the employee from achieving psychological success, the exhilarating sense of accomplishment that results only from achieving a task that entailed a reasonable probability of failure."[16] To do otherwise is to perform a disservice not only to that woman, but to all women and to the organization itself.

"Yes, we created some jobs," admitted an executive at a Midwest-based manufacturing company. "The divisions that did this got serious a little late about moving women into management. Typically the job would be something like a business planning manager. Because of the quality of the people we brought in, they saw that they were wasting their time and ours; the position really had no definite set of responsibilities. So they were quickly pulled into the next position vacancy that occurred. This had given the divisions maybe five or six months to assess the person and figure out the best fit. But we're a big company with a lot of opportunities, and we never should have done that. In a couple of cases, we lost people who took a tremendous cut in salary to get out. But job content meant more to them than money, and I'd have to say hats off to them."

So the woman should be a fit for a substantive position. Third, the standards by which the incumbent in the position is judged should be clearly defined and readily measurable, so ability can be demonstrated and recognized. "There is growing evidence that discrimination against females is most likely to occur in the absence of objective performance data or indications of competent performance," an academician pointed out.[17]

Fourth, before the selected individual has been extended an offer, she should be advised of the pluses and minuses of the situation for which she is being considered. She should have a full understanding of the amount of risk that she and the organization are assuming.

Fifth, the company should commit itself to providing the support that the woman will need if she is to succeed. This assistance might range from reviewing the treatment accorded her by her immediate superior in order to assure that it is free of bias in either direction, to making certain that sex-neutral language is used in corporate communications. No woman manager appreciates receiving an announcement of a social event urging that "you and your wife" attend!

"Especially in our early placements of women in management slots, we looked for a supportive environment," an officer of a West Coast company said. "We were not interested in setting a woman up for failure; we wanted to avoid positioning her where she'd have a better than even chance of defeat. We wanted to put her where there was a strong likelihood her capabilities would be allowed to develop. I think there's merit in that approach, for it helps to create a climate of receptivity elsewhere in the organization."

"Will I be the only one?" is a question management may hear from a female candidate for a "man's" job. Very few individuals relish being pioneers. If a woman is destined to be the first and only female to assume the post for which she is being considered, management should contemplate placing others in similar spots as quickly as possible so that none needs to suffer the burden of isolation. Males not appreciating the importance of this consideration might do well to envision themselves as the sole man in an organization of women.

"If you're going to socialize a group, it's better to do it with a greater number of people," commented a personnel executive with an Eastern seaboard company. "The most effective way to help women succeed in management is to turn the spotlight off. After all it's easy to say about one, 'Oh well, she's exceptional.' And if you bring the next 12 in one or two at a time, maybe they're all going to seem exceptional!"

However, another key official in the same city pointed out that learning from experience is not always easy. "Say you're a forty-nine year old white male whose attitudes are fixed, and who believes that women are inherently incapable of managing well and ought to be home taking care of the kids. Say you have those beliefs as strongly as a significant number of men still do, and I am a woman manager, and I become your peer or maybe even your boss. I'm just great, and you like me and you accept me in every important way; but the extraordinary thing is that your stereotypical feelings probably won't change! You may see several of us about whom you've relaxed all your traditional values, and you *still* won't generalize to women as a group. It's a very tenacious problem," he said, "because women managers are breaking down everything that the forty-nine year old male's home is built on; indeed, everything he believes in."

Most certainly, management should make plain to the organization and to the woman herself that she was selected on the basis of ability and not sex, and that she has the confidence and backing of management. As Kanter[18] showed, power depends on influence outside the work group and upward in the organization. The obvious support of management is crucial if a woman is to achieve power or the ability to make things happen in the corporate setting.

"We adopt a very no-nonsense attitude regarding our women managers' peers and subordinates," explained the vice president-human resources of a technical company. "We're not going to take a bunch of sour grapes. If subordinates don't want to work for women, it's goodbye, subordinates. If colleagues don't want to work with them, we'll get some new colleagues. We'll back a woman up just as we would any other manager. It's our job to make it go, and we're not going to blame the woman if people don't like her gender."

At another company a key official said, "On our performance appraisals is a question regarding one's ability to work with others. If someone — and it's usually a secretary—says he or she can't work for a female, then we respond that that's an indication the person isn't effective in work relationships, and it will hurt the performance appraisal. After that, they don't say they can't—they just say they don't like it." However, the situation *is* improving, he noted. A few years ago a woman manager at the company had to interview 18 secretaries to find one who would work for her; recently, she hired the second prospect.

"We're sensitive to the problems of the isolated woman," pointed out a manager at a major organization. "We'd like to avoid the 'only woman' situation, but we can't in every instance. We don't attempt to precondition the environment into which a woman is going. We simply stress to her and the organization that the reason she's there is her ability to get the job done. To a certain extent it's up to the woman to take care of herself. One discovered that several of her subordinates were calling her a derogatory nickname. She called them in and threatened them with a bad performance appraisal if they didn't stop." The manager smiled. "They stopped."

Of course, not every woman is troubled by being an exception. "Most of our women on the technical side don't think twice about it," said an official of a capital goods company. "They've been in that posture too long—first to enroll in engineering, first to get a degree in that field, and so on."

Some organizations fear placing women in certain positions because of an expected negative reaction from clients or customers. The vice president of a bank told me, "Sometimes customers object. When this happens, we simply say, 'If you can't do business with that employee and your objections are based solely on her sex, we're just going to have to lose your account. But if you go to other banks in this city you may well be assigned a woman by them!' I'll never forget the officer in our corporate banking department who was taking a woman with him in calling on an important new customer. He kept worrying about what that company controller would say, and how he'd handle it. Well, they got there, and the controller was a woman!"

## THE IMPORTANCE OF INITIAL PLACEMENT

Assuming an organization has few or no women within the management ranks, where should women be positioned initially?

There are those who contend it is not only desirable but necessary to the success of the effort to immediately place several women in high-ranking, very visible positions. Such placements will prove that no echelon is considered off limits, and the major battle for integration can be fought by more experienced troops. Further, the women can serve as role models for females in lower ranks who aspire to advance. Thus, the organization is more likely to retain its promotable women—demand for whom currently exceeds supply.

The caveat is to make certain that any highly placed woman is truly qualified. A sizable company in the East determined recently that its most senior executive woman was not performing satisfactorily and would have to be discharged. Line management's conclusion was confirmed by the review of affirmative action specialists, who wanted to make sure that the move 1) was a proper one and 2) would be handled in such a way that the organization would not suffer legal repercussions. When the AA officer examined the woman's file, he discovered three highly uncomplimentary reports from previous employers. These had been received after the woman had been hired and had never been acted upon!

The affirmative action officer's remaining concern was how women in the company might react to the discharge. He need not have worried; as he subsequently discovered, other women were well aware of the "role model's" incompetence and were relieved when she left since they felt she reflected unfavorably upon all other women in the organization.

In contrast to those who favor immediate placement of women in the upper echelons are those firms which emphasize promotion from within and rarely, if ever, go outside for any staffing beyond the entry level. These firms recognize that they may require a much longer time to advance women, but they feel that the burden placed on any outsider entering the higher ranks would be considerable, if not impossible.

"We're a technical company," a vice president of an Eastern manufacturer said. "Our disciplines are hard. Our women managers must be from the inside, just as our men managers are. Sure, we could hire some women from outside. But knowledge of the company is critical for success. Ninety-five percent of all our employees earning $50,000 or more have been developed inside." The company reserves a third of its entry level spots for women, who have been part of the management development program since 1970. "We have generated some stretch promotions for women—moved them ahead faster," the officer said. "But no faster than some men. We're fast-tracking the women at the speed of the fastest males."

Between these two positions are those companies which by and large promote from within, but which have a policy of bringing in a certain number of highly ranked outsiders as a deliberate means of avoiding inbreeding. Ideally, the number of these new employees would be sufficient to permit inclusion of more than one woman.

However, not all companies feel that suitable talent is available. "We have not been able to locate or, to this point, home-grow female talent for the most senior levels of the company," said a West Coast personnel officer. "We now have significant numbers of women who are in middle management, and we have others who are making that step to the senior manager level. While there aren't as many as we'd like, given the length of time we've been working on this they're moving very well."

If an organization does place women in uppper echelon positions, it should resist the temptation to turn them into showpieces, to be pushed into the limelight whenever it appears to be advantageous to the company. In all probability, the women executives will cherish whatever privacy they are able to maintain in the face of their avis rara status, and this unsought attention can be detrimental to their relationships with peers and subordinates as well as offensive to them personally.

In positioning females by function, organizations which remain unconvinced that women can succeed in nontraditional roles are likely to think in terms of those areas where the cost of failure would not be critical to the organization.

"Our philosophy has been that standards should not be compromised," emphasized a personnel executive in one of the nation's largest companies. "We also believe there is no need to compromise in order to advance women in management. Of course we have managers saying, 'We always used to choose the best qualified, but now we have to take a woman.' Well, the fact is that separating the qualified and unqualified is easy. But ranking the qualified? That's a crude measure at best, and there are lots of reasons for different outcomes.

"All I can tell you is this: we don't promote *anybody* who's unqualified—man, woman, white, or minority. And when managers say to me, 'We have to put women into jobs before they are completely qualified,' I reply, 'How many times have we put you in a job before you were completely qualified for it?' "

Said a personnel executive at a highly successful capital goods company, "Each person is looked at as an individual and progressed through a career path to the best of his or her ability potential. If it happens all the women end up in one function, okay. But by our recruiting and development program, women have become dispersed throughout the company."

Because of organizations' concern over their possible failure, women are often found in public relations or personnel which are considered by many companies to be less important and less demanding functions. Of course, the availability of women with public relations or personnel backgrounds is greater, and it's far more difficult to locate females for, say, manufacturing positions. But it can be done, as Ford Motor Company has proven with an innovative program.

The auto maker realized that historically most women college graduates had entered the field of education, and that many of them had risen to high level administrative positions with sizable management responsibilities. Recently, advancement opportunity in that field had declined, and many women in education had redirected their ambitions toward industry. At the same time, Ford had made only limited progress in identifying women for manufacturing positions either in management or grades feeding into management. Thus, a pilot program was initiated to offset a projected shortfall of women in this area of the company. It also offered an attractive career development opportunity for the women selected.

The project placed nontechnical, high potential women educators within four areas: industrial/process engineering, material control, production, and quality control supervision. The accelerated two-year development program is now fully implemented, and both the company and the women are pleased with the result. When the trainees' rotational assignments are completed at the end of 1980, a joint determination will be made as to appropriate long-range career paths in manufacturing.

Granted, women working in production management are still few and far between, but they do exist in other companies as well. They work for Boeing, Lockheed, General Electric, Merck, RCA, and Scott Paper, among others. Women are beginning to appreciate where presidents come from, and they enjoy the feeling of accomplishment that accompanies working at the heart of a manufacturing company. Results are immediate—and measurable.

Certainly, the aim of any organization should be to disperse women (and men) across functional lines broadly enough that no observer could conclude that sex-linked ghettos remain. But this objective has its cost. "We have found it very difficult to keep women in managers' functions which have been historically all male, technical and seen as 'man's work'," reported a key manager at one of the nation's leading companies. "Some women who have moved into such jobs have encountered rejection and even hostility. If they did not endure it, and some could not, the word spread; and other women became reluctant to risk such unpleasantness and anxiety. Frequently the attitudes and mind-sets of their male peers create the biggest barriers and discouragements for women moving into management."

He recounted the experience of one woman who was the first of her sex to join a group of aggressive, market-oriented sales managers. They did not think she "fit in." She was excluded from the informal discussions "from which we all learn so much that is important about how to cope with our jobs." When she had to ask for help, it was given reluctantly or with obvious resentment. Her peers made it plain to her that they expected her to fail; and eventually she did.

In contrast, a major transportation company has taken the attitude that if the selection is right, no "clustering" of women is necessary or desirable. "We don't want to create the impression that women need more support than men, or that we're willing to give them more support than men," an official told me. "I know it sounds like a sink-or-swim proposition, and I'm sure if you talked to some of our women managers, you'd hear some horror stories. But over the long term I'm confident that our approach will prove to have been the better choice."

In terms of positioning by location, it's admittedly more difficult to attract women to nonmetropolitan areas. If the females are married, suitable employment for their husbands may not be available. The choice is then between declining the opportunity, attempting a commuting marriage, and separating. Various women have opted for each of the three solutions. An airline has a female city manager in New England who commutes to Iowa on weekends to be with her husband. A Midwest manufacturer has a woman manager who left her husband, a retired military officer, when he refused to move after her job offer. "I've been following him all my life," she said. "Now it's my turn."

If the females are single, they find the nonmetropolitan location offers relatively few social, cultural, and educational opportunities. In addition, they consider the environment less receptive or even downright hostile to a career woman. ("Where can they go out at night and have a hassle-free time?" asked one personnel executive in explaining the difficulty.) Hence, in weighing career versus quality of life, the women may well conclude to confine their career to movement within or between major cities.

"We made a mistake when we put women into sales," pointed out an officer of a West Coast company. "We hired people here, or promoted clerical personnel. After training, we placed them in Baltimore, Pittsburgh, Gainesville; you name it. They failed in large numbers. What we discovered was that men are much more willing to relocate to further their careers. These young women were fond of California. So we changed our tactics; we now go to Pittsburgh, recruit a woman who's already in sales, send her through our training program, and return her to her home base."

A consumer products company also had problems with women on the sales force. Said a vice president, "Two resigned fairly early because we put them out in rural areas where they'd be sleeping in a different motel each night. They were being propositioned constantly by male salesmen from other companies! So we began putting females in metropolitan areas where they wouldn't be away from home overnight, and now 30 percent of our field sales force is women. Zone managers, district managers know they can do the job. They've had a chance to gain recognition for their abilities. And these weren't women with sales experience—mostly they're ex-teachers and former librarians."

"If we had it to do over, we'd watch location more carefully," admitted a key official of a Western company. "We lost a number of women who were assigned to small towns. But then any young, single person would have been a problem."

It has not been too many years that women have had jobs requiring travel. Organizations formerly held that it wasn't a good idea if women traveled alone, and an even worse idea if women traveled with male co-workers. Today, women are traveling and appear to have no objection to travel. Even companies which send male/female teams out on extended trips report no objections from spouses.

"Occasionally, we've had new mothers who asked not to travel for a while so they could spend more time with their babies," said a bank vice president. "But that has happened maybe half a dozen times, and we've got 12,000 women employees. Most of them jump at the chance to travel."

"Most of our women don't have a problem with travel," noted an oil company official. "Some women—particularly those who are a family unit's only wage earner—have difficulty arranging travel, but this is not a widespread difficulty. More frequently, there is no child involved or if there is one, alternate arrangements can be made for child care for short periods."

The chief executive officer of a major company recently met with a group of women employees. When asked why he had never had a female assistant, he pointed out that the two would have to work closely together, there would be considerable travel involved, and it obviously was not appropriate. The reaction of the group was immediate and forceful. When the next vacancy occurred on his staff, a woman was appointed.

On occasion the discrimination against women which epitomizes other cultures makes the placement of women executives a problem in certain overseas locations. "We have 10,000 or so people located outside the United States," pointed out an officer of a financial institution. "The overseas people never stay in one spot long, and there's some difficulty in placing women in Bangladesh or the Far East. But right now there are a couple of VP's in the Orient who are women. They must be the only women over there in such jobs. There's been a lot of resistance to them. But we do it nonetheless, then transfer them in a couple of years."

Except in such isolated instances, women have demonstrated their ability to succeed in any job, providing they qualify on the basis of competence and personality.

"Organizations are so cautious when they start hiring women managers that it's hard for them ever to make a mistake," declared a personnel executive at a New York-based consumer services firm. "My advice would be this: Don't be afraid to let women fail. Don't create jobs for them, and don't put them in what are viewed as easy spots. Spread them out in a variety of nontraditional roles and let them stand or fail on their merits. I've never heard of an organization being disappointed in a woman who was picked for her ability, rather than her sex. There may have been a case, but I doubt it very much."

An officer in a Midwest-based company added, "Our managers want people who can solve problems and produce results. If it happens to be a man, that's fine. But if it's a woman, that's fine too. And that's the ideal way."

## REFERENCES

1. Rosen, B. and T. H. Jerdee, "Influence of Sex Role Stereotyping on Personnel Decisions," *Journal of Applied Psychology* **59**:13 (1974).
2. Heidrick and Struggles, Inc., *Profile of a Woman Officer*, Chicago, 1977, 1978 and 1979, p. 3.
3. Rosen, B., and T. H. Jerdee, "Effects of Applicant's Sex and Difficulty of Job on Evaluation of Candidates for Managerial Positions," *Journal of Applied Psychology* **59**(4):512 (1974).
4. Shaeffer, Ruth G., *Staffing Systems: Managerial and Professional Jobs*, New York: The Conference Board, 1972, p. 22.
5. Miner, John B., "Motivational Potential for Upgrading Among Minority and Female Managers," *Journal of Applied Psychology* **62**:694–5 (1977).
6. Robertson, Wyndham, "The Top Women in Business," *Fortune*, July 1978, pp. 58–64.
7. Shaeffer, Ruth G. and Helen Axel, *Improving Job Opportunities for Women: A Chartbook Focusing on the Progress in Business*, New York: The Conference Board, 1978, p. 10.
8. Shaeffer, Ruth G. *Staffing Systems: Managerial and Professional Jobs*, New York: The Conference Board, 1972, p. 12.
9. "How Men Adjust to a Female Boss," *Business Week*, 5 September 1977, p. 94.
10. Lyle, Jerolyn R., *Affirmative Action Programs For Women: A Survey of Innovative Programs*, Report submitted to the Office of Research, Equal Employment Opportunity Commission, under Contract 71-45, 1973, p. 58.
11. Bowman, G. W., N. B. Worthy, and S. A. Greyser, "Are Women Executives People?" *Harvard Business Review* **43**(4):16 (July–August 1965).
12. Heidrick and Struggles, Inc., *Profile of a Woman Officer*, Chicago, 1979, p. 5.
13. Bayes, Marjorie and Peter M. Newton, "Women in Authority: A Sociopsychological Analysis," *Journal of Applied Behavioral Science* **14**(1):19 (1978).
14. Churchill, Neil C., "Analyzing and Modeling Human Resource Flows," in *Monitoring the Human Resource System* by Ruth G. Shaeffer, New York: The Conference Board, 1977, pp. 20 and 23.
15. Epstein, Cynthia Fuchs, *Woman's Place: Options and Limits in Professional Careers*, Berkeley: University of California Press, 1971, pp. 140–1.
16. Hall, Douglas T. and Francine S. Hall, "What's New in Career Management," *Organizational Dynamics* **5**(1):18 (Summer 1976).
17. Bartol, Kathryn M., "The Sex Structuring of Organizations: A Search For Possible Causes," *Academy of Management Review* No. 3, p. 811 (October 1978).
18. Kanter, Rosabeth M., *Men and Women of the Corporation*, New York: Basic Books, 1977, p. 168.

# 5

# Looking Inside

"We haven't had any EEO problems," declared an officer of a Midwest company. "I think it's because we've advanced women who seemed to have the qualifications as rapidly as they could be advanced."

An organization's prospects for promoting women employees to middle and upper echelon management positions depend upon the size of the female population, the technical and personal qualifications of those individuals comprising it, and the requirements of the organization. Obviously, companies with a large and able female work force dispersed in different functional areas are advantageously positioned, provided that the vast majority of managerial and professional positions do not require technical training.

"Two-thirds of our work force has traditionally been women," said a key official at a New York-based firm. "We had a large supply of well-educated, well-qualified women when we lowered the barriers, and a lot of them came through. We have never had to turn outside, never."

Another company in New York pointed out that of its director-level executives, many were women who had come up either from lower-level exempt positions, or from nonexempt posts. "A number of women really only needed a chance to assume higher levels of responsibility," emphasized the personnel vice president. "They were there; they were ready; we had a commitment to improving our EEO posture, and so they were selected." Yet many organizations in heavy industry will require a number of years before their hiring programs and training programs ready women for responsibilities in middle management or beyond.

## ADVANTAGES TO PROMOTION

All companies recognize the difficulty involved in searching for women on the outside; there aren't very many. And certainly the cause of equal employment opportunity is not best served by simply moving an experienced woman manager from one company to another.

"Some companies concentrate on bringing women in," pointed out a consultant. "There are others which attempt to take advantage of capable women within the company. The former are working on the numbers; the latter are saying, 'We're going to develop a source of talent we haven't drawn from before, but we're still going to build our management team as we have in the past.' Unfortunately, more companies seem to take experienced women managers from somebody else, because it's the easy way to get the government off your back."

Nevertheless, an increasing number of companies are desirous of utilizing to the fullest possible extent females who are already on the payroll, who know the company's business, and who have demonstrated their ability to succeed in the corporate environment. This is particularly true of companies which are experiencing stable or declining employment, where limited opportunity exists for recruitment from external sources.

"I would advocate developing the home-grown female executive," emphasized an officer of a Chicago company. "This is far better than attempting to buy some talent that someone else has developed or bringing in a woman who is capitalizing on her sex to get somewhere more rapidly. Our promotion-from-within policy has really paid off, not only with women but all minorities; our own people seem more ambitious, more solid, more capable of winning the respect of others in the organization."

Said the vice president of a West Coast company, "We stayed with women we knew. We tried to provide broadened exposure to new opportunities to women inside the organization, and they responded well to that. We did not go outside to seek women with a considerable amount of experience in our industry. There *were* no such women; traditionally, our industry had been very male oriented."

A New York-headquartered company initially identified 100 women employees who were considered to have the highest potential. "We divided them into four groups with specific objectives for advancing each tier within certain time frames," a kew executive explained.

At a transportation firm, a personnel specialist said, "We prefer to develop our own managers, give our own people first opportunity at management vacancies. Back in 1974, we required every manager to discuss career plans with each of his female nonmanagement employees to try to find some we hadn't found before who'd say, 'Yes, I want to be in management,' and who'd be viewed as having the potential. Currently, 13 percent of our management employees are female, and our 1981 target is 20 percent. We think we'll make that."

At one time, companies typically handled single-level promotions as a routine affair. The manager selected a subordinate on his own and had his choice confirmed by his superior. The personnel department was not involved unless its help was requested; candidates receiving consideration were likely to be those already known and well regarded by the hiring manager. Equal employment opportunity (EEO) considerations have led to a much closer involvement in the selection process by staff specialists. The roster of prospects has been broadened considerably so that well-qualified candidates not previously known to the manager can receive consideration.

While the final choice remains that of the supervisor, he receives suggestions from personnel, particularly in identifying female and minority candidates. This eliminates the "I couldn't find any" excuse which some line managers resort to out of bias or an unwillingness to expend the extra effort required to identify candidates other than while males. The review by personnel helps to assure that if no suitable female or minority candidates can be found inside, the search can be extended to persons outside the company.

"We have encountered the situation where a department chief will *insist* that there is no qualified woman to fill a key job," pointed out an East Coast personnel executive. "But, when faced with having to accept an unknown from outside the organization, he often is able to find someone inside."

At another company in the same city, a vice president told me, "When a job opens up, one of the first questions that's asked is, 'Is there a minority or female we could move into that position?' If there is, we attempt to do it. This system may not be scientific, but it works. Our results prove it."

As progressive firms know, promotion from within offers many advantages. Among these are lower cost, lower turnover of the most able individuals, heightened employee morale, and improved productivity. The negatives, if the program is not conducted properly, are lower morale due to unrealized expectations, and poor selection if availability transcends appropriateness as a consideration. Not everyone is qualified for advancement, even with additional training and greater experience.

Ultimately, organizations must concentrate their efforts on those of both sexes who have the essential talent and motivation.

## POSSIBLE PITFALLS

"Like a lot of corporations, we've made our mistakes," said a personnel executive at a large consumer products company. "In the beginning, we took some secretaries and put them into jobs without any training and without building a support system. They simply weren't prepared. I'll never forget one woman we promoted. She'd become an administrative assistant, an exempt job, after seven years as a secretary. Her first day in the new position she sat at her new desk in her new office for some time, waiting for someone to come in and tell her what to do. She suddenly realized no one was coming, so she came in to see me and said, 'Help me.' That's how we developed our program called 'The New Woman Manager.'

"We're living with our mistakes, and we're trying to work those people back into an environment where they will be comfortable. But we learned you don't put a mantle on someone and say, 'You are now a manager' and give that woman a budget to manage and people to supervise and a whole lot of other things."

Surveys have shown that many lower level employees—particularly women—believe no opportunities for promotion exist for them. In some cases this is undoubtedly true. One bank official recounted, "When we began looking for women to promote, we found some who had spent most of their time training other people to move up and had never moved themselves."

In some companies, employees remain unaware of openings and the procedures for applying. Employers are fearful that a higher level of employee knowledge would prove disadvantageous to the organization. One personnel vice president told The Conference Board, "We have some jobs that are much harder to fill than others . . . once someone accepts the assignment it wouldn't make sense for us to allow him to bid out of that job onto one we can easily fill."[1]

Ideally, however, an organization will make clear that every employee is to be given the opportunity to utilize his or her capabilities to the fullest extent. Certainly, job posting is an affirmation of this policy. "After we initiated job posting, we found that employees became far more self-directed in their career development," reported an official at a Midwest manufacturing company. "We feel we're going to have far more success in advancing women if we can get them to formulate their own goals and style of moving ahead.''

Increasingly, companies are assessing their total requirements rather than separating their needs into exempt and nonexempt categories. These firms have discovered that many opportunities exist for moving individuals from the nonexempt to the exempt category. ''Education was the root of our problem,'' recounted an EEO officer at an Eastern company. ''There's a very thin line between the executive assistant and the secretary; we required a college degree for the assistant which eliminated many secretaries who could do the job.''

Some employers continue to view the secretarial position as a dead end, and while raising the salaries of those who perform well in this capacity, never consider them for nonclerical positions. In fact, women in secretarial positions may be severely underutilized. For many age thirty-five or more, the secretarial position was the best available to a liberal arts graduate, even if she were Phi Beta Kappa.

''When we surveyed our employees,'' reported the EEO officer of a New York-headquartered manufacturing company, ''we found out that secretaries believed once you joined in that capacity, you never moved, even though you were a college graduate. And yet they saw the company was going to the campuses and hiring people for managerial and professional jobs. Well, we decided to make this company itself a campus. Everybody in engineering doesn't have to be an engineer; everybody in tech science doesn't have to be a physicist; there's a lot of room within functions for the nonmechanic. We'd had a good tuition refund program, but we hadn't sold it. The only beneficiaries had been the superstars. Now we've gotten away from that mentality, and we're broadening the base.''

In 1970, a group of eight senior secretaries in New York launched Atlantic Richfield's successful movement of women into management. Many of these women were degreed and felt they had the qualifications to move into exempt professional positions. They presented a position paper to management, outlining recommendations to enhance the career potential of female employees. The following year, one of the group was promoted to Equal Opportunity Coordinator, with special emphasis on women's programs. Within 18 months she was elevated to Manager of Equal Opportunity Affairs. She noted at the time that she had been promoted more in a year and a half than she had been in the preceding 20 years.

Said the vice president of a diversified New York company, ''A lot of women who are now in management were secretaries in 1965 or even

1970." However, this depends on the company. A consultant pointed out, "I think it is unrealistic to say, when all of the male managers in an organization have to be graduates of the Harvard Business School, that your are going to take a woman who's spent her first ten years in the company as a secretary and transform her into an executive."

An EEO officer at a transportation company declared, "The transition to management from being a secretary is one of the most difficult I have ever seen. In fact, it is even more difficult for a secretary to be successful in her own organization. She may have to leave the company to lose the stigma of the typewriter."

Confirming this view, The Conference Board pointed out that "first impressions tend to be lasting, and it is sometimes difficult for an employee's previous boss, peers, and other work associates to adjust their perceptions of that individual to fit a major change in her role in the organization. Some companies report that a 'rite of passage' to the new status—or shifting the woman to a different part of the organization— has proven helpful."[2]

## IDENTIFYING "PROMOTABLES"

The accessibility of information regarding promotability of employees varies sharply from company to company. Some firms possess a computerized personnel data system which makes available a wealth of data on employees. This system is used to generate candidate lists as vacancies occur. A bank, for example, launched its program of promoting women by running a printout of all female college graduates working in clerical positions. If their performance was satisfactory, the women were interviewed to determine what their ambitions were.

Other companies have only limited information or limited access to it and may be required to take an inventory manually to identify candidates for promotion. One company reported, "Right now our information is in crude form. We've put the system in place just within the last couple of years. We did the exempt level first, and now we've extended it to nonexempts: what their background of experience is, their education, how they're appraised, whether they're mobile, and what their language capability is."

A consumer products company sent corporate personnel people to the operating companies to talk with women to determine their abilities and aspirations. "It was the very first time anybody had gone to where the action is to find out what people wanted to do," a vice president noted. "Our purpose was to help line management identify women candidates for positions, and we accomplished that. As slots become available, we know who out there is ready to fill them. It was personal contact which was key; I don't think you can do it all from a piece of paper."

Many companies conduct performance appraisals for a variety of reasons, including an assessment of promotability. Some cover employees at all levels; others have appraisals only at certain ranks. A Conference Board survey of nearly 300 companies found that 71 percent have appraisal systems for their middle management employees but only 55 percent do for top management.[3] Usually the appraisals are conducted by the immediate superior but may in certain companies and in certain functions be the result of the pooled opinions of co-workers. These may include the superior, higher-level managers, peers and lower-level workers.

An Eastern seaboard company's talent inventory program calls for group appraisal by 5 to 7 peers and subordinates and the immediate supervisor. "We give the appraisers a list of 40 to 50 behavioral statements generated by the critical incident technique which describe management performance. The appraisers indicate whether these statements describe the individual. We have done studies of those appraised and when the subjects are categorized by level of management there is no significant difference in the way women as a group are measured, compared to the total," a key official pointed out.

"We've had a rather sophisticated performance appraisal system for about 25 years," a bank officer explained. "When it became apparent that women should be in management positions, we began to look at the women who were rated 'outstanding.' Whenever we've promoted a woman, she's always been the best qualified. She's met the same standards as anyone else."

Since certain appraisal systems have been found discriminatory in court cases, it is important that the plan employed be a defensible one. According to The Conference Board, the system must be reliable (yield consistent data) and valid (measure what it is supposed to measure); it must be job related, standardized in its form and administration, and be practical.

Many companies wish to weigh not how well employees have performed on the jobs they have held or hold, but rather how they are likely to perform in the positions for which they are being considered. Too often, the company's best salesperson has been elevated to become the worst sales manager. Rather than rely exclusively on inventories or appraisals, thousands of companies have developed assessment centers in which outside experts or company management work in teams to evaluate the performance of employees in simulated work situations.

Some use assessment merely for training, but others rely on the technique to identify promotables. "In our company salary is tied to appraisal, but promotion is tied to potential; and we determine that by assessment," an East Coast personnel executive told me.

Employees can be chosen through self-nomination or identification by supervisors. The typical center may require as much as a full week's time of 6 assessors and half a week's time of their 12 candidates.

Advantages of the assessment center concept are several. First, the assessment of employees depends upon a panel of trained individuals who pool their judgments. Hence, a more realistic evaluation is likely. Second, the assessment center makes clear to the entire organization the importance top management accords to executive selection. Third, the assessment center helps train managers to be better developers of their own people by teaching them to observe behavior.

"We put our assessors-to-be through three days' training," noted a key official of an East Coast organization. "During that time we eliminate the business of 'he seemed to' or 'she looked like'; managers are forced to think in behavioral terms and to rule out prejudice. Some of our managers have said being an assessor was the very best experience they ever had."

Negatives are the cost involved (although certainly less than poor selection and turnover) and the lack of meaningful results, unless the contents of assessment relate to the realities of the job for which the candidates are being considered.

Assessment may be particularly helpful to women. "Assessment is an enabling mechanism in building up our pool, so when there's a vacancy to be filled, there's more chance a woman will be among the qualified candidates," pointed out a personnel executive at a major corporation. "But there's more to it than that. When someone does well in assessment, there is an acceptance of that person that otherwise might be absent. Let's face it; there's a natural skepticism on the part of middle-aged or older men as to whether a woman is competent. A successful assessment experience can mitigate that doubt."

American Telephone & Telegraph, a pioneer in assessment, has included women since the early sixties, first separately and since the late sixties, in mixed groups. The company's assessment activities include a leaderless group discussion, a business game, an in-basket exercise, an interview with an assessment staff member, and participation in a variety of tests and written exercises. Like their male colleagues, women are rated on leadership, career ambition, inner work standards, decisiveness, energy, flexibility, judgment, and communication skills.

AT&T has found that assessment results correlate with management progress of both men and women. (The results do not determine progress since assessment results are not retained for more than a two or three year period, and subsequent supervisors are not aware of performance at the center.) In the latest reported year, nearly a third of women attaining top rating in assessment had reached the third level of management, while fewer than one in 10 remained at the first level. In contrast, 56 percent of the lowest rated women were still at the first level, and only 4 percent had advanced to third level.

AT&T staffers point out, "Since the proportions of males and females who do well in assessment centers are nearly identical, the assessment-center method appears to be a logical means for providing equal opportunity to women for promotion into management positions and advancement within managerial levels."[4] In addition, assessment centers have the approval of the EEOC and can be used as evidence when evaluations are questioned in court cases.

Some critics contend that centers basically measure interpersonal skills, and that these can be rated by other, less expensive means. However, certain companies utilize assessment centers both as a management selection and development tool. Hence, half the employee's time at a center is devoted to assessment exercises, and the remainder is limited to training designed to shore up weaknesses which have been brought to light. The combination serves to make centers more economical.[5] There are hundreds of companies which retain consultant psychologists or rely on staff psychologists to conduct in-depth evaluations of individuals to determine their suitability for hire or promotion. Interviews conducted by Rohrer, Hibler & Replogle, the largest organization in psychological assessment, take up to three hours and concentrate on five areas: intelligence, emotional maturity, skill with people, insight, and organizational and supervisory ability. Sears has had a psychological assessment program for more than three decades. Each year staff psychologists give tests to 7000 employees and applicants seeking executive posts. The tests measure emotional strengths, mental ability, social skills, and breadth of interests.[6]

Certain organizations have utilized "temporary assignments" to evaluate promotability of employees. Under this plan, individuals may be advanced to new jobs and given whatever on-the-job training is required. If after a certain period the individuals are adjudged to have successfully assumed the responsibilities of their new positions, they remain in the posts. However, if the employees fail to measure up to expectations, they are returned to their former positions.

"To improve our percentages early in the game—nearly ten years ago—we decided that each division would take a number of women and minorities and put them in on-the-job training programs which varied by division," recalled a vice president of a diversified consumer firm. "In six or nine months, depending on the degree of difficulty of the job, if they made it, they stayed. We would give a secretary, for example, a lower-level management job. We had an awful lot of women with college degrees who were typing."

Another strategy to evaluate promotability is the internship. Individuals are assigned new responsibilities for a portion of their time, perhaps one day weekly, while remaining in their customary slots for the remainder. Once again an evaluation is made after a set interval, and the individual either remains in the lower level job or is promoted to the higher ranking position.

"My former secretary was an intern," explained a personnel officer. "One day a week for 26 weeks she went to another division of the company and sold. Each division had a couple of interns, either women or minorities. We started in 1970, and fairly soon we began to develop a pool of trained people. I'd advise any company to do that; it's easy to set up. But you'll have to change the mind-set of the men. They're likely to think a woman can't lift a wastebasket, can't travel, can't write a memo, or whatever. You've got to change that mind-set—or no matter how good the woman is, she's not going to make it."

Should a woman not prove suitable for the position to which she has been promoted, she may be moved to a mutually agreed upon fall-back position. A number of companies are adopting a fall-back plan, which reduces risk both for the organization and the employee. The company promises a job equal in standing and pay to the one the employee agrees to assume, should the move not prove to be a successful one. This strategy can be particularly advantageous in the promotion and retention of women, who may be less confident of their ability to succeed in a pioneering role.

Through job enrichment, any organization can offer an employee a greater challenge in his or her current position and perhaps encourage the employee to consider promotion. The individual can be given increased responsibility, increased authority, and greater opportunity for direct contact with upper echelon executives inside and outside the organization. However, care must be exercised not to run afoul of the law. "Job enrichment used to be practical, but now you could get an 'equal pay for equal work' suit; that's the negative side of the new legislation," commented an EEO officer in New York.

## OVERCOMING RESISTANCE TO PROMOTION

In selection of those to be promoted, organizations must exercise both good judgment and appropriate restraint. Employees should be encouraged but not pressured. A good employee who is promoted may become a poor employee; or a contented employee who is promoted may become a dissatisfied employee, to the organization's disadvantage. Even if such an employee is salvaged by being returned to his or her former position, the morale of that individual, and indeed of all employees, may suffer as a consequence.

"The flavor of our company is that you seek you own advance; nobody is going to tap you and say you're on a fast track. We use self-nomination to identify managerial candidates," emphasized the vice president of a large technology company on the East Coast. "We've let people step forward and then provided them with the opportunities to grow."

However, in an unfortunate incident at another billion dollar company in Chicago, a college-educated young woman who served as secretary to a top manager one day expressed to her boss an interest in moving up. He immediately arranged for her to become a trainee in Personnel. The company not only lagged in affirmative action but had no development process in place. So it was not surprising that a readily available female would be advanced on inadequate criteria: first, the company's need to show some EEO progress; and second, her expressed interest in management.

Less than a year later, she returned at her own request to the secretarial ranks. Her reason? "If I'd known being a manager involved all that travel, I never would have accepted in the first place!" (The travel had amounted to one week.) Since there were other women in the organization with a desire to advance and a far better understanding of managerial requirements who had not been offered a similar opportunity, much ill will resulted.

Occasionally, employees prefer to stay where they are because they view their nonmanagement jobs as more attractive either on the basis of money or of job content. A vice president-human resources at a technical company said, "Our biggest problem is with bright, energetic, able women who entered the clerical ranks, have gone to the top there, and don't have any training to equip them to do other things. They wind up as executive secretaries, and they don't want to relocate. That means there aren't many positions available to them in our company.

"If they were willing to become personnel clerks, they might advance as others have eventually to become managers of personnel at a division. There's a career track that would take them to a $40,000 income level. But they'd have to take a cut to start, and they've got a $15,000 standard of living they can't get out of. We're hoping to train some of these people to become inside sales service people. That isn't high paying, but it would be a little more money, and it might be more satisfying to them than pounding a typewriter. But from there you'd go to outside sales, and they lack the technical knowledge.''

A consultant has found in a number of client companies that ''the biggest problem in trying to move executive secretaries to middle management positions is their reluctance to make the switch. They like dealing with competent, decisive, highly successful people. To deal with clerical types and all the pettiness you find there—they just don't want to do it. They look upon it as going down—not in terms of money or even in terms of status, but in terms of people and situations they'd deal with.''

This view was confirmed by an officer of a West Coast company who noted that a secretary to a senior officer who had been put into a lower level professional job, ''was bored stiff and left the organization to become a secretary elsewhere.''

Regardless of how the promotion-from-within program is communicated, or how employees are evaluated and selected, there must be adequate support for those designated as promotable or the effort will fail.

Many organizations at an early stage institute career counseling for all employees to determine their abilities and ambitions, to jointly decide on target positions, and to determine what self-development or training is needed to qualify the individual. Such specific counseling is of far greater value than generalities, both to the organization and to the individual. In planning his or her own career by objectives, the employee assumes greater responsibility for progress and is less likely to blame the employer for lack of advancement. The program is also helpful to both the employer and employee in identifying those who have plateaued, so the employee is free to consider an interorganizational move while his or her chances of accomplishing one remain good. The counselors in some companies are supervisors, in others, members of the personnel staff or even outside consultants.

''We're one of the few corporations in the country which has training programs for nonexempts,'' proclaimed a personnel executive with a consumer products organization. ''As part of the program, the employee is supposed to have a development discussion with his or her boss. The boss and the employee fill out a form which analyzes the requirements of the job and the employee's skills. Then the two review where the employee is performing well, what skill gaps exist, and what plan to institute to exploit talents and to improve skills. Many of the women are terrified to approach their bosses, so we do a lot of counseling and coaching.''

Some companies fear management development, believing that the narrowing pyramid does not permit promotions for everyone. Why build up hopes?[7] In truth, when inadequate development exists, the ablest persons—and those the organization would most like to keep—are the ones most likely to leave since they experience the greatest ease in doing so. However, under a proper development program, the highest rated employees can be moved ahead appropriately and retained. In addition, upward mobility will prove possible from a larger number of positions providing career paths are reassessed.

AT&T found that women who had undergone assessment and been recommended for promotion were more likely to remain on the payroll than those who were not recommended. And AT&T discovered that among the recommended women, management progress also influenced turnover: only one-tenth as many women who reached the third level of management left the company compared to those who remained at the first level.

Of course, not every employee wishes to assume greater responsibility. Even many women who are qualified for bigger jobs are reluctant to accept them. In a study of 160 women in a variety of occupations in different companies, 100 perceived themselves as "promotable." But when asked how the new position would differ from their present responsibilities, most saw the promotion in negative terms. A majority (63 percent) termed the added responsibilities, longer hours, or additional travel as drawbacks. Only 25 percent noted benefits such as greater respect or personal development, and just 6 percent mentioned an increase in salary.

Said the study's author, "They view promotions as a series of demands on them which benefits the organization rather than as positions which can make a positive contribution to their lives." Indeed, 47 women said they would refuse promotion. Women over 40 and those in traditional female occupations such as clerical or sales work were most likely to reject opportunities for advancement.[8]

"There have been some women who basically have said, 'I appreciate your considering me,' " pointed out a personnel executive at a petroleum company. "But they've added, 'I'm very happy doing what I'm doing, and I don't want to do anything different or anything more.' "

At another company which also experienced declinations, an officer pointed out, "What we think we want is sometimes different from what we want when we have the option of getting it. Some women over the years found they could do their boss's jobs. But when the option was presented, I was surprised at how many didn't want it; they just wanted to know they could have it."

However, many qualified women need only receive encouragement from management to accept and perform well in more demanding jobs. "The secretary to one of our vice presidents was very concerned about leaving a secure situation for a promotion," pointed out an EEO officer at one of the Fortune 1000 companies. "She agonized for days. Finally her boss said, 'I think you can do that job and do it well; but to make you feel better, I promise to keep your old job open for four months.' In my opinion that was really above and beyond his call of duty; but she then went to the new job, and of course she did very well, as he had predicted." With career counseling and the availability of necessary training, the hesitancy of such women can be overcome.

"I've heard a few stories of people who really didn't want to move, and we've had one or two instances of people who moved to management from secretarial jobs and asked to go back," reported a personnel vice president at a promote-from-within company. "But they're the exceptions. In fact it's more that women are pushing us to find jobs for them faster!"

Despite their best efforts, organizations sometimes do find women who have been promoted wishing to return to what they were doing previously. This is a problem in particular for the airlines in promoting flight attendants to supervisory slots. However, this difficulty applies to attendants of both sexes; the work schedules of attendants are too favorable to forsake, especially for those who have other business interests.

The EEO manager at one of the nation's largest companies declared, "You can't expect people who've occupied the same role for 25 years to feel totally confident about moving into another job. So we provide counseling. By surveying managers we found out the minimum number of credits needed to get into accounting, for example. But clerical women in their forties were intimidated at the thought of applying to college for the first time in their lives. So we got catalogs, helped them fill out admission forms, furnished the tuition money, and they went off to night school. And they got good grades, and the payoff for them was even greater than the promotions they won; it was an enhanced self-image."

But an EEO officer in New York reminded, "If you establish training programs, you have to be very careful you aren't establishing unrealistic expectations as part of the process. That can very easily happen."

Employers pay all or part of the cost of job-related training offered by the American Management Associations or other organizations, or even all or part of any enriching course, whether or not job-relatedness can be demonstrated. Not only is there a trend to 100 percent reimbursement, but more and more organizations are furnishing money at the start of a course so that employees need not commit their own funds even for a short period.

"We've got three women right now at the Simmons College program," reported an officer of a New York-based consumer products company. "We're now expanding that so women at the manager and director level have their choice of going to Harvard's Advanced Management Program, or the Sloan program, or the one at Stanford. Through our tuition refund program, we've encouraged women to take college courses. And we've had a fairly high level of participation in various outside seminars. We try to identify specific needs on an individual basis."

A bank in the East offers core courses toward an undergraduate degree right on its premises to encourage clerical employees to qualify for better jobs. Many companies offer a variety of training courses for different levels of management and for skills required in particular functional areas.

The vice president of a promotion-from-within company in the East advised me that the organization offers technical skills training at the division level, and both middle management and executive training at the corporate level. "We get twice as many requests as we can satisfy," the officer noted. "There's been a tremendous growth in training requests by nonexempts who want to advance to exempt jobs. Most but not all are women. Next year we're going to offer a presupervisory training program to help them."

Many companies undertake a special tracking of women to assure that appropriate developmental opportunities are made available to them. Their progress and pay in relation to men of similar training is watched closely to be sure no inequities exist.

For any promotion-from-within program to operate at maximum effectiveness, organizations must reward the development of subordinates. Otherwise, managers may be prone to keep the most talented and pass along to others the less able, without attending to the needs of either group.

One successful program of promotion from within is that carried forward by General Foods Corporation.[9] In 1973, GF's management appointed a task force to increase promotional opportunities within the nonexempt group of jobs, as well as to find a way to open exempt opportunities to secretarial, clerical, and technical employees. Members included both personnel specialists in employment, compensation, and organization development, and several long-service employees who had already been promoted from the nonexempt ranks. The task force developed "Upward Mobility," a career management program which has been carried out by existing staff with no increase in personnel budgets and overhead.

The first step of the task force was to identify those with skills and interest in moving. Selected were long-service nonexempt employees who had had few if any chances for advancement. In addition to training sessions to improve such specific skills as oral and written communications, Upward Mobility encompassed:

- Self-assessment workshops to help employees evaluate their own strengths and weaknesses and pinpoint development needs.
- On-site courses to make available convenient college training.
- College orientation sessions with representatives of 20 area schools to provide employees with information on programs, course offerings, and schedules.
- Job fairs to furnish information on roles and responsibilities of various departments of the company as well as jobs within those departments.
- Job clinics permitting managers to describe the activities within their areas and requirements for specific jobs.
- Goal-setting workshops to assist employees in setting realistic career targets and developing plans to accomplish their goals, including help with resume preparation and interviewing techniques.

Two placement systems were established, one for nonexempt positions and the other for exempt slots. Job posting was utilized to make known nonexempt opportunities on a corporate-wide basis, while the task force received notice of all lower-level professional openings and identified candidates for interviews. Later, job posting was extended to these positions as well. Indeed, the company utilizes an open-information approach, sharing with employees job descriptions, specifications, and salary grades and ranges, plus job opening information. Thus, the program addresses the five competencies termed "most basic" for career growth: 1) self-appraisal, 2) occupational information, 3) goal selection, 4) planning, and 5) problem solving.[10]

Within two years of the start of the program, the entire nonexempt population had been invited to participate in Upward Mobility. A majority expressed interest, 25 percent actually participated, and half of the participants have taken part over an extended period. The company makes clear that there are no guarantees for advancement, and employees appear keenly aware of this fact. Yet the program has thus far permitted promotion of nearly 200 nonexempt male and female employees to exempt ranks.

"At first we went outside for women," said an officer of a giant consumer services organization. "Later we started looking inside, and we found we had an extraordinarily well-educated group, even of clerical people. A high percentage of our secretarial force has college degrees. Now we are dedicated to filling 70 percent of our jobs from within. Each group, each office, each function is responsible for establishing training programs for their people, in keeping with specific career paths they've formulated. Any company that ignores its own people has got to be crazy; you just can't waste the resources you've got or spare the extra time training people from outside."

What's more, prospects for success are much better if undue reliance is not placed on bringing women in from outside. When The Conference Board asked companies about their programs to improve job opportunities for women, the following record of success and failure resulted:

|  | SUCCESSFUL EXPERIENCES | DISAPPOINTING EXPERIENCES |
| --- | --- | --- |
| Bringing in women as new employees | 24 | 44 |
| Upgrading, transferring or promoting present female employees | 29 | 26 |
| Both | 44 | 20 |
| Other or no answer | 3 | 10 |
|  | 100% | 100% |

The Conference Board noted that the emphasis "on *both* initial hiring and internal movement of women in the successful cases" seems "to signal reliance on an ongoing, managed process rather than on special programming."[11]

## REFERENCES

1. Shaeffer, Ruth G., *Staffing Systems: Managerial and Professional Jobs*, New York: The Conference Board, 1972, p. 42.
2. Shaeffer, Ruth G. and Edith F. Lynton, *Corporate Experiences in Improving Women's Job Opportunities*, New York: The Conference Board, 1979, p. 23.

3. Lazer, Robert I. and Walter S. Wikstrom, *Appraising Managerial Performance: Current Practices and Future Directions.* New York: The Conference Board, 1977, p. 8.
4. Moses, Joseph L. and Virginia R. Boehm, "Relationship of Assessment-Center Performance to Management Progress of Women," *Journal of Applied Psychology* 60(4):529 (1975).
5. "How to Spot the Hotshots," *Business Week,* 8 October 1979, p. 62.
6. Koten, John, "Psychologists Play Bigger Corporate Role in Placing of Personnel," *Wall Street Journal,* 11 July 1978.
7. Shaeffer, Ruth G., *Staffing Systems: Managerial and Professional Jobs,* New York: The Conference Board, 1972, p. 44.
8. Albrecht, Maryann, "Women, Resistance to Promotion and Self-Directed Growth," *Human Resource Management* No. 17, p. 12 (Spring, 1978).
9. Duval, Betty A. and Roslyn S. Courtney, "Upward Mobility: The GF Way of Opening Employee Advancement Opportunities," *Personnel* No. 55, pp. 44–7 (May–June 1978).
10. Hall, D. T., *Careers in Organizations,* Pacific Palisades, CA: Goodyear, 1976, pp. 181–5.
11. Shaeffer, Ruth G. and Edith F. Lynton, *Corporate Experiences in Improving Women's Job Opportunities,* New York: The Conference Board, 1979, p. 23.

# 6

# *Looking Outside*

Success of corporate efforts to recruit women will depend upon management's commitment to achieving results, credibility of the company among women, establishment on a continuing basis of relationships with sources of female talent, and the effectiveness of those individuals responsible for the recruiting process.

Why do organizations look outside for experienced women executives? For a variety of reasons. In some cases it's "a lack of sufficient time to grow our own," so the proper level of experience isn't available inside. Fifteen or 20 years are required to develop a senior executive, and companies have had women in the pipeline for ten years or less.

"We go outside for women, particularly in those areas where we don't have women coming up," said a manufacturing company personnel executive. "Engineering and manufacturing are the areas where we need more women. We got one woman engineer out of government who's already saved the company several million dollars. She's been with us just a year and a half and never had any business experience before, but she's been identified as high potential. Lots of women in government and education are stifled. They're not necessarily there because they're complacent. It's because those were spots where they could see opportunity as they were beginning their careers."

Sometimes companies go outside because the particular kind of background sought is not present in house. "We have hired a large number of people from the outside over the last three to five years because the nature of our business was changing, and we really didn't have the proper talent inside," pointed out a bank official. "This was also the time of affirmative action, and we simply tried to insure that we were getting women to consider through referrals, executive search, and other means. We have done pretty well in hiring women at the management level, recognizing that there are few available outside with significant experience. We've remained flexible and have taken a number of women from government.''

On occasion, the move to recruit experienced women is due to failures in the existing recruitment and development program. Perhaps women have proved to be inadequate, or they have left for better opportunities elsewhere. Demand for experienced women managers seems to outstrip supply by a considerable margin. ''When we've given out recruiting assignments for women, we've paid a premium, no question about that,'' said an officer of a technical company. ''You find the best person you can, and she commands a price in excess of the average man. And that's a problem.''

Are women who are brought in comparable to men? Apparently, stringency of standards depends on level. A personnel executive in durable goods admitted, ''Quite frankly, we hire women without experience in our industry at a higher level position than we ever would a man. And they simply can't perform as well as someone who has known the business for some time. But I've seen the opposite phenomenon in hiring for even better jobs, paying up to $60,000. There the company is looking for women with superlative skills.''

A consumer products company officer seconded this view. ''We don't exercise sufficient care in bringing women into entry level sales jobs, and we've made some mistakes that have slowed us down. But when we went after a woman to assume a vice presidency, the screening was so thorough that there was very little question remaining about the capability of the individual.''

However, some companies make it a point not to impose extraordinary standards even in recruiting women for highly visible positions. ''We're looking for women with undergraduate degrees in engineering coupled with MBAs,'' pointed out an officer of a technical company. ''We're not a bank which has a lot of jobs where how bright you are or how good your interpersonal skills are might be the key factor. Unfortunately, there just aren't many women who fit our description. The first one we found we brought in as assistant to the president. She wasn't flashy, just bright and unassuming, and she did quality work. I think it was a plus she wasn't superbionic, so we don't have that standard to make others perform against.''

The head of personnel in a heavy industrial company explained, ''We initiated a program of going outside for people with four or five years of experience following passage of the Civil Rights Act. Since 60 percent of our manpower demands are technical, we looked for staff additions—medical, law, accounting, finance, and computer science. We've had mixed success. We've picked people carefully for their qualifications so they'd have credibility. But in order to be a full-fledged manager rather than a specialist, you have to understand our company. And that takes closer involvement in the guts of the business.''

A representative of a consumer services organization said, ''Our first high-ranking woman was recruited from outside. She was superior to all other candidates and could run circles around her subordinates. For a short time we had our one woman vice president who was invited to the dinners before the board meetings and otherwise performed as *the* woman executive. But we quickly brought in a number of others at high levels to build a mass. That kept people from saying, 'This is our woman; aren't we good to have one.' And we paid the women equally. No premiums, which would have destroyed our salary structure. We simply paid them what we would have paid comparable men. Then we started bringing in women at other levels, and now we have a real pipeline.''

Some firms target specific jobs for women (usually those which are likely to offer the greatest number of prospects) while others would consider women candidates for any vacancy. Those who favor the former plan feel that a concentrated effort is the only sure way of finding and hiring females. It's so much easier to identify suitable male candidates, they emphasize. So few middle and upper echelon women have had an opportunity to gain experience comparable to that of men, that any panel of ''best qualified'' candidates is unlikely to include any females.

A West Coast vice president pointed out, ''With the pressures that are on us today, we really do need women. So we focus our recruiting efforts on them; if we don't, the jobs inevitably will end up in the hands of males. It's so much easier to find men, but we're trying to move on two fronts. We're attempting to identify women in the organization and offer them special development to move them along as fast as we can. The second thing we're doing is earmarking jobs for females and not settling for the expedient thing when we go outside. But I should point out, we have never sacrificed standards in order to put a woman in a position, and we would not do so to get a woman.''

''Especially if you're looking for an experienced woman, you're seeking a rare commodity,'' emphasized a personnel officer at a New York-based company. ''The scarcer the commodity, the longer the lead time. It may take six or even seven months to find the right woman. If you wait for a job to come up, there's so much pressure to fill it that it's difficult to see a reasonable selection of women. The thing to do is to decide when jobs are in the budgeting process. If I'm going to add five jobs next year, I can earmark certain ones for a woman.''

And a consultant told me, ''Some people say, 'We've got to get our numbers up.' They go outside because they haven't developed the pool. They try to find women already in management positions, and then they may have to design jobs to allow those women to work out.'' In contrast, those who insist on women candidates as well as men feel it's preferable from the company's standpoint to pick from a roster of ''qualified'' individuals of both sexes for every position. Further, they emphasize that any other course would be illegal: either ''discrimination'' or ''reverse discrimination.''

A vice president-personnel in New York told me, ''When we go outside, we hire the best executive we can find. It might be a woman, but we don't deliberately go out to find a woman—absolutely not! In fact, we don't go outside very much. Probably 70 percent of our jobs are filled from within. We never say, 'Let's go get that woman because she's a terrific woman, and it will help our numbers.' Our numbers have been pretty good all along.''

One company said, ''In bringing in women from outside, we wanted them to be as good or better than anyone on the inside. And yet we tried to take care not to get overqualified people. We've subjected them to no special pressure, but we've given them no quarter either because they're women.''

Where experience is not a factor in selection, women may well prove better. Indeed, a Midwest company declared that more than half of its MBA hires are now women, ''and they are on average superior to the men.'' In all probability it is still the case that the women seeking this degree are more highly motivated than the men. Even now, new male MBA graduates outnumber females six to one. When the number of students of each sex enrolled in graduate business schools is approximately the same, there is unlikely to be any discernable difference in the ability or motivation of males and females.

## WHERE TO SEARCH

In another generation, searching for female executives may very well be analogous to recruiting males today. Now, however, the dissimilarity of the talent pools makes the process distinct with each sex. The most important difference, of course, is the number of people in the pool. Males in management positions in the corporate sector outnumber females roughly nineteen to one. Not only are women executives fewer in number, but they are concentrated by level, industry, function, and location.

Organizations need to take a hard look at the odds before embarking upon a lengthy and costly search which may prove fruitless. In the first place, women are disproportionately represented in the noncorporate sector. As a consequence, prospective employers should consider at the outset whether a corporate background is essential or only preferred. Women in consulting firms, for example, often are closely familiar with the corporate world through their work with clients, even though they may have never been on a corporate payroll. And women from government or education may have the desired skills as well as the flexibility to adjust to the business environment.

A survey of women officers at America's 1300 largest companies showed that there was one for every 1.6 nonindustrials (banking, diversified finance, insurance, retailing, transportation, and utility) but only one for every 3.7 industrials.[1] However, the largest organizations are more likely to position women at the middle and upper echelons than are those of lesser size. The giant firms are most image conscious and also subject to the greatest government pressure.

If experience in a particular field is key, recruiting organizations should note that certain industries are female intensive while others are male intensive. Indeed, just five industry categories—finance, insurance, real estate, retail trade and nondurable goods manufacturing—account for three of every four working women in the latest census.

Women represent more than 77 percent of the apparel industry's work force, 63 percent of those in banking and 56.5 percent of the workers in leather and leather products. At the other extreme, females represent only 5.8 percent of the employees in construction, 8 percent in mining and 9 percent in primary metals. Even though women are found disproportionately at the lower levels of female intensive industries, there is nevertheless a far greater incidence of women at all levels of these fields. The proportion of women managers and administrators in the female dominated industries is 23 percent, compared to 6 percent in male industries. Women represent 25 percent of professional and technical slots in female intensive fields and just 10 percent in male industries.[2]

In terms of functional areas, women are more often found in marketing, finance, personnel, and public relations than in general management, research and engineering, and manufacturing. But the picture is changing.

"Sure, we experience difficulty in finding women for technical jobs," confessed the head of human resources for a male dominated business. "In any given year there are not nearly as many women chemical engineers coming out of schools as there are men; there aren't as many mining engineers or petroleum engineers or geologists. However, we see a greater availability of women in those disciplines now; more and more females are looking at these specialties as viable career options.''

Said a key executive at an East Coast company, "Societal changes have made it a lot easier to find women physicists, mathematicians, or construction engineers. That makes our recruiting simpler.''

Executive women are most often situated in major metropolitan areas, not only because the life style is more appealing to them but because the community's receptivity to women in nontraditional roles is far greater. A woman earning $50,000 is not the exception in New York and is admired for her success. In Anytown, USA she might be the only female at that income level and viewed as a freak by her co-workers and neighbors. Women officers are also more frequently found on the coasts than in the Midwest and South-Southwest.[3] Both seaboards are typically more receptive to societal trends than other parts of the country.

"The cream of the woman crop is in the New York market," pointed out a vice president of a company located in The Big Apple. "There aren't that many New York-headquartered companies left. Because we decided to stay, we've got a lot of very good people to draw from.''

How should organizations look outside for women executives? They should either utilize internal recruiting capabilities or an outside consultant. The former course is preferable, for those inside know the environment in which the selected individual must succeed far better than any outsider could, however familiar with the organization. If the proper resources in terms of experience and time availability are present in the personnel function, the line manager need not take time away from his primary responsibilities to do the job himself.

However, if the necessary expertise and/or time are lacking on staff, an executive recruiting consultant is called for. Indeed, because of the special difficulties involved in searching for women, organizations which rarely if ever call upon outside help in their recruiting activities may retain consultants to assist on such assignments.

The advantages of using a consultant are several. The saving of management time is key; usually, the manager's involvement is limited to the several hours expended communicating with the consultant at the beginning and during the course of the search, and the several days needed for interviewing and evaluating those individuals who have been prescreened by the expert. Usually, the consultant is able to work more rapidly than management since the specialist probably has been involved in a number of similar assignments. In any event, he or she can quite easily tap knowledgeable sources in appropriate industries, functions, and geographies. In certain instances, the consultant may even know of prospects as the assignment gets under way.

An organization may feel it will be able to save money on a do-it-yourself basis, only to discover after considerable unanticipated outlays that a satisfactory solution to the project is impossible. In contrast, cost of using a consultant is predictable, and search firms of highest rank have similar fees. No reputable consultant will guarantee results, but those who do not find satisfactory solutions to an overwhelming majority of client problems do not prosper.

One of the key pluses in using a consultant is the breadth of the search process. Due to time pressures, unfamiliarity with search resources or other causes, management is limited in terms of the individuals who can be considered for any opportunity. In contrast, the consultant searches widely, nationally or even internationally at the middle and upper echelons, taking full advantage of sources cultivated over years of activity.

Finally, there is the matter of preserving confidentiality for both the hiring organization and the executives who are candidates. Often companies do not wish their identity known during a search. Public knowledge might at worst reveal that an organization is entering a new market or could at best attract a substantial number of unsought applicants. Thus, companies find it advantageous to retain a consultant who can work in the organizations' behalf without identifying an employer except to those few individuals selected as candidates.

Women candidates, particularly those at the middle and upper echelons, also are concerned about confidentiality. Few would deem it advantageous for their own employers to know that they are exploring another opportunity. While candidates are quite willing to place their trust in search consultants whose very survival depends upon an unblemished reputation for confidentiality, they may be reluctant to entrust their fate to companies whose representatives' respect for nondisclosure has not been tested.

## CHOOSING A CONSULTANT

If an organization decides to retain a consultant for a specific assignment, it usually does so on the basis of prior work done for it by that search firm. However, this may not be a satisfactory approach to use in initiating a search for women executives. Not all organizations, even those knowledgeable in other areas, are competent to complete such an undertaking.

Should the organization turn to a consulting firm which specializes in searching for women, rather than an across-the-board firm which identifies both men and women? No, not necessarily. The primary considerations are the quality of the search firm and its ability to get the job done. The client-to-be organization first needs to assure itself of the consultant's reputation for integrity and professionalism and then turn its attention to appraising the firm's ability to perform in a specialized area.

A company on the West Coast told me it retains a search consultant to look exclusively for women, but that its choice is a general firm "because we found a particular person there who can do that job very well for us." However, the vice president added that "referrals remain the best employment source that any company has."

Several years ago I met with a woman employed by a consumer products company based in the Twin Cities. Although I knew enough of her background to know that our firm had no assignments at that time which would be appropriate to her consideration, she urged the get-together. Perhaps there would be such an opportunity in the future, she pointed out, and she definitely had decided to leave her company.

At our meeting Ann Collier (not her real name) told me she had been contacted at home just the previous week by a woman hired by Collier's company to identify a vice president. The recruiter and Collier had not been in touch for several years, but the recruiter insisted that she was qualified for the situation. The consultant identified the client organization and outlined the opportunity to Collier. When she asked if Collier were interested, Ann replied, "But I'm *already* with (name of company). However, I didn't even know such an opportunity exists. Of course I'd be interested!"

The recruiter hastily replied, "Oh, my, I didn't know you were with (name of company) now. I can't suggest you as a candidate, or I wouldn't get my money!" And with that she hung up.

"Can you imagine my company hiring somebody like *that* to represent us in the executive marketplace?" exclaimed Collier. "What do you suppose is wrong with management?"

Collier has since joined another billion dollar corporation, as she hoped to do. She might have been a qualified candidate for her former company's officership, and she might not have been. Her ex-employer however, had overlooked the importance of identifying a representative who knew how to perform professionally, as well as how to locate women.

Recently, a woman attorney in San Francisco was interviewed by a male executive recruiter. He asked her several questions concerning her personal life which were, as she pointed out to him, illegal. His response was that she had better answer what he asked if she wanted to be considered for the opportunity. Not only is she unfavorably disposed toward the recruiter and the company he represents, but she is considering bringing suit. The organization retaining the consultant may not be aware of the recruiter's actions, let alone sympathetic to them, but the company is destined to suffer the consequences of its representative's conduct.

A sizable technical company told me, "We don't specify women on our searches. We tried using a search firm specializing in women, but they turned up people who weren't competent. However, our focus remains on promoting women. Right now the market is hot for successful women. Other organizations are paying a premium for our women and for our minorities too."

The EEO officer of another technical company said, "I told managers I would help pay for a specialty recruiter out of my budget; that made it impossible for them to turn me down. But the managers wouldn't hire the people the recruiters came up with. They thought they weren't right. But the fact that those firms proved availability made the managers then go out and find their own women. One manager told me he couldn't do it when I reminded him he was slated to hire six females. He said he should have to hire only one. He'd been in this business a long time, he told me, and he knew that women simply weren't available. Well, that was eight months ago. He's since hired not six but seven. Thanks to our offering the specialty firm's services, he's been able to find more on his own in this last year than he'd hired in the preceding six."

In selecting a consultant, an organization would be well advised to interview several firms. The client should determine whether the various contenders are competent to perform successfully at the level and in the function and industry under consideration. Many more consultants can perform satisfactorily at the lower levels than at the middle and upper echelons of management, where considerably more adroitness is required. The client will wish to explore what searches for women the firm has completed, and what resources it has to tap the woman talent market. The hiring organization should make certain not only that the recruiter possesses the know-how and desire to search for women, but that the firm will represent the client well in its interface with women as the client's representative. Further, the firm's good reputation should be recognized widely. Women are less familiar with particular firms than are men, but a growing sophistication among females leads an increasing proportion of them to reference-check recruiting organizations before pursuing opportunities.

Not very long ago, I talked with a woman officer of a New York company. She mentioned that she had received a call from a male representative of a major recruiting firm on the West Coast. "He was calling to get my thoughts on an assignment he had to find a woman," she noted. "I was amazed at how uncomfortable he was in talking with me. He was absolutely discombobulated in trying to deal with me as a professional woman as opposed to a female. Yet he had been recruiting with a leading organization for about 20 years."

As is true in any search assignment, the client organization should assure itself that both the firm and the individual assigned to the project are what is needed to get the problem solved. Since the client representative and consultant will be working closely together, a satisfactory chemistry must exist between the two. Once the consultant has been determined, it is key to success of the client-recruiter partnership that the company avoid competing with its representative. All leads which come to the attention of the company should be furnished to the consultant for follow-up and evaluation.

Regardless of the firm selected, should the consultant searching for women executives be a woman? To say that this is so is to further the erroneous concept of the segregated labor force. Those searching for women need not be female, any more than those searching for men have to be male. It is the experience and personal qualities of the recruiter that count.

Yet, a vice president-personnel in New York asked, "Who can do better in finding females than a female search firm that's good? We gave a search for a woman to a general firm, and it took a terribly long time. They kept coming back and saying, 'We can't,' and we'd keep saying, 'Oh, yes you can.' Finally we did get a woman for our treasury function from one of the banks. The attitude of some of the male searchers was not very positive. I think they felt if they told us they couldn't find anybody that we would accept that."

Said an oil company officer, "The ideal world would be to go to a general search firm when you're looking for women. But the first five candidates might be white males. I'd say start with a well-respected, general search firm, and if you see it isn't producing results, go elsewhere. I think the large, well-established firm is better able to turn up good candidates than some of the new, specialized consultants. They just don't have any candidates above a certain salary level."

## SPECIFICATIONS COME FIRST

The first step in the search process, whether conducted internally or in partnership with a consultant, is to prepare detailed specifications for the position. Included should be title, responsibilities, reporting relationships, compensation range (including base, any incentives, perquisites, and benefits), the minimum experience requirement in terms of function, industry, and possibly geography, preferred educational level and personal qualities. Specifications should be kept as broad as possible, particularly when looking for women. Otherwise, the organization will overlook people who could do the job and narrow the choice unnecessarily; or, even worse, the prospective employer will end up not being able to identify anyone to fill the position.

Consideration of personal qualities should be limited to those bearing on ability to perform the job; to do otherwise in searching for women is to expose oneself to charges of sex discrimination. Clearly, if a prospect proves inordinately shy and is unable to lift her eyes to meet those of the interviewer, it's a good bet she's not the right person to assume the title vice president-consumer affairs and appear as the company's representative on radio, television and before a variety of community groups. However, irrelevant considerations often enter into the picture.

On one of our assignments for a billion dollar corporation, a vice president voted against extending an offer to a woman candidate for a key financial post. He pointed out that "something must be wrong since her husband is so much older than she is." Fortunately, the thinking of higher ranking management prevailed, and the candidate was hired. She turned in an outstanding performance.

After the specifications are formulated, the decision must be reached as to who will conduct the search. The designated individual must then develop a timetable. In the typical search for candidates of both sexes, three months are allowed for completing the assignment. This means that the selected individual, after giving notice, will not be available to the hiring organization for at least four months from inception of the search. When only women candidates are being sought, even more time must be allowed due to the scarcity of the prospects. Six months might be required to bring together the proper panel.

Next, the searcher should determine where his candidates are most likely to be in terms of function, industry, location, title, compensation, and target companies. If the hiring organization is conducting its own search, certain firms are likely to be placed off limits due to outside director affiliations, customer relationships, or other considerations. If a consultant is doing the work, employees of other clients will be unapproachable.

Rather than writing letters, which are more time-consuming and far less productive, the searcher should then begin telephoning both sources and prospects. In looking for women, the most likely sources are other businesswomen, both inside the hiring company and outside, who are in the same function and/or industry or geographic area. Men should be queried as well, but total reliance on the "Old Boy Network" won't produce results. I've called male sources who have assured me that *no* woman could fill any job at the level I've described!

The searcher can obtain names of sources and/or prospects in membership directories of functional, industry, and geographic associations of businesswomen or groups of both sexes. Trade magazines, again by industry, function, or location, can be helpful in identifying female prospects. The faculties of graduate business schools, particularly those offering executive programs for middle managers, can also be useful in identifying women to be approached. A personnel executive at a Midwest company advised that she keeps a file of women "who are being recognized" which is divided by function. This gives her a running start when the company decides to undertake a search for an executive.

The searcher should recognize that women usually are both more security conscious than men and less familiar with the search process. In telephoning the typical male, I find him ready to explore any situation which appears to be attractive in terms of challenge, scope of responsibility, title, reporting relationship or compensation. He believes he's qualified, whether I do or not. On the other hand, the average woman is quick to tell me that she isn't qualified for the opportunity I've described, even when I have every reason to believe she is.

On one occasion, I talked with a woman in Texas about a position as vice president of public relations as a rapidly growing Midwest company. Our client was several times larger and much more dynamic than her employer, which she served in the capacity of director of public relations. "I don't think I want to make a change," she said. "My boss, the president, treats me like a daughter." I pointed out to her as tactfully as I could that he was most certainly a parsimonious pater since she was earning at least $10,000 less than anyone else I had encountered with similar responsibilities in a company of like size. "Oh, that doesn't matter," she responded. "I don't need any more money than I'm making."

In another misadventure, I met with a woman in New York on the same assignment. She had served for 11 years as assistant director of public relations in a billion dollar company. When I first contacted her, she had expressed great enthusiasm for pursuing my client opportunity, and certainly her experience was a fit. During our get-acquainted dinner meeting, she regaled me for two hours concerning the underutilization of her abilities. Her boss, she emphasized, got all the credit and all the money. Yet, she felt she was to a large degree doing his job for him. She was sick of the injustice, sick, sick, sick. Finally, when she paused for breath, I filled her in with a description of the very attractive situation I was working on. "Don't you agree that's a good fit for your abilities and aspirations?" I asked. "When can you travel to see the client?"

She hesitated. "I really don't think I should go," she replied. "I don't feel I'm ready for that job yet."

Today, several years later, she is still in the assistant position, and I'm sure she will retire out of it. Underutilized? Yes, but by her own choice.

The client rejected an able and ambitious woman candidate because she lacked a degree and then refused to consider males. Instead, the company promoted a woman who had previously been considered too weak to be a candidate. She lasted less than a year.

Even women who are graduates of the Harvard Business School sometimes display less than expected career drive. One of those with whom I spoke recently was loath to consider a situation I described, saying that what she was doing was "okay." It was not until I reminded her of the reasons for her considerable investment of time and money at HBS that she was encouraged to consider accelerating her career progress.

Since there are so very few women at the middle and upper echelons of management beyond the age of 40, businesswomen are prone to manifest the same concern with quality of life considerations that typify the younger executive in general. Furthermore, it remains the case that even those women who are exceptional from the standpoint of education, experience, and potential have not done sufficient thinking about their careers and are less likely to consider where an opportunity might lead them than they are to question where the position is located. For all of these reasons, the searcher must be prepared to act as more of a salesperson than is required in the ordinary assignment. Career counseling must play a large part in the search process for women.

The searcher is also more likely to face hard questions up front than he is in the normal assignment for both sexes. Women who are contacted may ask whether this is a position slated for a woman, or whether both men and women are being considered. If it proves to be "for women only," their next query is whether the job is one of substance or something that has been created only to satisfy government requirements. They may also question what the climate for women is within the hiring organization. Prospects will seek to learn how many women managers and professionals are already employed by the firm, at what levels, and in what functions.

The individual conducting the search should have as his or her goal sufficient telephone screening to minimize the number of personal interviews to be conducted. In the typical search for both sexes, the searcher might count on meeting with six to twelve individuals after talking with 50 to 100 by phone. However, in searching for women only, a searcher may be forced to make 200 calls before being able to assemble a list of four to six who are suitable and can be persuaded to interview.

In meeting with prospects, the searcher must get essential information without violating the law. The next chapter covers interviewing in detail. The searcher also has a responsibility both to the organization he or she represents and to the prospects to discuss as candidly and comprehensively as possible the pluses and minuses of the position, the company, and the industry of which it is a part. After concluding the interviewing, the searcher should hope to have a minimum of two candidates to be considered for the position. He may have as many as four, depending upon the stringency of the requirements and the attractiveness of the opportunity. He should confirm the degrees claimed by the candidates and conduct at least one reference check of each, in person or by telephone. His referencing must be performed in compliance with privacy laws and should be aimed at confirming or denying the prospect of the candidate's success in the new position and new environment.

## CAREFUL SCREENING REQUIRED

Unfortunately, both for themselves and the women involved, companies are often so eager to hire women that they do not consider their candidacies as carefully as they do those of men. Having decided that the vacancy is one that "a woman" can fill, the company forgets that woman "A" is of superior intelligence while woman "B" is merely above average, that woman "C" has demonstrated strong leadership skills while woman "D" has never supervised anyone but a secretary. Not all will fit the requirements and quite possibly none will. If this proves to be the case, others must be sought or the specifications altered, but hiring an unqualified woman does not serve the cause of equal opportunity.

As soon as the panel of candidates is set, the searcher should arrange for interviews to be conducted by appropriate members of management as rapidly as possible. Especially with women, it is important not to let the interest of candidates flag due to delays. The searcher should also furnish candidates with appropriate materials concerning the company and the position. This will help the women formulate the questions to be asked during subsequent interview sessions and will also assist company representatives in evaluating the quality of candidate preparation.

Of course, those meeting the candidates should be provided in advance with materials concerning the women's career background and education, as well as the searcher's assessment of their applicability to the position. Those who will be meeting the candidates should also be briefed not only on effective interviewing, but in regard to the law. Amazingly enough, I still hear frequently from women of illegal questions asked during interviews, even by personnel people who should know better. At worst, such ignorance can lead to a suit; at best, it will make an unfavorable impression upon those who have been brought as far as the interview stage by a considerable outlay of time, effort, and money. Ideally, the decision will be made within a short time, and the organization will assume responsibility for developing a program to integrate the new hire into the organization. This will be especially important if the woman is the first or one of the few in management.

The searcher should send a letter of thanks to all those whose assistance was sought during the course of the project, advising them of the outcome. He or she should also maintain a periodic check with the candidate and the hiring manager to assure that the new association is mutually beneficial and to help correct problems before they develop into insoluble ones.

In looking for women, should an organization use advertising instead of search, in addition to search, or not at all? Advertising is always of limited help in recruiting management, for it typically attracts those looking, who are not necessarily those best qualified. In addition, advertising becomes progressively less productive as the rank of the position rises. Not only are those qualifying for positions at the higher levels far fewer in number and not as easily reached by a mass medium, but top management is unaccustomed to making career changes by this means. For the senior level, either executive search or personal contact is the typical route to a new position.

Advertising is particularly undesirable in looking for women. Those who advertise are forbidden by law to say ''women only'' even when that's what they mean. And women are far less likely to respond to ads than are men, even when the ''Equal Opportunity Employer, Male/

Female'' tag line is included. Even for those areas of business where women are concentrated, advertising won't work. Women as we have noted must be attracted to opportunities.

Ideally, employers recruiting on the outside for experienced talent will in every instance consider both men and women as candidates. This course minimizes the possibility of committing an illegality on the basis of sex. But more important, such a procedure permits consideration of top talent whatever its gender and encourages females who are suspicious of "women's jobs."

One woman vice president summed it up well when she told me, "The only time I hear from recruiters is when they are looking for a woman and want me to suggest someone or are looking for a woman and think I might be interested. Sometimes I get calls concerning an opening in a different function and a highly dissimilar industry. The presumption, I suppose, is that a woman would know all other women. Why am I never called about positions in my own industry or my own function where 'just people' are being sought? I know a lot of able men, and I'd be more than happy to suggest them. And why do I never hear about an assignment which is right in terms of my experience, without it having to be reserved for a woman? I'm not afraid to compete with men. Goodness knows, I've been doing it all my life, and I haven't done too badly, even against sizable odds. Anyway, I've had it. The next time a recruiter calls me about a 'woman's job,' I'm not going to say I'm interested. I'm not going to suggest anyone else. Instead, I'm going to tell him to shove it!''

## REFERENCES

1. Heidrick and Struggles, Inc., *Profile of a Woman Officer,* Chicago, Illinois, 1979, p. 1.
2. Shaeffer, Ruth G. and Helen Axel, *Improving Job Opportunities for Women: A Chartbook Focusing on the Progress in Business,* New York: The Conference Board, 1978, pp. 10 and 11.
3. Heidrick and Struggles, Inc., *Profile of a Woman Officer,* Chicago, Illinois, 1979, p. 1.

# 7

# Selecting Women Executives

Too many members of management are poor interviewers, although relatively few would concede this fact. The vice president of a major company reported that male managers in his organization, when first confronted with the possibility of interviewing female prospects for positions in management, complained about the amount of time assigned them. "They said they didn't have any problem spending an hour with male prospects because they could talk about sports," he pointed out. "But in interviewing women, the men claimed they ran out of subject matter in 20 minutes." Obviously if managers are devoting that much time to extraneous topics with either sex, the selection decision is basically "seat of the pants." While no choice is 100 percent sure, the more relevant information that is obtained in the interviewing process — and the more astutely it is interpreted—the more likely a successful outcome.

To be effective, interviewing requires preparation. The manager must review in advance both the job specifications and whatever material is available on the candidate so that he or she can decide what requires amplification or discovery.

The resume itself can reveal much about the individual to be seen. Both the data and their form of presentation represent the interviewee. While an excellently done vita does not guarantee a superb candidate, a poorly prepared resume should be cause for concern. Aside from such matters as misspelled words and errors in grammar and punctuation, all of which are found even at the middle and upper levels of management, a resume speaks of its subject by what is included and what is missing.

There seems to be an inverse correlation between length of vita and size of accomplishment. At the same time, omission of certain details may evidence a character fault. Any time period unaccounted for in career background should be investigated. A missing degree designation or date (Yale University, 1970, or Elmhurst College, B.A.) all too often masks a failure to matriculate, let alone graduate. Of course, women candidates may have gaps in their career experience due to familial obligations. If this is the case, the subject's community responsibilities should be explored in greater detail to determine their application to the hiring decision.

Many males feel uncomfortable interviewing females simply because such occasions are unusual. The men wish to act appropriately but aren't sure what the proper posture is. "We didn't prepare our managers properly for interviewing, and they didn't know what to do," said an official in a male-intensive industry. "They didn't know whether to stand up, light cigarettes, and open doors, or not."

Should the male interviewer treat a woman candidate as he treats women in social settings, or should he relate to her as he does to secretaries in the office? The answer, of course, is in neither way. To the greatest possible degree, women candidates for executive positions should be treated in the same manner as male candidates. An officer of a West Coast company contended, "We shouldn't make an executive woman feel different by treating her protectively. If a person is working as a professional, we should treat that individual on a professional basis. The fact that it's a man or a woman shouldn't make any difference."

The interviewer should be friendly, relaxed, nonauthoritarian, and certainly not condescending. He will refrain from calling the woman candidate pet names and will avoid referring to his secretary as "my girl." If interviewing in the office, he will pick a private place free of interruptions for the meeting. Otherwise both he and the subject can be distracted, to the detriment of the interchange. Further, since the interviewee is being asked to reveal much of herself, she needs assurance that no eavesdroppers are party to her disclosures. An open door or partial walls will make her responses guarded.

If interviewing out of town, the manager will pick an equally appropriate setting—possibly a private room at one of the airline clubs or space at the offices of his recruiting consultant. He most certainly will not invite the woman to meet him at a club which does not admit women members and has separate entrances, elevators, and dining rooms for "ladies."

## THE INTERVIEW PROCESS

The interview process itself should be the same for both men and women candidates. The form selected may be directed, nondirected, or a compromise of the two. While there are those who recommend a highly structured interview which asks the same questions of all candidates as a protection against discrimination charges, this is not feasible at the management level. On the other hand, the completely unstructured interview is difficult for the manager of average skill to employ to good advantage. Therefore, the best choice seems to be a guided interview which is dedicated to covering important topics within a designated time frame but allows the flexibility that an evolving situation demands.

The manager must decide in advance how much time to allow. Since some individuals prove more difficult to read than others, he should set aside two hours, although no more than 90 minutes may be required to reach his goal. With women as with men, he should let his mind remain open until the meeting is concluded. Some interviewees start slowly and build; others make a tremendous initial impression but appear less suitable with the passage of time. Unfortunately, there are interviewers who make their minds up within the first several minutes of the encounter and then spend the remainder of the interview seeking substantiation for that initial impression.

On the basis of the 90-minute time span, the interviewer should block out certain periods for soliciting various pieces of information, as well as a portion for providing the candidate with information and answering any questions she may have. The interviewer is concerned with two principal areas: the career experience and the personal qualities of the candidate. The former must be applicable to the job under consideration, while the latter must match not only the requirements of the position, but the environment into which the successful candidate will be placed. The personal characteristics should jibe with the values of the corporation and those of the immediate superior as well.

The manager must refrain from making assumptions based on gender before meeting the candidate, as well as during the get-together and in the evaluation process. As one corporate equal employment opportunity (EEO) officer put it, "We pay our managers to make subjective judgments, but in the human relations area their subjective judgments must be based on objective facts."[1]

"We were interviewing a female candidate for a position in our organization just the other day," commented a woman executive. "One of my male associates had seen her and said she was too aggressive. I asked, 'What does that mean, *too aggressive?*' As it turned out, he meant too aggressive for a woman! People think of male characteristics and female characteristics, and they don't think of management characteristics. Therefore, interviewers think it's wrong for a woman to display the same traits that a man in management does. They haven't been exposed to enough women managers to get over that as yet.''

Her view is supported by researchers who have found a significant bias against selecting women for managerial positions. For example, when asked to make selection decisions among candidates for management positions whose descriptions differed only by sex, undergraduate business students were prone to favor males over equally qualified females.[2] Lowest acceptance rates and poorest evaluations were given female applicants for "demanding" managerial positions. And professional interviewers, in another study, preferred males to females for a managerial position when asked to rate and rank bogus resumes, which systematically varied applicant sex.[3]

"What we need to do," said an officer with an Eastern seaboard company, "is to look at the attributes required for success on the job and forget about the sex of the candidates involved!" Yet, there is evidence to indicate that only when an applicant is seen as overqualified is sex-role incongruence accepted.[4]

A woman executive in the East complained, "I don't know why it's so much harder for men to interview women than men—why can't they ask the same questions and get the same information? I've been in interview situations where I've been talked down to. It would never happen if I were male! The interviewers ask the most insignificant things. *I'm* the one who has to bring up the hard questions.''

The discomfort that many males feel in interviewing women probably accounts for the above woman's experiences as well as the results of a survey of Penn State women students in technical fields who were undergoing campus interviewing. A third of the women found company representatives to be condescending or sarcastic. "One company came right out and said they didn't think a woman should be in research," reported one student. Indeed, 60 percent of the women felt they had been discouraged from pursuing employment because of their sex. Almost half the women reported a discussion regarding their ability to cope with male counterparts, which recruiters suggested would "be at least challenging, if not impossible.''

Some of the women were interviewed by female recruiters, and 80 percent of the students rated the women corporate representatives better:

"definitely more professional," "much more probing," "more honest, open, and receptive."[5] Other observers have found women to be egalitarian interviewers, who do not devalue either those of their own sex or males.[6]

Certainly, the male interviewer should never decide for himself that the woman is too fragile to assume a production management responsibility in a dirty and noisy factory environment, or that she is carrying too many home responsibilities to take a crammed briefcase with her each night. And it is illegal for him to conclude that she must be eliminated from consideration because peers, superiors, subordinates, and clients or customers would not be willing to accept a woman.

The first order of business for the interviewer in facing the candidate is to set the stage for a pleasant conversation. The manager may or may not select the candidate, and the candidate may or may not choose to join the organization; however, whatever the outcome, the interviewer should establish and maintain a cordial relationship with the individual he's meeting. He should be as concerned with furthering his own image and that of his organization as the interviewee is in making a favorable impression.

If the interview is conducted in an office, the manager should refrain from sitting behind the desk; this will foster a sense of equality. By maintaining eye contact, displaying a sense of humor, and evidencing his interest in the subject, the interviewer can relax the candidate and himself. His responsive face and deferential ear will encourage commentary vital to the goal of selecting the right individual.

Needless to say, the interviewer will exercise care not to display sex bias. This still happens, however. A female MBA in Chicago recently was told by a corporate personnel man that her salary target was too high "for a woman." During the course of her job search, a second male interviewer asked her, "You're not one of those women's libbers, are you?" And still another questioned her about her contraception practices.

Even remarks by an interviewer which do not touch on illegal areas can be totally inappropriate, of course. Another woman recently underwent a job interview in Cleveland. "You wouldn't believe the questions he asked me," she recounted. "I'm 49 and I look my age, but not any older. I've had gray hair since my twenties, and so I've given up coloring it. Well, the interviewer asked me why I let my hair remain gray and didn't I think it would look better colored. I had been undergoing a heavy travel schedule, and I was tired when I met with him, no question about that. He looked at me and remarked that my eyes were somewhat bloodshot. He told me it was particularly important for women to watch their appearance. 'I don't know whether it's fatigue or drugs or what, but you should do something about your eyes,' he told me.''

Many companies offer training in interviewing for managers. Commonly, the instruction centers on the selection interview and focuses on legal and illegal queries. A leading transportation company counsels managers on interviewing by means of audiovisual presentations and a newsletter which highlights the ''how'' of bias-free interviewing. ''We give examples of questions to be avoided,'' a personnel officer said, ''such as 'What is your husband going to say if you work late?' Of course there's an art to interviewing that the average person doesn't even understand. One of the major pitfalls here is that the managers want to do too much of the talking.''

A bank officer declared, ''Some illegal questions still get asked from time to time, but we try to make sure they don't. Subjects can be gotten at in a nondiscriminatory way. After all, if you want to know if a woman will travel or work overtime, all you have to do is ask her. You don't have to inquire whether her mother is available to take care of the kids! We communicate our concern in a variety of ways—a manager's guide, meetings, supplemental written instructions. We cover everyone who's involved in talking with women, from college recruiters and employment office personnel on up.''

A Midwest-based manufacturing company which does little in the way of training nevertheless requires every manager to undergo thorough interviewing instruction. ''We've had no discernable difficulties,'' said a personnel staffer, ''but don't you know, even now somebody may be saying, 'And how many children have you got?' '' An executive in New York admitted that despite an in-house course on selection interviewing for line managers, ''We still have a terrible problem.''

Another Manhattan-based organization runs training workshops that have proven quite successful. ''We put finance, marketing, and engineering managers who do college recruiting through a two-day session,'' noted an officer. ''We hire a few college students to come in and serve as guinea pigs so the managers get to practice. At the end of the course, the students form a panel and furnish us with a critique. Believe me, you learn real fast when all of your errors are exposed that way!''

## STAYING WITHIN THE LAW

Some companies use, as a basic guide to staying within the law, this axiom: If you'd ask a man the question, ask a woman. This doesn't always prove to be good advice, since some interviewers ask males illegal questions. It's dangerous, for example, to ask either a man or woman date of birth or age in advance of employment. A better guide would be this: If the inquiry is truly job related, feel free to ask it. Unquestionably, the best procedure is to know the law and to stay within it.

Said a consultant, "I know male managers who interview women and are afraid to ask them anything. Really, the restrictions are no greater in interviewing women than men. The males are just more uncomfortable in talking with females. Some of the managers in these days of government regulations and pressure groups become extremely cautious. They suspect they're being set up for a suit by any member of a protected class who comes in." While there are those who believe it's impossible both to avoid illegalities and to find out what must be known, this is not so. A greater degree of adroitness is called for, but the interviewer can still get answers to his job-related concerns.

The vice president of an oil company noted, "We train our interviewers, both those who are full time and operating managers who do it on occasion. We counsel them as to what they can and can't ask, but we have not shied away from as many questions as other companies have. There are firms that won't ask a woman her marital status, and if she has a spouse, what he does. We approach that topic in a different way. We'll inquire if she has any relatives who are employed by a competitor or any company with which we do business and if so, in what capacity. While we're exploring conflict of interest, we'll also ask if she has any relatives on our payroll, and if so in what capacity. There are certain working relationships we avoid: a spouse, parent, or child is not permitted to work in the direct management line of the family member; and we don't want to hire a woman as an auditor if her husband is one of our disbursement officers."

It's important for the interviewer to get answers to considerations key to the candidate's appropriateness. And he can do so, while staying within the law, as the following examples demonstrate.

IMPROPER: Does your husband object to your traveling on business?

PROPER: Are there any personal considerations which would prevent you from doing the traveling this job calls for?

IMPROPER: This job calls for long hours, as you know. Are you going to be able to arrange suitable care for your mother all the time you're gone?

PROPER: Are there any personal considerations which would prevent you from working the number of hours this job calls for?

IMPROPER: How are you going to be able to relocate? Isn't your husband's career tied to Los Angeles?

PROPER: Are there any personal considerations which would prevent your relocation to Denver?

The interviewer should keep careful notes of responses made to such questions. If the candidate is hired and fails to live up to her answers, appropriate action can be taken. Record keeping proves helpful in the event of an investigation.

Table 7–1 specifies safe and unsafe questions. In determining how the woman got where she is today, the interviewer will wish to learn as much as he is able concerning her family background, education, work history, and personal situation. He will find, if he conducts himself in a friendly and interested manner, that the interviewee may well volunteer items which legally cannot be sought. She may furnish marital status, number and ages of children, husband's education and occupation, and even information on her childhood circumstances. Further, questions which might have appeared threatening at or near the beginning of the session may evoke a ready response later on. Queries concerning compensation and personal assessment are examples.

Many authorities on interviewing advise taking notes throughout the course of the meeting. One piece of research on interviewers showed that managers missed an average of half the items of information concerning the candidate after viewing a selection interview on videotape.[7] However, note taking should be avoided unless the manager is able to perform the task without distracting either himself or the interviewee.

Some experts suggest that the notes deal not with additional factual information gleaned, but with the interviewer's impressions. If this advice is followed, however, the manager would have to conceal his notes. At best this is a distraction and at worst a deterrent to disclosure. By debriefing immediately following the interview, the manager should experience no problem in recording personal characteristics germane to the evaluative process.

## THE "LEARNING" PORTION

In the "learning" phase of the interview, the interviewer should ask open-ended, value-judgment questions without telegraphing the responses he prefers. He should make his inquiries as clear and as concise as possible. The freer the responses of the interviewee, the better. The

Table 7-1. Safe and Unsafe Interview Questions

| TOPIC | INQUIRIES |
|---|---|
| Name | Safe to ask name; unsafe to ask about a change in name, or to ask for a former name |
| Marital Status | Unsafe to ask marital status, marriage plans, present or planned children |
| Birthplace | Safe to ask interviewee's place of birth; unsafe to ask that of parents |
| Residence | Safe to ask current residence and length of residence in city and state |
| Race | Unsafe to ask |
| Religion | Unsafe to ask religion, church attended, or name of religious leader |
| National Origin | Unsafe to ask |
| Age | Unsafe to ask |
| Education | Safe to ask schools, degrees obtained and years granted |
| Foreign Language Capability | Safe to ask foreign language capability but unsafe to ask how capability came about |
| Career History | Safe to ask past employers, years of association, positions held, responsibilities and compensation received. |
| Assessment of Strengths and Weaknesses | Safe to ask |
| Career Ambitions | Safe to ask |

manager learns relatively little from a "yes" or "no" answer. However, he should not allow the candidate to digress into irrelevant subject matter. Her observations, opinions, and judgments on meaningful matters are what he seeks.

Some managers waste their time and that of the candidate by simply going over facts spelled out on the resume. Instead, the interviewer should seek in examining career history to learn what the woman has liked and disliked about the positions she's held, what she's accomplished in each, her perception of her strengths and weaknesses, and her view of her career future.

Bernard Baruch once commented, "Most of the successful people I've known are ones who do more listening than talking." Nowhere is listening more important to success than in interviewing. Yet, due to nervousness or ego considerations, the inexpert interviewer can become loquacious. Ideally, the manager should let the subject talk 85 to 95 percent of the time. The manager's contribution to the conversation should be limited largely to supportive comments which demonstrate attention and interest and encourage the subject to keep talking. Phrases such as "Isn't that interesting," "I can imagine how you felt!" and "You're certainly to be commended for that!" are most useful. Certainly, the manager should keep his opinions to himself and never evidence surprise or displeasure at what he hears. There is absolutely no advantage to expressing his own views unless they are in keeping with those of the interviewee.

The manager needs to concentrate on the meaning of what is said and what is not said. As the interview proceeds, he should decide which thoughts should be stored for future reference and which may be discarded as unimportant. Although he must manage the interview to make certain that all of the appropriate ground is covered, he must never appear hurried or anticipate the subject's response or his own next question. Since the mind works four to ten times faster than most people speak, it's easy to miss an important point made by the subject if her response is not heard in its totality.

Occasional pauses are desirable. They serve to make both parties to the conversation feel less pressured and may elicit some significant information which otherwise would never have come to light. Most interviewing counselors feel that a special effort must be made to ferret out unfavorable information since the subject is desirous of showing herself to best advantage. However, it rarely proves a problem to obtain negatives if the interviewer has been successful in establishing rapport. For most people, there is nothing more welcome than an all-too-rare opportunity to talk about themselves. With proper encouragement, nine out of ten subjects prove so anxious to talk that they will present a well-rounded picture, unknowingly or even knowingly. If by some chance the interviewer does not get the information that he seeks, he should press until he does. Vague or unclear responses are no more acceptable from a woman than they would be from a man.

Interviewers should remember that women are probably not as accustomed to the process as men for at least two reasons. First, it has only been over the past decade that women have been sought for managerial and professional positions. Second, because of lower career aspirations as well as a perception of discrimination, women have not pursued opportunities as frequently as men.

A male subject in an interview assumes, without evidence to the contrary, that he will receive consideration on his merits and if selected will be permitted to advance within the employing organization as far as his talents permit him to go. In contrast, a woman may question at the outset how the interviewer himself feels about women. Will she be given proper consideration as a candidate? When satisfied that no prejudice against her gender exists there, she may wish next to explore the commitment of the organization.

She may wonder if she is being considered because she is a woman. If this is the case—or she suspects that it is—she will question whether her qualifications will permit her to succeed in the post for which she is being considered. If she becomes convinced that they will, she will want to know whether the post is one of substance or a created "woman's job." If the task is real, she will seek to learn whether the possibility of upward mobility is present. She will, in other words, be doubtful about many of the considerations that her male peers take for granted. If the female candidate fails to state such concerns, it is not inappropriate for the interviewer to cover the subjects. He may affirm the organization's commitment to equal opportunity and name some of the more highly placed women within the company, as well as the firm's overall progress in moving women into management.

"I've met a lot of women in my recruiting," pointed out a personnel executive in the Midwest. "Personally, I'm turned off by any woman who's more interested in the women issues than the job issues. I don't think I feel any differently about that than line management does. I think all of us expect some questions such as how many women and at what levels, but it gets down to the manner in which the questions are asked."

One particular concern of the interviewer in interfacing with women is to detect those who are overly sensitive to the specter of sex discrimination. "We have a few who read sexism into everything that happens to them," commented one manager. "I sure wish we knew how to weed those people out before we hire them."

"Generally, the women who fail are the ones who see ghosts everywhere," a high-ranking female executive pointed out. "They can't deal with the interrelationships. They are very smart in most cases, but sometimes they think they're smarter than the men they work for when they really aren't and are overcompensating for their insecurity. And they make issues of things that aren't really important. For example, at a meeting they'll get up to get themselves some coffee. A male will say, 'Would you pour some for me?', and the woman will reply, 'No, why should I?' That's silly—the men will pour for you if you ask them, so why the big deal? I'd say instead of saving themselves for the important issues, they become so difficult to work with over little things that others don't have any energy left to concentrate on their jobs. And it ends up nobody will have anything to do with the women. You simply have to recognize, man or woman, when your style is not acceptable in the culture of an organization."

This is not to say that only one style is correct. Another executive pointed out a classroom exercise in which males and females lock arms in a circle, and an outsider is left to his or her own devices to get inside. "Invariably," she noted, "men will use force to break through. Women on the other hand will talk their way in. But what's the difference? They both end up inside which is where they're supposed to be."

An East Coast executive emphasized, "At this stage in the evolution of females in business, an unlikeable male is probably more acceptable in terms of getting ahead than the female who has difficulty getting along. Her problem is compounded by her being a woman; I don't know why."

An officer of a West Coast company said, "I see a difference in women managers in terms of age. The older ones have overcome a lot of obstacles in their careers. They've struggled with nonacceptance, and they've had to make accommodations to the male-oriented business world. If they experience slights, they can shrug them off. But younger women seem to make an issue of everything. Lots of their complaints are unimportant from a male point of view, and this tends to impede progress toward equal opportunity. The men think, who needs these problems?"

## THE "TELLING" PORTION

In the "telling" phase of the interview, it is incumbent upon the manager to describe both the pluses and minuses of the position, insofar as he is able. He should also outline the advantages and disadvantages of the environment from the subject's point of view. If the woman would be the first female at her level, at least in her location, this point should be communicated. Some women will count the pioneering role as a plus; others won't be concerned about it, but more may be dubious about the additional pressure such uniqueness imposes.

Since in all probability the manager will not have decided, on the basis of an initial meeting, whether this candidate is the answer, he should endeavor to maintain the individual's level of interest without overselling. Unlikely prospects can be discouraged without being eliminated until a conclusion has been reached. The interview should be ended in the same gracious manner that characterized its start. The manager should explain when and how the subject will be hearing from the organization, and this commitment should be kept.

Before arriving at any conclusions regarding his selection for a middle or upper echelon position, the interviewer may wish to see candidates twice or even three times. He may wish the subject to meet with one or more other individuals who would be important to the successful candidate's progress. Seldom do different interviewers display complete agreement, and the diversity of views is helpful in weighing pros and cons regarding various candidates.

Ability coupled with motivation in the proper setting equals a successful performance. Probably the biggest mistake made in selecting a woman for a key position is failure to consider whether her personal characteristics are appropriate to the organization. Admittedly, there is limited availability of qualified women, and companies may be eager to add females to the management ranks. However, to select a woman who doesn't fit the environment is to doom the match to failure. If the firm is a large, conservative organization, an impatient woman is no more appropriate than a hard-driving man. And in surroundings where a high degree of personal commitment is called for, a low-energy woman is as out of place as a lethargic man would be.

"I try to be very up front," said a personnel executive at a manufacturing company, "and give candidates a clear impression that I'm more interested in their making the right decision than I am in their joining our company. There have been some that I've dissuaded; I didn't think they'd be happy. And it had nothing to do with their being women."

Unfortunately, it is still the case that women's backgrounds of experience and progress in compensation cannot be compared with those of men. Any woman older than the early thirties is unlikely to have been exposed to the same career opportunities as her male peers. If her education is not particularly appropriate for business, the lack may have stemmed not from disinterest in the field as much as serious doubt about return on investment. If her experience is not as broad, it may be because she was channeled into a specialty and found no way of breaking out. Further, since women typically began their careers at a lower salary than males and did not progress as rapidly, they remain lower paid. Career progress of females, in other words, should be evaluated in light of difficulties encountered and overcome.

Said a consultant, "The incident in a person's career is not important; it's how the individual responded. Did it represent an opportunity or a trauma? Did the person take advantage even of a negative situation and grow from it, or was she defeated by it? Sometimes with a woman you have to look more at potential than career track record."

At a New York-based company, an executive commented that "whatever are established as qualifications for a position, you should use for women, although perhaps a little more creatively. For example, if male candidates have had ten years or so of line management—two years in this plant, two years in that plant—well, you're not going to find many if any women with the same experience. But if you think about what it is that those male managers gained from their exposure and try to find women who have obtained the same thing in another way, the likelihood is the woman can succeed."

However, it's possible to be too creative. At a transportation company several women had been considered for a director level position "and the vice president to whom the position reports very much wanted a woman in the job," explained a personnel executive. "We finally decided that none of the women had reached the point of taking the step. That probably sounds like a chauvinist rationalization, but I think it will take those women two to three years more to prepare themselves. We ended up with a man in the job. I really felt we would be doing the women a disservice if we deprived them of additional developmental experience. When you see people who have been one year in an assignment before they move onto another where they again spend a year, you know that eventually they're going to have problems functioning effectively. This is not exclusively a female manager problem. We're running the same risk with some of our young males who are moving awfully fast."

On the personal side, there is no need in selecting a woman to sacrifice intellectual efficiency, emotional maturity, physical stamina, human relations skills, or ability to organize and direct. Like men, women in management should possess the appropriate human qualities: they control their emotions rather than letting their emotions control them; they are able to deal with people at all levels; they understand themselves and they understand other people; they can strategize, plan and execute, providing leadership, support, and constructive criticism to others. If any necessary difference does exist between women and their male colleagues, it may be that women require an even stronger spirit of independence. Men are lauded universally for succeeding in business; no conflict exists for them. It remains a far different story for women.

It is still the case that interview evaluation forms being used for hiring decisions rely on too many subjective impressions which cannot be substantiated. The more explicit the job specifications and the more closely the evaluation form is tied to the career experience and personal qualities needed for success in that position, the more demonstrably bias-free will be the employment decision.

Some business people conclude that selection of a woman automatically means that the "best qualified" procedure was not followed. Such an assumption clearly is unjustified. It has developed from the propensity of certain organizations to select women without regard to their qualifications, or in spite of them. "The key to the whole issue of equal opportunity is whether you're bringing women in based on qualifications. If the peers don't see the competence, they'll be upset," emphasized a personnel executive at a petroleum company. "I think the selection process is crucial. You've got to select women on their merits, just as you presumably do with men."

## REFERENCES

1. "Acting Affirmatively to End Job Bias," *Business Week,* 27 January 1975, p. 98.
2. Rosen, Benson and Thomas H. Jerdee, "Effects of Applicant's Sex and Difficulty of Job on Evaluations of Candidates for Managerial Positions," *Journal of Applied Psychology* **59**(4): 512 (1974).
3. Dipboye, Robert L., Howard L. Fromkin and Kent Wiback, "Relative Importance of Applicant Sex, Attractiveness, and Scholastic Standing in Evaluation of Job Applicant Resumes," *Journal of Applied Psychology* **60**:43 (1975).
4. Cohen, S. L. and K. A. Bunker, "Subtle Effects of Sex-Role Stereotypes on Recruiters' Hiring Decisions," *Journal of Applied Psychology* **60**:571 (1975).
5. Driscoll, Jeanne Baker and H. Richard Hess, "The Recruiter: Woman's Friend or Foe?," *Journal of College Placement* **34**(4):48 (Summer, 1974).
6. Feather, N. and J. Simon, "Reactions to Male and Female Success and Failure in Sex-Linked Occupations: Impressions of Personality, Causal Attributions and Perceived Likelihood of Different Consequences," *Journal of Personnel and Social Psychology* **31**:20 (1975).
7. Carlson, R. E., et al., "Improvements in the Selection Interview," *Personnel Journal* Vol. 50, p. 271 (1971).

# 8

# *Attracting Women Executives*

Whether an organization seeking women for its management team is able to attract candidates from outside will be dependent in part upon the corporate image. If one single communication may be said to represent the corporation more than others, it is the annual report. A variety of audiences, ranging from prospective investors to would-be employees, gains an impression of management's philosophy and the company's style from this document. In reviewing the report, women will conclude that a firm either represents a supportive environment, affording a climate conducive to realization of their career objectives, or a setting that is unlikely to be suitable.

Specifically, the women might observe how many females are pictured, how many of these are portrayed in nontraditional roles, and how many women in the middle and upper echelons of management are represented. Also, readers might review whether the company alludes to women specifically in discussing equal opportunity efforts, and if so, whether numerical results are cited.

A review of one hundred annual reports of some of the country's largest industrial and nonindustrial companies showed that very few devoted attention to women in management. Eighty-five percent of the books contained pictures of women, with the number ranging from 48 to none. Only 38 percent of the reports showed females in nontraditional roles; the others limited their photographs and illustrations to women as housewives, women as mothers, or women as clerical workers.

In a majority of cases, any female pictured in a nontraditional role was a member of the board of directors. However, Chessie System devoted half a page to pictures of nine female employees at work. Entitled "More Women Are Moving Up the Ladder at Chessie," the feature included a supervisor of station operations and an inspector of police, among others in nontraditional roles. Only five other reports depicted women in middle or upper echelon management posts. Of these, one showed two vice presidents and a director, another had three middle managers in a training class, two showed middle managers on their jobs, and the last depicted a female business owner as a customer of the annual report company.

Forty-one percent of the companies referred to their equal employment opportunity (EEO) activities and made specific reference to women in doing so. However, the proportion of firms specifying the number of women in management and professional roles was very small, representing just eleven percent of the total. Only two companies presented detailed information on both number of women and percent of women found in each of the EEO-1 categories and compared current standings with earlier figures. More frequently, organizations referred to sizable percentage gains without including actual numbers.

Of course, other publications can be just as important as the annual report in portraying the company to women. Recruiting brochures, employee handbooks and corporate magazines designed for external as well as internal audiences should feature both men and women in a variety of roles. "We have a magazine that goes to all domestic employees and to opinion-molders—elected officials, college presidents, people like that," said a personnel executive at a New York-based company. "We have consciously done many feature stories on women and minorities in management; out of eight issues a year, at least two covers will be this type of story." A leading bank devotes one issue of its magazine each year to senior-level women employees, primarily to demonstrate to lower-level women that their opportunity to progress is limited only by their ability and ambition. An industrial firm uses reprints of similar magazine articles, accompanied by reprints of advertising featuring women, as recruiting aids.

However, at least one major company is concerned about the possibility of visible talent being wooed away and endeavors to avoid all external publicity concerning managers of both sexes. Unquestionably, women in "men's jobs" attract press attention, but it is not always completely favorable. A recent wire story revealed that the sight of a female in the cockpit crew had caused a few fearful passengers to change flights. And a *Business Week* article on industrial saleswomen pointed out that customer resistance is not uncommon, at least initially.[1] Perhaps fear of unfavorable investor, customer or simply public reaction leads some companies to downplay new roles for women in their organizations. But others feel differently.

"Our management is convinced we have a good story to tell. We take a high profile regarding the hiring and promotion of women," one of the nation's largest companies reported. "We were part of an article in *Fortune* on the progress of women MBAs, and we've had other publicity we did nothing to generate," a consumer products vice president related. "There's an awareness that women are doing well at this company, and recruiting is not a problem."

A key manager at a service organization said, "In our advertising as well as in our employee and recruitment media, we assiduously strike a visual balance between sexes and among races. We have undertaken to play a rather prominent role in the community insofar as changing existing sex stereotypes is concerned. We do more than we need to do in order to keep a minority applicant flow coming our way. We have a lot of influence in locations where we're the sole or at least the major employer. We have accepted the changing of stereotypes as a societal obligation, as well as a legal one."

In advertising, both the medium and the message influence the impression made on women by the corporation. What, for example, did an automotive company gain by running in a woman's magazine an ad touting one product as a car only a man could appreciate? Companies cannot be expected to create new stereotypes—portraying all women as executives—but they can recognize that a majority of American women are working outside the home, and that many more intend to enter or reenter the work force. They should also acknowledge for their own benefit that females buy cars, liquor, and stereos as well as cosmetics and clothes. In advertising, companies might occasionally depict women in nontraditional roles—blue collar, white collar or managerial and professional. It seems all too seldom that an airline advertisement shows a woman business traveler, an insurance company depicts a female with briefcase among the waiting commuters at a train station, or a toiletries company features a woman jockey winning a race. And only one clothing store has used the *Wall Street Journal* to advertise special facilities for the woman executive shopper!

Recently, the U. S. Civil Rights Commission reported that "the portrayal of minorities and women on television hasn't improved in recent years." The commission noted that women are cast in a disproportionately high number of "immature, demeaning and comical roles." White female characters are most often cast as someone between 21 and 30, and the report claimed, "Women are increasingly being stereotyped on television as sexy girls."[2] More than a third of the females are depicted as unemployed or without any identifiable pursuit. "Most others are students, secretaries, homemakers, household workers or nurses. For every woman who's in law enforcement, at least two are criminals," a commission spokesman emphasized.[3] Perhaps a sponsor departing from this pattern would find increasing acceptance by women of its company and products or services.

Institutional or image advertising can make plain that companies welcome female talent; however, the implication should not be that women are sought because they are women. "I don't want any ads that say we want women," a female personnel executive declared. "I want our ads to say we hire without regard to sex and mean it. Women resent being picked because of their sex or in spite of it."

An officer at a consumer products company explained, "We do a lot of institutional advertising which runs coast to coast. A lot of it is recruiting oriented and runs in the major women's magazines. We're involved with a number of women's groups nationwide. Our recruiting people are male and female. We're known as an organization that is oriented toward females. We have more of a problem attracting males because they think that top management comprises a lot of women, which isn't true, at least at this point."

Echoing this sentiment, an officer of another consumer products company declared, "Our problem is with men who are interviewed on campus by a woman—a line representative, possibly a brand manager. If the men pass muster, they come in here and are seen by the recruiter's boss, who also may be a woman. And they end up wondering if there is any opportunity for men in this company."

## SUPPORTING WOMEN'S GROUPS

A number of firms support women's organizations in a variety of ways. In addition to financial contributions, companies provide speakers for meetings and personnel to serve on boards and committees, as well as making the corporate presence felt at affairs staged by the organization. "We want people to realize we mean it when we say we're looking for women for our company," an East Coast executive explained.

Such actions not only make obvious corporate support of progress for women, but also provide access to knowledgeable sources regarding female prospects for employment with the company. "The women we hire from outside have come from other companies and by referrals from the women's organizations we work with," said an officer of a conglomerate.

"We use them as feeders, our liaison to find out where people are located."

A personnel executive in the Midwest said, "We look at a long list of women's organizations, but we scrutinize very carefully those we donate money to." Said another corporate representative, "When you start giving out money, word spreads fast. Women and proposals appear left and right. We make on-site visits to see what organizations are all about."

One company emphasized, "We look for programs that are aimed at developing women in nontraditional fields to make the community richer in female resources." However, another firm takes a broader view; an executive explained, "The groups we support are working in behalf of the Equal Rights Amendment, removing sexist language from text-books—lots of different areas. We feel we must be involved with the women's movement generally, and this is strongly supported by our top management. Of course some companies are afraid of dealing with women's organizations for fear they'll be a focus of unfavorable actions later. They don't want to call attention to themselves. Our feeling is, if your record looks good, and you've done all you possibly can, then you need have no fear about reaching out."

Many companies encourage their women executives to act as role models by assuming a high profile outside the organization as well as inside. "Our women are encouraged to be active in organizations of their choosing," noted an executive at a manufacturing company. "First they join their professional societies, and then the women-only group in the field. There's an obligation there—the women's groups have younger memberships, and it's a mentoring role for our people."

An officer of an Eastern company pointed out that "one of our vice presidents was honored by an outside organization last year. Our chairman was present at the award ceremony and made a speech which has been quoted a lot. I think our stance relating to women in manage-ment is becoming very well known."

At another organization in the same city, an officer said, "We are often asked to speak about what we've accomplished. In fact one of our female personnel executives has appeared this year at several schools and at other companies, telling them about our program to advance women. We're very proud of what we've done."

A bank in another city explained that women employees are encour-aged to become active in women's organizations. "In addition," pointed out a personnel officer, "our foundation supports women's groups— everything from a rape crisis line to assistance for women who want to return to the labor force. We picture women in our annual report and commercials; we recruit at women's schools, and we advertise in women's publications. Some time ago, we won the account of one of the nation's leading women's organizations, and we still have it.''

Of course, it's highly advantageous for organizations to avoid discrimination charges because of the unfavorable publicity, as well as the considerable expense involved. Yet, court records demonstrate that tens of thousands of discrimination charges have been brought over the past decade against companies of every size by individuals and groups of employees.

Some charges, though, are more harmful to corporate image than are others; those involving the greatest number of people and the broadest charges, resulting in the most sizable settlements and widest publicity, rank as most damaging both to bottom line and to reputation. For instance, a class action suit filed by 13 women in behalf of 10,000 employees resulted in a multimillion dollar judgment against one of the country's largest banks; news of the case appeared in the nation's press over several years.

The women claimed virtually every possible form of discrimination: in recruitment, hiring, job assignment, compensation and benefits. One well-publicized piece of evidence concerned a job-seeking woman who sent a copy of her resume to the institution and received a reply indicating that no openings existed for someone with her background. However, a short time later, she sent the same resume using initials rather than her first name and in return received a letter addressed to "Mr. _____,'' requesting that she come in for an interview. Such publicity can be harmful to recruiting and to business long after the suit is settled.

## THE ROLE OF RECRUITING

The effectiveness of any company's campaign to attract women executives will stem in large part from the nature of recruiting activities. In campus and work place recruiting, organizations should use both women and men as representatives and be certain that all are properly trained in the way to interface with female prospects. ''We have special training for all our recruiters,'' explained an executive at a sizable company, ''whether they are new or experienced. An important part is an update on EEO law. We review questions to ask and questions to avoid.''

Organizations may need to include women's colleges or coed institutions with large numbers of women students in addition to traditional sources. Many women's colleges are now supplementing their traditional liberal arts curricula with business-oriented course work. A survey conducted in 1977 found that close to one-third of women undergraduates at 67 women's colleges were majoring in business administration, management, or economics.[4]

"We've done some institutional advertising, we've done some recruiting at women's colleges, and we have paid special attention to women at schools which have good technical programs," recounted a petroleum executive. "We make a special point of seeking out the women and asking them to interview with us. That's a fairly common practice among companies like ours, since we're competing for a very limited commodity."

In affirmation, an official at another company in the same industry noted, "We recruit at 189 colleges. Our representatives are responsible for seeking out the most competent people to be found on campus. We go after the students; we don't let the students pick us."

In seeking experienced managers and professionals, prospective employers should consider placing ads in previously untried publications, such as those issued by women's professional societies. Companies would also do well to place emphasis on recruiting employees of firms known to hire women but not to offer them appropriate promotional opportunities.

For the last 15 years, Ford Motor Company has conducted a College Roundtable Program. Participants include officers and managers (among them blacks and females) and thousands of students and faculty from various colleges in the area surrounding each roundtable site. All expenses are paid by Ford. The objective of the two-day forum is to initiate an exchange between campus and company and to attain a higher level of understanding of business, the automotive industry, and Ford. A sizable number of questions relate to women's issues. Other companies, also taking a longer range view than immediate hiring needs, are working with colleges and even high schools to channel women (and men) into business careers. Managers—both male and female—act as executives in residence, as guest lecturers and as speakers on Career Day panels.

"If we're going to have a broader participation of women in our company, we'll need female engineers," said an executive at a capital goods company. "We send our women engineers out to high schools as part of our outreach effort to talk to girls about how great engineering is, and that it's the wave of the future for females. I don't believe they're responding; I guess we just don't know how to do it. Maybe its presumptuous to think we can change society because we need engineers. It's still the case that women would rather work for a glamour business than for us. And they certainly prefer glamorous locations to the small towns in the Northeast, South, and West, where our facilities are located.''

Each year, a sizable New York-based organization brings to the company two dozen female college sophomores who are liberal arts majors to spend a week, all expenses paid. ''A lot of these women are uncertain what to do when they get out of school,'' a personnel executive explained. ''We give them a chance to find out firsthand what some of the options are. They are able to meet one-on-one with people in areas the students think they might be interested in and find out what such a job is really like. That helps them to decide whether to take particular courses or to go on to graduate school. We tell them, go back and share with your classmates what you found out. Whether your opinion is good or bad, it's your responsibility to let others on campus know what you think. The students hold conferences, write articles for campus newspapers, and some have even invited us to visit and talk to student groups. They ask tough questions, but many of them end up deciding all of us are more real than they thought we'd be.''

Many companies, particularly those in the technical area which have experienced considerable difficulty in locating women scientists and engineers, offer scholarships in nontraditional specialties as well as internships and co-op programs. ''We have a special program for women and minorities,'' pointed out an oil company executive. ''We'll take them while they're still in high school or between their freshman and sophomore years in college. We try to identify the mutual fits before graduation.''

An officer at a high technology company said, ''We started an intern program last summer. Our strategy, of course, is to attract some of these people as employees. One young woman worked on an important project and made such an impressive contribution that she was called back after she'd returned to school to serve as a consultant. We flew her in to attend a national meeting of our managers.''

Some firms participate in job fairs along with other companies; at such get-togethers, working women are able to meet company representatives and learn of the opportunities employment at the various concerns offers. Other organizations sponsor meetings of their own for undergraduates. In collaboration with the Center for Research in Career Development at Columbia University's Graduate School of Business, Citibank sponsored a Business Career Forum for 240 sophomore and junior college women from twelve traditionally female schools. The first half of the all-day session featured women in a variety of occupations who discussed how they combine business and personal lives. The remaining time was devoted to representatives of six schools offering MBA programs. Highlights of the day were recorded in a brochure, entitled "Getting Down to Business," which was made available to interested parties.

"Women we interview ask what women are in our organization and in what jobs," pointed out an officer of a New York company. "It's nice to be able to say we have them and to tell what they're doing." Nothing is more telling in its impact on women executives than the company's record of success as indicated not only by the number, but location and level of women employees. Another key consideration is the view of EEO held by both men and women workers. Given a choice, women would prefer to join a company where all employees—females and males—feel they are treated fairly, and where there is no perceptible backlash problem. This means the equal opportunity program must have been soundly conceived and executed with considerable care.

In fact, confidence in the fairness of the company transcends the number of women already in management as the ultimate factor determining whether a woman candidate will accept a managerial or professional job. As an executive in a male-oriented industry explained, "We get the more able, more confident women because there are no role models. The women we attract either think the environment is okay, or if it isn't, that they'll be able to change it. Certainly, the women we hire aren't shy, but they're smart in how they handle things. I suppose the best description for them is 'pleasantly aggressive.' "

An executive at another male-oriented company noted, "The last thing talented young women MBAs want to do these days is join a female-intensive company. They want to be in a male industry where the pay is better and the problems are more complex than those encountered in retailing or insurance. Many of them have an interest in international issues, so that adds to our appeal. And if you're corporate staff, not having a technical degree doesn't matter. Of course there was a time when getting to the top in a technical company meant you had to be an engineer. Now, however, there are many more financial, personnel, and legal experts in key roles. The world has changed, and a person must understand the external environment and how to interface with it."

## DETERMINING THE OFFER

Once the strong interest of the prospective employee has been aroused, the offer she receives will either sway her to join the firm or to turn away from it. Obviously, both financial and nonfinancial factors must be acceptable. The title and responsibilities of the position offered the candidate should reflect her abilities and aspirations. Compensation should be in keeping with the job: not less because the woman has been underpaid previously, and not more because she is a scarce commodity.

In the early seventies, entry-level women engineers were being offered stock options, monthly salaries $200 to $300 higher than those offered white males, and placement on the payroll for six months before graduation.[5] Many companies are still paying premiums for women with technical training while others which refuse to counter with similar offers sometimes, but not always, lose out. Any remaining disparity in pay by sex is likely to prove a short-run phenomenon, since the number of women enrolled in mathematics, physical science, and engineering courses is skyrocketing.

"There's a good supply of women engineers now," said an official of a technical company. "We're able to apply the same standards as we do for men." And a personnel executive in the East pointed out, "As recently as the early seventies, women were less than one percent of engineering enrollment. Now at some undergraduate schools there's one woman for every four men! The message is out: If you're a woman engineer, you're going to get a job. I think a lot of the activities we've engaged in—visiting campuses, giving out grants—have played a part in this transformation."

A vice president in heavy industry said, "I think premium payments are tapering off. There are companies which still offer them; we tend not to. I think women, by and large, have become somewhat more mature in approaching the pay question. Many of them say, 'I'm not about to be bought. I want a job that has meaning and money that's comparable to what my male counterparts are getting. An extra $2,000 isn't going to be enough in itself to attract me.' And that's a refreshing thing to see happen."

But a manufacturing company official noted, "We pay well and make no bones about it. I'd have to say, that has proved to be one of the most useful tools for us in recruiting women engineers. Sure, grade point and class standing are important in determining offers for every one. But at times we've paid more to get a woman."

If possible, the compensation package for experienced women managers and professionals should be tailored to the candidate's preferences, as is true with males. Particularly if she is single and more highly taxed as a result, the woman may prefer a club, car, or other perk to additional cash income. If she is a mother, she might welcome partial subsidy of her day care expenses more than the additional life or health insurance available at her level. Of course, it is illegal to discriminate on the basis of sex in either pay or benefits, so whatever is provided to a woman should be equal in value to that accorded a male of the same rank.

"If we are recruiting one-half of a two-career family, we'll try to hire both of them if we can," said a manager at a technical company. "If that's not feasible, we hire one and find a job for the other. And this is true regardless of location; you can find a job for a qualified person almost anywhere."

However, one observer of 'spousal nepotism' pointed out the practice has mixed results. Said Carnegie-Mellon professor Arnold R. Weber, "The cost of the tied transaction may include the compromise of selection standards, the loss of morale on the part of other employees who perceive an erosion of the merit principle and complications introduced into future promotion and transfer decisions. Conversely, the availability of a joint unit of supply may make available to the employer talented individuals who otherwise would escape his recruiting net." Weber suggested that "when the employer is in hot pursuit of a candidate and must respond to the job needs of the spouse, the availability of the second position should be disseminated through normal labor market channels and the spouse evaluated in relation to other prospects."[6]

The attitude of the recruiter can influence the woman's career decision. If the corporate representative is careful to provide a balanced picture of the opportunity and shows concern for the candidate's future, whether within or outside the organization, the woman will be much more likely to accept an offer.

"In bringing women in from outside—men, too, for that matter—we take pains that they know what they're getting into," a petroleum company executive said. "We're a paternalistic industry, compared to others, and some people just don't belong in that kind of an environment."

A bank officer said, "We're fortunate in being able to attract women. This is an industry—especially in lending—which offers high visibility and broad exposure to business. An individual can move rapidly as sole performer, and women are looking for this. There's no waiting for chairs to open up. And if the best qualified are hired, 50 percent of the professionals in banking will be female."

An officer of a food company noted, "In a company such as ours, people are like swimmers—they peak at 40! We have division vice presidents and others a step below that who are in their late twenties and early thirties. Women can see they have good opportunities here."

An official at a female-intensive organization reported, "The concerns of women are very much the same as those of men. They care about work satisfaction, working environment, remuneration, and opportunity to get ahead. They want to do their thing and be rewarded for it, just as is true of men. We have enough women here that it encourages more to come. There is less reason to suspect tokenism where there are numbers to support the opposite conclusion."

However, many other companies indicate that women express concerns which men do not. "I think women suspect—and rightly so—that they're going to have to be better and work harder than men," said a vice president in New York. "They have more questioning attitudes about their advancement over time. Men think they'll perform and be rewarded. I don't think women take this for granted. They may feel they'll have to be special to move up the ladder."

Said an executive at another firm, "Women want to know how females have progressed in the company. They want to know how many are in the executive ranks and how many women get promoted in a year. We assume they're asking other companies the same thing."

A woman executive in a male-intensive company said, "Women who are considering joining our firm ask to talk to a woman if that invitation isn't extended to them. When they get to my office, they close the door and say, 'Okay, you can tell me how bad it really is here.' "

At a giant technical company, an official commented, "Women want to talk to women who work here, and we refer them to people who will tell good stories so they don't learn much. But there is a general perception on the outside that changes are going on for women at our company, and it may not be a bad place to come to. In the past, our reputation hasn't always been so good, but that doesn't seem to be working against us. Maybe that's because there aren't many firms which can boast of better histories. Now, if in fact things *don't* get better for women here, it's going to wreck our recruiting business. That's because other companies *are* making progress, and we won't be keeping pace."

## REFERENCES

1. "The Industrial Salesman Becomes a Salesperson," *Business Week*, 19 February 1979, p. 109.
2. "Women, Minorities Still Out of Focus on TV, Agency Says," *Wall Street Journal*, 16 January 1979.
3. Nunez, Louis, "TV Image of Women: Distorted," *Chicago Tribune*, 25 January 1979.
4. Rankin, Deborah, "Business of Women is Business," *New York Times*, 30 April 1978.
5. "Acting Affirmatively to End Job Bias," *Business Week*, 27 January 1975, p. 94.
6. Weber, Arnold R., "Spousal Nepotism," *Wall Street Journal*, 17 September 1979.

# 9

# *Developing Women Executives*

Organizations are paying increasing attention to employee development. Once left mostly to chance, or at best limited to certain levels and to individuals tagged as superstars, now the developmental process has broadened. It may include both exempt and nonexempt ranks, but in any event is no longer restricted to those few employees who show greatest promise.

At one time, women were excluded from management development programs. Most females lacked the extent or type of education commonly considered appropriate for upward mobility, since their families and they themselves had been reluctant to invest sizable sums in their schooling. Women were seen as wives and mothers to the exclusion of work outside the home. When females did enter the labor force out of necessity or choice, they were consigned to dead-end jobs whose earnings plateaued rapidly and were barred from opportunities to progress to more responsible, higher-paying positions. It was assumed that women were only temporarily in the work place and therefore had no desire to advance. Any training females received was to improve their performance in their present jobs, not to qualify them for promotion. More recently women have become career oriented, and some have prepared themselves academically for management roles.

"Remember how it used to be?" a female executive asked. "Your high school counselor wanted to know your plans for the period until you were married. College was a way of filling the waiting time. I didn't know what to study, and my school recommended interior decorating or dress design.

I didn't have talent for either, but that didn't matter! Now it's so different. Women are saying, 'Even if I do get married, I'll probably work the rest of my life—what should I be doing to prepare for that?' "

A study of women officers of major organizations showed that 42 percent hope to advance to a higher position, while 34 percent would move to another company if blocked at their present employer. Only 24 percent anticpate staying in their present position for the remainder of their career. Younger women, degreed and already the most highly compensated of the group, display the most ambition.[1]

## EXCLUSION OF WOMEN

Unfortunately, some organizations remain convinced that women do not desire advancement, and even if they did, would prove to be a bad investment because of poor performance or failure to stay in the labor force. Thus, even today, women are excluded from certain development programs.

A recent study of nearly 2000 members of the American Management Associations showed that 70 percent of the employers represented have a formal management development program, but 58 percent consider only a limited number of women qualified for development. Lack of education, experience, motivation and career commitment were cited as principal problems. While 4 percent of the organizations include women on a quota basis as representatives of a minority, another 12 percent do not admit females. The vast majority of firms— 70 percent—say women are permitted to participate in management development "as discovered." Relatively few companies (9 percent) specifically recruit women for developmental activities. It is not surprising that 30 percent of the firms have less than 1 percent female representation in their management cadres, and 58 percent have no more than one woman out of every 20 managers.[2]

Companies are required by law to provide equal opportunity, not only in employment but in development. Indeed, it is in the best interest of the organizations to afford the same developmental opportunities to employees of both sexes to improve the quality of the management team. "Every person with career ambition should have lots of help," a senior executive emphasized. "We've always done it for males—sent them to schools. Now we realize that women should be encouraged as well. There is no different development or training program for women; they don't need any special help. All we're doing is saying, 'Okay, now the door is open to everybody.' I think that's all that's required for women to make full, fair and equal progress in the organization.''

"We're probably stronger on management development than most,'' pointed out an executive with a major oil company. "Our line management spends a lot of time on personnel matters. We had to look further down in the organization to identify promotable females and minorities, but now some have surfaced and are known.''

The development program must incorporate instruction for managers in development matters since the major responsibility is theirs and not that of the training specialists. Developers must not only be prepared for their task, but must be rewarded for the time and effort expended in "growing" their people. Development cannot be viewed as a distraction from the manager's true priorities; it should be included in appraisal, and performance in this area related directly to compensation.

One New York-based company incorporates on its appraisal form a question relating to the individual's development of women and minorities. In addition to the superior's efforts, in-depth counseling for promising women (and men) is provided by an outside consultant. Each employee in the program receives up to 60 hours of personal counseling over a six-month period to equip him or her for greater responsibilities. "The consultant doesn't really find dissimilar problems between white males and minorities,'' a company officer reported. "They just find more of them among women and blacks.''

Effective development, of course, is not mass produced but treats each individual's needs as unique. The company which views "all women" as needing a particular course or "all supervisors" as requiring a certain experience is doomed to waste development dollars. The most effective program is one which affords a variety of opportunities and communicates these fully to the organization. Employees should recognize that development cannot be provided by others nor serve as a guarantee of improved rank or increased salary. Individuals should be encouraged to devote the time and attention required for self-improvement, but with assurance of no other reward than personal growth.

A 16-page booklet on the subject furnished to employees of a giant technical company concludes, "Employee development planning is not a guarantee of promotion, transfer, or any other specific result. It is, however, a helpful process for any employee who wishes to guide the future rather than allow things simply to happen. Should you wish to participate, you'll find your manager supporting you, providing assistance, and wishing you success.''

## SUPERIOR'S SENSITIVITY NEEDED

Development of women executives requires special attention, simply because the ranks of such women are so sparse. The women's superiors must be sensitive to the need for integrating them into the organization to the fullest possible extent. Particularly if the women are the only females or among the very few females in a work group, they may be ignored or excluded by peers and subordinates made uncomfortable by their presence. Hence, the women's opportunities for informal development will be highly restricted, and perhaps even their ability to do their jobs will be jeopardized.

The superior's first task is to make clear to the woman and to her co-workers that she is being judged on the same basis as others. Management skills are asexual, and no one has ever demonstrated that the sexes have different management styles, let alone results. While the standards for a woman's work should be no higher, they certainly should be no lower.

One of the nation's largest companies named a woman to a senior vice presidency, with responsibility for a staff function. Unlike others at that rank, she was not permitted to have an impact on the organization. Instead, she was used as a "show woman," being limited to external duties of little significance. After demanding and failing to receive a chance to contribute, she resigned. To judge a female by a double standard is to insult her and destroy her ability to gain the respect of the organization.

The superior should assume that a woman's abilities and interests are not unlike those of a male who has attained similar rank. Rather than being overly protective, the superior should demonstrate confidence by allowing her to accept the same risks as others. To be developed successfully, the woman, like any newcomer, "must be provided with opportunities to achieve and master new skills. This fosters a positive self-image and provides the employee with the means for repeated goal attainment."[3] Like a man, a woman won't become a good manager without making decisions and learning from mistakes. Despite the manager's feeling of being "on the spot" with a rare commodity as a subordinate, the superior must assume the risk of her failing rather than doing her job for her.

"I think I ask women to perform more independently than male subordinates," said the vice president-human resources of a Midwest company. "Initially, they seem more tentative than men of similar age and experience. Females have been sheltered. When they get in a work situation, they sometimes like to have the boss handle the tough problems. I'm really interested in the women learning that they can do it themselves. I want them to know that their successes *are* their successes and not due to my intervention. If I shelter them, I won't grow real managers. They'll be limited in their scope and their effectiveness.''

Being the only or one of a few women at a middle or upper echelon job is stressful; a supportive relationship with all levels is what any female manager would welcome. But failing to obtain this, she cannot survive without the support of her superior. If bias against women is present in the environment, the supervisor must insist that behavior not reflect this feeling. There may be some in the work group who adhere to the trait theory: management requires masculine traits; for a woman to succeed as a manager she must fail as a woman, or if she remains feminine, she must fail the requirements of her job. These persons must be counseled to treat the woman as an individual, not as a sterotype. Her manager can help by being openly supportive of her and by passing around among staff members such stereotypically female tasks as note taking at meetings.

The superior may need to caution the woman encountering resistance that performance will prove more than clashes with superiors, peers, and subordinates. She will need to develop her own style of handling possible inequities in a noncombative manner. Such savoir faire is exemplified by the former public relations director of a New England company. She was promoted to the directorship when her boss was recruited away. The first and only woman manager in her old and conservative company, she nevertheless was invited to attend the weekly management council meetings in which her male predecessor had participated. At her first get-together, the chairman and chief executive welcomed her, and one of the members handed her a notepad. "We always let the newest member take notes," he pointed out, and she hesitated only a moment before assuming the secretarial role.

She continued to take notes for several months. At that point a newcomer joined the council. Once again the chairman welcomed the addition. Then he turned to the first item of business. "Just a minute," said the public relations director, rising from her chair. She marched around the table to the new man's place and handed him the notebook. "We always ask the newest member to take the notes," she smiled. She has since been recruited away herself and now serves as vice president for communications at a larger company.

Development opportunities for women should be as varied as those offered to men. Periodic rotational assignments between line and staff responsibilities, cross-functional transfer or movement between head-quarters and field operations will give women a better understanding of the company's operations.

"Every manager is charged with identifying the promotable females at position X or above," the head of EEO at a large technical company explained. "They specify what training it will take to get the women to the next job and map out their paths—one year for certain and tentatively for the next five years. Through corporate monitoring, we're going to see that these women get their cross-functional training."

A female official of a manufacturing company declared, "One of the most attractive features about this company, unlike others in our industry, is that we develop across parts of our business. You might be in one area for a year and the next year move to another. It certainly increases the opportunities for advancement."

Female executives might be given temporary assignments working on projects for senior executives or be included on any task forces, not just those dealing with EEO or "women's concerns." They might be named to a permanent or ad hoc committee or to a junior board of middle managers studying top management concerns and providing recommen-dations for review by the upper echelon.

A woman executive at an East Coast company recalled a co-worker who had complained, "I'm on three task forces and I can't get my work done."

"I responded, 'You've got your priorities wrong. Those task forces are where you ought to be. You'll learn new things and get great visibility. Look around and delegate some of your desk work.' Well, she obviously thought I was crazy. But about a month later when I saw her, she was on cloud nine. An officer had seen her functioning on one of those task forces and had called to suggest she apply for a posted job. It was a nice promotion, and she got it."

## OTHER DEVELOPMENT POSSIBILITIES

On their present jobs, in addition to coaching by superior and co-workers, women managers could be offered such developmental assign-ments as preparing reports for presentation to peers or higher-level management, or undergoing assessment. In the past, men have often been assigned detached services, assuming a leadership role in charitable, civic or governmental activities. Such an experience would not only be broadening for women executives but would emphasize to the community the corporate commitment to equal opportunity and familiarize opinion-molders with the contribution which can be made by women in leadership roles.

One possibility is the President's Executive Interchange Program which permits middle managers from industry and government to work in the opposite sector for a year. More than 400 men and women have participated since the program began in 1969. Exposure to national issues and the governmental process should prove especially valuable for tomorrow's top manager. Women executives might be named liaison to an association, or one of the association's committees. They could be encouraged to join and participate actively in professional organizations comprising both sexes or only women, which center on their functional areas of expertise or their level of management.

Certainly, women executives should be included in training sponsored by the company. Such training is widespread today; 610 companies surveyed by The Conference Board reported more than $2 billion in direct expenditures on courses. Three of every four companies provide some in-house instruction, 89 percent have tuition aid or refund programs, and 74 percent authorize some employees, principally managers and professionals, to take outside courses at company expense during working hours.[4] Larger companies in particular are increasing the participation of women in company courses, which seek to increase effectiveness at managing people, to enhance functional abilities, or to improve personal skills. And most women are receptive to the opportunity since they perceive enhanced prospects for promotion.

An executive at an Eastern firm pointed out, "A company should review its records of training to assure that men and women are participating equitably. Management training for men and women should be the same, but it will probably be necessary to provide basic background for women which is taken for granted by men. Women have not been trained for jobs they were never expected to attain. Courses on management skills are important, as well as information courses about the work of departments which have been traditionally male."

While a wide variety of courses is offered by outside organizations in terms of content, duration, faculty, location and cost, quality of these varies. As a consequence, organizations are well advised to obtain verification of value before investing employee time and company money. Appendix III provides information on a number of courses designed for women or on the subject of women in management. In addition to training courses, many companies encourage employees to participate in college courses, either to learn specific skills in certain areas or to pursue an undergraduate or graduate degree.

"Our organization's senior management group believes in education," a woman vice president told me. "They think having a better educated work force is advantageous. There is a very loose interpretation of our educational assistance policy; we'll pay for virtually anything. If you want to take a course in art or music, we'll say fine; we'll pay for it."

Another company in a suburban location has arranged for course work leading to degrees at two different universities to be held right on its grounds after hours so employees don't have to travel to the city to continue their educations. In fact, a number of corporations have cooperative agreements with colleges to grant credits for in-house courses whose primary aim is to upgrade job skills. However, the opportunity to receive credits may encourage employees to seek further study and this is a plus for the company. Corporate courses for college credit range from "Elements of Supervision" at John Hancock Mutual Life Insurance Co. to "Introduction to PDP-11 Peripherals" at Digital Equipment Corp.[5]

Simmons College in Boston developed for the National Association of Bank Women a three-year course to enable women managers to earn undergraduate degrees and qualify for advancement. In addition to the usual course work, the students are exposed to skills training geared especially to them: assertiveness, teamwork, delegating authority and career planning. The women are able to remain on their jobs, taking two two-week management institutes annually but otherwise attending school close to home.

Many leading graduate schools of business now offer an executive program leading to an MBA degree on an accelerated schedule. Typically, such sessions meet weekly, alternating Fridays and Saturdays, for two years. Attendance is limited to middle managers, who usually are sponsored by their organizations. Representation of women is much higher than even a few years ago.

Organizations selecting women executives for in-house or outside training must decide whether to offer courses designed especially for women, or to enroll women in classes for both sexes. One course, entitled *Women in Business*, is conducted in-house by a Midwest company. Aims are to improve the self-image and self-confidence of women; to create a climate of professional support among women; to provide exposure to resources within the company and the community for further education and development; and to discuss career planning.

A leading bank has developed an advanced opportunities program for middle management women. Outside speakers are brought in and technical mentors assigned to ready the participants for senior management. "Out of this group, we hope we'll get candidates for senior vice presidencies," a personnel officer noted.

However, a personnel executive at a New York company declared,

"In the area of management training, we've resisted the idea of special courses for females and minorities. Rather, we present programs designed to impart knowledge, and if any individual—regardless of race or sex—needs that help to do his or her job or prepare for a bigger responsibility, he can go." Women-only training is obviously better for those who feel ill-at-ease in a learning situation with men. Also, women may not have had any other opportunity to interface with women in comparable positions and find this experience a supportive one. But women-only instruction is not advantageous for more confident females who have no wish to separate themselves from their male peers.

## APPRAISAL CAN BE TOOL

Performance appraisal is an important development tool, if properly used. On too many occasions, however, it serves as a way of substantiating a salary increase that has already been decided upon. The courts have found performance ratings to be discriminatory when they are based on subjective and ill-defined criteria; when they may have been affected by sexual and/or racial bias; when they were not collected and scored under standardized conditions; when content was not based on careful job analysis; and when they were not shown to be job related through proper validation studies. Therefore, organizations must provide raters with a standard of significant performance factors against which employees' records can be judged.[6]

"There's nothing like a manager's knowing that he can be the subject of a suit to help encourage him to do his documentation in a diligent fashion," a West Coast executive told me. "Ordinarily, appraisal is a task that managers by and large avoid. They don't like to discuss why they're giving such and such a raise. EEO has provided us with the stick to make managers more conscientious about appraisal."

A company on the opposite seaboard noted that not until 1976 had a career appraisal program been initiated for all exempt levels. Late each year, all 7500 exempt employees establish goals with their supervisors for the coming 12 months. Twice annually progress is reviewed. "We started this program because we were concerned that we weren't properly and objectively evaluating all of our people," a vice president indicated. "Women applauded the program, as did blacks."

Some male managers have claimed that they hesitate to appraise women subordinates since females cannot accept criticism easily and may burst into tears at the first negative comment. Their companies indicate that this stance is viewed as a "cop out," probably reflecting that the appraiser is not competent at his task with either men or women. "Originally there was a lot of speculation that you couldn't be candid with women; there'd be an emotional display," confessed an officer of a food products company. "That hasn't proved out. We have some men who cry bigger tears than most of the women."

Said a consultant, "I would venture that if you examined all of the performance appraisals done last year in the 500 largest corporations, you'd be surprised. Except for those companies which really force a ranking, you'd discover 50 to 70 percent in the above average to excellent range. That indicates to me that managers don't like to tell people working for them that they're not doing well and has nothing to do with women in particular."

And the head of human resources at a technical company exclaimed, "Certainly people in this company aren't going to break down in tears; that's the last thing I would worry about. If women can do the jobs we're asking them to do, they're tough enough to take criticism."

Appraisal should be especially valuable to a woman who, because of her minority status, may be less confident of her performance. She may require feedback more frequently, but if the appraiser displays the sensitivity due any subordinate, she will welcome suggestions for improvement.

One study showed that males who have negative attitudes toward women in management tend to attribute success of females to luck or lack of challenge in the job. On the other hand, males who have positive attitudes are prone to credit the success of women to ability or effort.[7]

Companies with which I spoke insist that no differences exist between appraisals of men and women. No allowances are made, they maintain, for differentials in education, career experience, or societal conditioning of women. But there are those observers who say women executives are rated lower than men because they are not expected to do as well. There are others who claim women are appraised better than they deserve to be when doing a good job, simply because this is so unexpected. Laboratory and field studies have served to substantiate both opinions. In any event, investigators have discovered that evaluations of females are higher for those performing a "feminine" task than for those perceived as performing a "masculine" task.[8] This does not auger well for the female manager unless her appraiser remains unaffected by stereotyping.

According to a majority of companies, the management-by-objectives approach to appraisal is most desirable since it involves the subordinate in the process from inception and allows mutual agreement as to how the individual's performance is to be judged. MBO is undeniably job related and difficult to contest. The negative is that a manager may slavishly adhere to predetermined objectives even under changed circumstances, to the disadvantage of the organization.

"We've improved our evaluation forms," reported an officer at a Midwest company. "They're more structured in measuring performance against objectives jointly set by the manager and employee. This has tended to do away with the 'my boss has it in for me' reaction that used to arise. Now, our managers are appraised in part by the quality of their evaluations, which must be reviewed by the manager's boss before being shared with the employee."

When the appraisal is conducted, it is important for the development of the subordinate that both positive and negative feedback be included. Remarks should be based on behavior, not values or personalities. Suggestions for improvement should be definite, not couched in generalities. When a woman fulfills performance expectations, she should be praised and given enlarged responsibilities and/or increased compensation, just as a man would. Reward for accomplishment will lead the women to even higher aspirations and greater accomplishment.

Ideally, the appraiser will share his or her assessment of the subordinate's potential with the individual being evaluated, and together the two can consider the subordinate's future. Perhaps it will be possible to agree upon the next two jobs to which the subordinate can aspire, and what will be needed in terms of training or experience to qualify.

"We're trying to get our employees to take a more active role in their own development," an executive at a financial services organization said. "What we do is open up opportunities for them and give them all the help they should need in terms of recognizing their shortcomings and providing the training to get them ready for the next job. We've established counseling sessions at least once every quarter, where the subordinate's plan of action for his or her career over the next year or two is reviewed by the manager. We look at what specific managerial or technical skills he is lacking, what training courses he needs to take. We also set up special job assignments for people who maybe need just a six-week transfer into a different discipline."

Assessment, as noted earlier, may be utilized in development. When centers "are used in this way, the emphasis is on feedback of results to the employee following the assessment experience. In a feedback session, a trained staff member points out the candidate's strong and weak points, illustrating them with examples of the candidate's behavior in the assessment activities. After the employee understands and accepts the feedback, the discussion turns to counseling and planning for future training experiences and developmental assignments that would lead to a particular target job in management.''[9]

Ideally, any organization will not have preconceptions as to which jobs are appropriate for a woman manager and which are not, but rather will treat her career strictly in accord with her merit. She will be advanced in the same manner as her male peers, neither faster nor slower than her abilities permit. This course reduces the prospect of both discrimination and reverse discrimination charges.

"We have not purposely accelerated the progress of any women," an executive at an oil company said. "They are progressing at the same rate as their peer group. Trying to telescope their experience would assure a certain level of failure. We leave people in positions long enough to let them learn from their mistakes. And women would far rather get a promotion because they're qualified, than because they're part of a 'special program.' Hostility comes from favoritism."

Help with career planning is even more crucial for women than for men. Because of preemptive family obligations or because of a perceived lack of opportunities, females have less frequently laid plans for their working lives than have males. A recent study of 1200 senior officers, nearly all of them male, showed that two-thirds of the most mobile had endeavored to follow a career plan over the years. Furthermore, those following a plan tended to earn more money.[10] However, even at the officer level, only 40 percent of female managers engage in career planning.[11]

A major financial institution offers both management and nonmanagement employees a career management program, all expenses paid over two weekends. The program is conducted by an outside consultant at a local hotel, with some 60 employees in attendance at each session. "There have been many networks established as a result of this program," an officer pointed out. "Employees get together and try to assist each other in career-related concerns. We were worried that people would be expecting to move up rapidly, and we wouldn't have enough opportunities to satisfy them. Instead, career management has made many people realize that the timetables they had set were too short. Or they have concluded that they'd really rather grow in the jobs they already have."

## THE ROLE OF MENTORING

Also of special importance to the woman executive is mentoring. Cut off from all or most other females by rank and from male peers by sex, she needs the support of a teacher for psychological as well as career reasons.

A recent study showed that two of every three senior executives have had a mentor, and those who have earned more money at a younger age, are happier with their career progress, and derive somewhat greater pleasure from their work. Although females constituted less than 1 percent of the senior executives surveyed, all of them had had a mentor. In fact, women tended to have more mentors than their male counterparts, averaging three teachers to two for the men. Although the women had women mentors more frequently than men did, nevertheless seven in ten of their mentors were male. Nine out of ten women had formed relationships with the mentors in the work setting, rather than school, family, or community, and the majority began during the sixth to tenth year of the women's careers.[12]

According to 331 women executives participating in a University of California/Los Angeles research project, "the most important kind of mentoring assistance . . . is encouragement . . . sharing belief in the protege's abilities and potential."[13] Mentors can be particularly helpful to a woman who may lack role models and be less sure of her abilities and the appropriateness of her behavior in the predominantly male corporate setting. Men are able to learn the "rules of the game" over lunch at the club or in other social settings which are not as accessible to women, either by male exclusion or female reluctance to intrude. Hence, on-the-job help becomes all the more important to the female.

In some organizations, mentoring is recognized as so important that mentors are assigned to each upwardly mobile manager. But the importance of sponsorship, or the support of one or more influential individuals in the corporate hierarchy, cannot be overlooked. A major bank, for example, initiated an executive sponsor program. Senior vice presidents are required to act as sponsors for women and minorities, to make sure that there are no roadblocks to their progress. In other companies, however, sponsorship develops on an informal basis and comes about either at the instigation of the sponsor or the individual seeking a "godfather."

Clearly, the immediate supervisor makes the best mentor, since that individual is closest to the protegee and has the best opportunity to observe her and her environment. In addition, the immediate supervisor's support is most important, since he or she stands as the gatekeeper to greater opportunity within the organization.

Upper echelon women make good mentors and/or sponsors for aspiring women in management, but they are not always present in the organization. Even if they are, they may hesitate to serve as mentors/sponsors for females for one of two reasons. First, they may be insecure regarding their own minority status in the organization and unwilling to foster any career but their own. ("I got where I am by virtue of my talent, but now they're advancing any woman.") Second, they may be resentful of the lack of help they themselves experienced in moving ahead and unwilling to extend to others an advantage they never had. ("I made it on my own; let her do the same!") One organization reported that its first woman officer, a senior vice president after 40 years' service, feels that today's women "want to move too fast."

A personnel executive in New York pointed out that "the more successful the individual, the greater the tendency to withdraw from sex identification. It's looked upon as sort of an 'I'm aboard mates, pull up the ladder' point of view. But I don't think that's it. I think a woman who's successful realizes that if she spends a lot of time beating the drum for other women, she somehow becomes suspect to the other executives who are white males."

Fortunately, this thinking does not appear to be widespread. At CBS, fourteen women in managerial and professional positions volunteered as "career advisers" when the organization began a training program for minorities in 1973. They have proved to be much in demand. At another company, a woman manager made mentoring of two other females a part of her goals for the year and asked to be held accountable for her results. Both protegees received promotions. And a woman executive in the Midwest meets with every newly appointed woman manager of her company, offering to be of help.[14]

At a large consumer products company, women vice presidents "are continually involved with other women in the structure," according to the vice president-personnel. "The others will call and ask to see them. Then the officers will tell them 'Here's the way I think this company works; here are the kinds of things you've got to do in order to be promoted. Please come back and talk again any time.' " He continued, "They've met with the women's group in the company, too. It's not anything that's been encouraged by management; it just happened. The officers are interested and approachable, so they've been a big help to other women."

A woman mentor not only serves as a role model but can bring to the relationship a better understanding of the particular problems that a woman faces in management. However, an upper echelon male can be even more helpful to a woman manager on the way up, simply because he may be more powerful than any woman in the organization. He can not only teach but be an effective sponsor as well.

"There are five or six older men in our company who have done a super job as sponsors for women," a female executive in the Midwest noted. "But I haven't seen the sponsor thing having an unusual impact; the women have gotten where they are by performance."

Some males are reluctant to undertake the mentor or sponsor role for a woman because the relationship might be interpreted as a sexual one. "It's easier for me to be a mentor to a male 20 years younger than I am, than to a female," declared a vice president-human resources at a billion dollar corporation. "I can say to my wife that I'm having dinner with Jim to talk about his career, and she'll say fine. They I say that I'm having dinner with Doris to talk about her career, and my wife may say, 'Why don't you have lunch with Doris?' And if Doris is a nice-looking 25-year-old, you can end up having a problem with the subordinate, with the spouse, and with yourself."

A female executive in the Midwest emphasized, "I see some women managers who are very bright and talented, but their progress will be short-lived. They're confusing business and pleasure; it doesn't work. If the focus is strictly the job, the women will get their mentors."

"There's a danger to having a sponsor," cautioned the vice president-human resources of a New York-based company. "I think some women fear getting too closely identified with one executive, male or female. If that person gets fired. . . . "

An organization may utilize a psychologist to meet with women executives and those of either sex who are most important to the females' success in order to facilitate mutually rewarding relationships.

And occasionally, organizations identify one individual to fulfill the mentoring role with a title such as "Manager of Career Development for Women." The incumbent not only serves as a teacher and supporter for women wishing to advance but also acts as a nominator, making certain that the organization does not overlook feminine talent when appropriate openings occur.

"I publish a promotable list once a year," a personnel executive told me. "What I do is go into our main personnel system and look at women and minorities who have been in a certain grade for X amount of time, have not received a promotion, whose performance is at a certain level, and who have expressed an interest in moving ahead. Publishing the list prevents managers from hanging on to people and keeping them in a grade."

Unfortunately, women do require more assistance in promoting their careers than do men. Males are seldom loath to take the initiative in seeking their own advancement. They expect promotion and, if blocked, turn to an executive recruiter to accelerate their career progress. Women, in contrast, wait to be discovered, feeling that those who perform well will surely be rewarded. If overlooked or ignored by their employer, women may accept their fate rather than consider an interorganizational change. This stance, which is often misconstrued as a greater degree of loyalty, might more accurately be described as lack of initiative.

One researcher studied the career progress of a group of 21 female managers in Boston over a ten-year period. All but one of the group were single; half had graduate degrees, and only one lacked a baccalaureate. The majority did not advance significantly in their corporate positions during the decade. The researcher examined various possible causes for the "shelf-sitting" and found the women "tended to be strongly wedded to their work, to the job itself, and to professional performance. This dedication, however, was not paired with an overriding ambition to rise higher."[15]

As another observer has pointed out, "Individuals with a strong motivation to management tend to move up faster and are more likely to perform effectively in managerial positions. This conclusion is supported by at least 15 independent studies. . . . " However, this researcher found "no support for the view that females who enter upon a managerial career have less motivation to manage than males."[16]

A woman executive pointed out, "For the first time, we really see a market for our talents. Up to now, if you succeeded in one company, it was a fluke—you were lucky. Now that's not true. You recognize, 'I'm doing well here—I could succeed at IBM, too.' I think we'll see the full impact of that in the next five years or so."

## INTRACOMPANY GROUPS

Another way in which women can receive mentoring help is through formation of a formal or informal intracompany organization for women managers. Some firms oppose this idea, fearing that the group might become militant or serve as a precursor to unionization of white collar workers. In other companies, however, the concept is encouraged. The idea may originate with management or with women themselves and may be funded by the company or supported by member dues.

One successful intracompany organization is Women United. More than 200 women managers of United Air Lines are members. WU originated with and is financed by its membership. The group holds three company-wide meetings annually in various locations, as well as interim regional get-togethers; all subject matter is work related. Emphasis of Women United is on self-improvement of members and increased knowledge of the company. In addition, the group stands ready to provide input to management when appropriate, in relation to the hiring, developing, and promoting of women. Members feel both program content and exposure to co-workers have been valuable, particularly in such a geographically dispersed organization. Some nonmembers, outnumbering those who joined 3 to 1, feel that affiliation with an all-women group would be a negative. However, management regards the organization as a plus for the company, and senior officers have served as speakers.

An officer of a West Coast company told me there were several informal groups of women at various locations which meet on the premises during lunch hours. "We do not discourage that, and in a subtle sense we may encourage it," he pointed out. "When a member of management is invited to talk, he does so."

An official at a major New York company recounted that a female managers' organization at headquarters had staged a job fair. Members holding different positions had been on hand to explain what was involved in their assignments. "Both men and women came; it was extremely popular," he noted. "We were embarrassed that we had never thought to offer employees such an opportunity."

Another large firm reports an internal women's group which conducts management development/training programs. "We furnish the facilities and the time for them to get involved in these kinds of programs," the vice president-personnel said.

At still another company, a discussion group of 30 women "spread like wildfire" and now includes both men and women. "They get together and talk about their jobs in management," reported a woman executive. "Early on one of the company lawyers got very nervous and told the CEO what was happening. All he said was, 'Great!' In some other companies, women's groups formed to exert pressure. Ours was not created out of anger or desperation and has received full support from management."

At a New York-based company an executive told me, "Here people tend to segregate by rank more than by sex. It's hard to get the secretary concerned about the same thing as a female sales representative making $28,000 and wondering whether to accept the Chicago job or not."

A woman executive at another Manhattan-headquartered company reported, "We have enough women at the vice president and director level that it's not necessary to form a separate group. Just in going about your business, you're going to find yourself dealing with women a lot of the time."

Despite the greater acceptance of females into management development programs, a recent survey of women managers showed the greatest perceived barrier to progress is the belief held by most companies "that a man is a better investment for potential managerial training than a woman."[17] Middle and upper echelon managerial and professional positions require sufficient education, significant experience, and developmental opportunities. In the past women typically have had none of these. Now, the education of females is not only more extensive but business oriented. Discontinuity of employment has been minimized, bringing the work lives of married women closer to those of their male and never-married female counterparts. All too often, only management development is missing from the ingredients needed to prepare for promotion.

"Where I see our program really needing to improve, where I guess discrimination still exists, is in assessment of potential and developmental assignments," a woman executive told me.

There is no longer reason to shunt women into specialties, where no bridge leads to progressively more responsible positions. Undoubtedly some women will decline developmental opportunities, just as some men do. But with either sex, the choice should be that of the individual. The organization should not decide, without regard for ability and desire to contribute, that some individuals will be helped to advance while others will not. The continuing shortage of management talent makes this approach indefensible as a business decision, as well as illegal.

## REFERENCES

1. Heidrick and Struggles, Inc., *Profile of a Woman Officer* Chicago, 1979, p. 4.
2. Burrow, Martha G., *Developing Women Managers: What Needs to be Done?* New York: American Management Associations, 1978, pp. 3 and 10.
3. Terborg, James R., "Women in Management: A Research Review," *Journal of Applied Psychology* 62(6):651 (1977).
4. Lusterman, Seymour, *Education in Industry,* New York: The Conference Board, 1977, p. 11.
5. "Company Courses Go Collegiate," *Business Week,* 26 February 1979, p. 90.
6. Schneier, Dena B., "The Impact of EEO Legislation on Performance Appraisals," *Personnel* 55(4):25 (July–August, 1978).
7. Garland, H. and K. H. Price, "Attitudes Toward Women in Management and Attributions for Their Success and Failure in a Managerial Position," *Journal of Applied Psychology,* 62:32 (1977).
8. Taynor, J. and K. Deaux, "Equity and Perceived Sex Differences: Role Behavior as Defined by the Task, the Mode, and the Actor," *Journal of Personality and Social Psychology* 32:381 (1975).
9. Hall, Douglas T. and Francine S. Hall, "What's New in Career Management," *Organizational Dynamics* 5(1):19–20 (Summer 1976).

10. Johnston, Thomas J., "Mobile Managers—Well Paid and Discontent," *Harvard Business Review* **55**(5):7 (September–October, 1977).
11. Heidrick and Struggles, Inc., *Profile of a Woman Officer*, Chicago, 1979, p. 4.
12. Roche, Gerard R., "Much Ado About Mentors," *Harvard Business Review* **57**(1):24 (January–February 1979).
13. Phillips, Linda, UCLA Career Development Research Project, 1977, p. 2.
14. "Women Finally Get Mentors of Their Own," *Business Week,* 23 October 1978, p. 74.
15. Missirian, Agnes K., "The Female Manager as a Shelf-sitter," *Human Resource Management No. 17, p. 30 (Winter 1978).*
16. Miner, John B., "Motivational Potential for Upgrading Among Minority and Female Managers," *Journal of Applied Psychology* 62(6):691,6 (1977).
17. Badawy, M. K., "How Women Managers View Their Role in the Organization," *Personnel Administrator* No. 23, p. 65 (February 1978).

# 10
# Retaining Women Executives

The president of a major bank points out that level of demand for bright career women results in "a greater tendency for a woman to get outside alternative opportunities than for a man."[1]

An oil company reports, "Our turnover of women is higher. We've lost some to other companies. There are organizations paying a premium for women."

"Sure, over the past ten years other employers have been way ahead of us as far as hiring women is concerned," notes a manufacturing executive. "But after a couple of these firms hired them, and the women completed their two or three year training programs, the companies reassigned them back where they started from. That made the women susceptible to other offers. Now a number of them with all that good training are working for us in middle management slots." Obviously, organizations must not only attract and develop women but retain them if they are to be successful in utilizing the female resource. Because experienced women professionals and managers remain in short supply, companies should exercise particular care to keep those in whom time and money already have been invested.

Historically, women have been perceived as being more loyal to their employers than have their male counterparts. "I see a greater sense of corporate identity among women," commented a representative of a consumer services organization. "There's still more reluctance to change companies. Maybe it's a feeling of 'I've made it this far here; I'd better not take a chance somewhere else.' A woman has a harder struggle, no question about that." However, this viewpoint is changing with the improved climate for women in business. Now, women rank as candidates for a substantially greater number of opportunities and are more likely to be receptive to them than even a few years ago. The pace of intercompany change among females is quickening. Certainly, those who have made one move are more amenable to considering another.

What do managerial and professional women want? Basically, the same things as men: responsibility, challenge, opportunity for advancement and appropriate compensation. But, more than this, females want to be treated as individuals and not as stereotypical women. They seek evaluation on merit, not on sex.

All too often, organizations concentrate their efforts on bringing women in or promoting women already in the work force. The companies may or may not provide awareness training for male managers and/or female managers to ease the assimilation process. However, no efforts are made to assure that the women executives are receiving as much support from superiors, peers, and subordinates as are males; and females in nontraditional roles clearly need that help.

A survey made just a few years ago of line managers and clericals at seven major companies showed that both women and men tended to see males and females as noncompeting components in the labor force. The study's author noted that "every male line manager as well as every EEO officer concurred with the idea that women can be moved into management only in situations where they are 'smarter' or more competent than their subordinates. These interviewees, however, did not consider these criteria necessary for effective performance by males in management." The majority of managers thought that sex-linked worker traits exist, that women are less career oriented than men and that workers have trouble accepting females as supervisors. The author added that "less than 5 percent of the workers interviewed believed that line managers as a group were supportive of equal rights for women in their company."[2]

Relatively few organizations appraise their managers on retention of women subordinates; thus, while significant numbers of women are hired or promoted into the middle and upper echelons, the total at these levels may remain static or even decline. For this reason, the more sophisticated affirmative action programs are designed to encourage not only hiring and development, but retention of women as well.

"We watch over individual promotable women from the standpoint of the boss-subordinate relationship," explained a key official at a consumer services company. "After all, the role of the boss is key to her promotion."

To remain satisfied, the woman must find that her expectations concerning the position she has assumed are realistic ones. If they are not, she will conclude the job was misrepresented. She should be positioned in a meaningful role which is appropriate to her interests and abilities. If a competent female is underutilized, she will lose interest rapidly, not only in her work but in her employer. Occasionally, an able woman is placed in an unsuitable role because the employer "wants a woman" in a particular function, level or location. Under such circumstances the female is no more likely to succeed than would a male.

"That first assignment is so important," emphasized a personnel executive in a consumer products company. "Getting the person into a position that parallels her strong suit is critical. She must gain respect, prove that she belongs; she'll succeed if she can show results."

The woman must have the support of top management, which should back equal employment opportunity (EEO) on a continuing basis. Regular review of appraisal, training, compensation, and promotion of women is key. If the attraction and retention of women managers and professionals does not remain a priority of senior managers, attention down the line soon will vanish.

"It's a continual struggle to make sure you're doing the right thing," emphasized a vice president of a New York company. "Progress is never as fast as you want it to be, but the commitment is there. And our performance (at least since 1972) shows that dedication has counted for something."

Said an officer at another company, "We've been pounding the EEO drum for ten years. The chairman lectures every chance he gets. We've had an internal measurement system at every echelon for almost a decade."

A survey of nearly 1500 women managers, when compared with a study of males, showed that more females felt they lacked top management support, could not advance (although 82 percent of the women wanted to do so), and were not looked upon as members of management.[3]

One female manager in Philadelphia clearly lacks top management support. She is never invited to meetings with her superiors although her predecessor, as department head, was. "She sometimes feels like such an outsider that she backs down when she shouldn't," a male middle manager commented.[4]

As psychologist James R. Terborg of the University of Illinois points out, "New employees of either sex must be socialized properly if they are to fit with the established functioning of existing work units and if they are to develop into contributing members of organizations."[5]

Ignoring the sole woman by addressing executives as "you fellows" does nothing to enhance the female's confidence level and sense of belonging! However, it can be just as harmful to a woman's success to pay her inordinate attention. Singling her out will stir resentment among her co-workers and damage her acceptance. Calling upon her to serve in public as "show woman" or proof of the company's success in equal employment will probably arouse the woman's anger or undermine her confidence. She may feel she's on display as a woman when her competence should be recognized, or she was picked because of her sex alone and really lacks the ability to do the job. The woman must have the support of her immediate superior, who more than any other single individual will be responsible for her success or failure. Of course, the superior may not personally support the entrance of women into management, but he does a disservice to his company and to his own career if he allows his prejudices to affect his actions on the job. The superior must back the woman publicly and privately by word and deed, seeing that corporate policies on equal opportunity are followed in respect to all conditions of her employment. He should invest whatever time is necessary to make her feel more at ease in her role, but also, he should criticize her for her weaknesses as a manager. He should do his best to make the woman aware of the behavior which will be rewarded by the organization, advising when conformity is required, preferable, or unnecessary.

Certainly, the superior should expect the woman to succeed. With executives of both sexes, others' expectation of success or failure can become a self-fulfilling prophecy. In particular, it is those women without role models who benefit substantially from their bosses' "you can do it" outlook. Of course, the supervisor will prohibit overt prejudice in the workplace; just one instance can result in an investigation or court case. He should resist the human tendency to hope problems will go away. Instead, he must effect a just resolution.

## NONSEX SIMILARITY IS KEY

Perhaps the superior's most important contribution to assimilation will have taken place in the selection stage. For a woman to relate to her colleagues, all differences other than sex should be minimal. The female of similar date and place of birth, socioeconomic class, education, marital status, and career experience, will doubtless receive the best reception from co-workers. Even so, because of bias or a feeling of discomfort with the unfamiliar, peers may ignore a woman in the work group and withhold information vital to her functioning. The superior must be alert to the propensity of others to exclude the woman manager from meetings and from memos "because we didn't think she'd be interested."

To be fully effective, a woman must be able to interact freely with co-workers. Yet, more than a quarter of nearly 1500 women managers interviewed felt they were not receiving the same kind of informal training as their male peers. Comments ranged from "I am excluded from the lunch bunch" to "I can't tap into the male pipeline."[6] Thus, women often lack knowledge gleaned from those more experienced in the what, when, and how of the job.

Uncooperative co-workers can prove devastating to even the most able and ambitious woman. Those who oppose her will seek reasons for their animosity; both the woman's functional skills and personality will be placed on trial. She may be distracted from her work because of tension in her interpersonal relationships. In addition, she may have already had many battles with parents, school counselors, professors, and even spouse and children over her executive ambitions. The supervisor should be sensitive to her situation and counsel her appropriately.

Continued unfamiliarity will only exacerbate prejudice. The superior should do everything possible to integrate the woman into the work group. He or she can encourage cohesiveness by the development of teams, task forces, or committees so that the success of others is tied to the success of the woman.

Women must be accorded worth equal to that of their male colleagues. Insofar as possible, the working environment should be the same for men and women; unfortunately, exceptions usually spell degrading treatment for the female. A retailing manager in New York reported that the young woman delivering the mail addressed her by her first name. "She always uses 'Mister' in talking to the junior executive across the corridor even though I am clearly senior to him," the manager added.[7]

The superior should make certain that forms of address relate to rank, not to sex. If clericals are required to call male managers "Mr." females should not be addressed on a first-name basis. Sex stereotyping may prove more of a problem with nonexempt females than with males at any level of the organization. In addition to the "She's one of us because she's a woman" outlook, there's "If she's a manager, why shouldn't I be one too?" which can cause difficulty for both the female manager and the organization.

"In those instances in which sex stereotypes are operative, women may be evaluated along the dimensions of sex and position while men are evaluated according to position. Consequently, the behavior and/or performance of women can be out of role by sex and in role by position, in role by sex and out of role by position, out of role by sex and position, and in role by sex and position," points out Terborg.[8] Thus, women in management can find themselves on the horns of a dilemma in terms of how they are viewed. Females are apt to be subject to as much criticism if they display the traits of a manager as if they do not, since management attributes are thought of as male. If the woman appears to lack "tough-mindedness," she may be criticized for a management weakness; if she does display this quality, she may be condemned for acting inappropriately as a woman.

The superior should take the lead in minimizing the importance of the woman executive's sex in her on-the-job treatment. The woman wants to be regarded as a human being, or a manager-woman, not as a mother, sister, or sex object. An officer of a New York bank reported, "There are guys who come in here and say, 'I want this; I want that,' and I have to say, 'Hey, wait a minute. You can't talk to me like that.' I've got to make them understand they're not talking to their wives.''[9]

A woman will not benefit even from sincere compliments about her beauty, charm, or dress as much as she will from deserved praise about her job performance; she will not find someone holding her chair or lighting her cigarette as helpful as the sharing of technical information that she needs to do her job.

Certainly, she must not be made to feel that she is representing her entire gender as an interloper in alien territory. In some organizations, the executive woman may be asked in meetings to express "the woman's point of view"; customers, clients or subordinates-to-be may be "warned" that they are being asked to deal with a woman, and the female may be singled out for introduction to visitors as if she were a curiosity. ("Nobody likes to be thought of as somebody you'd go to the zoo to look at," emphasized a woman vice president.) Joking references may be made to "our token female" or "our lady manager," and she may be "complimented" on her ability to "think like a man," although concern may be voiced that she has been given too much responsibility "for a woman." Such episodes characterize an unsupportive environment which virtually assures the woman's failure.

Of course, it is only recently that women have been viewed as equals in American society. John Adams's wife wrote entreating him and other drafters of the Declaration of Independence to "be more generous and favorable" to the ladies "than your ancestors . . . Remember all men would be tyrants if they could. If perticular care and attention is not paid to the laidies we are determined to forment a Rebelion and will not hold

ourselves bound by any Laws in which we have no voice or representation." He responded that rather than be subjected "to the despotism
of the peticoat, I hope General Washington and all our brave heroes
would fight."[10]

Little more than a century ago, a Supreme Court justice, in upholding
Illinois's refusal to license women as attorneys, declared that a female
was not at liberty to adopt "a distinct and independent career from that
of her husband."[11] Now, however, the Supreme Court, Congress, and
the Executive Branch affirm the equality of women. Language should
reflect these changed circumstances. The generic "he" serves to relegate
females to second class status and is as inappropriate as a generic "she"
for references to both sexes.

In order to minimize the "think manager-think male" link in the
organization, top management should establish a policy for written
communications, as many companies including Bank of America and
Mobil Oil Corporation have done. With women heavily represented in
the world of work, such terms as "manpower planning" and "workmen's
compensation" are no longer appropriate.

"I feel very strongly about the use of neutral language," stressed a
female consultant. "The only way images are going to change in people's
minds is if the language changes. If we continue to refer to the CEO as
'the man' and the manager as 'he,' the image will remain exclusively
male. The organizations which write memos referring to 'wives' rather
than 'spouses' are slapping their women employees in the face."

Use of male references to mean both sexes should be eliminated;
whenever possible, genderless words should be substituted, rather than
awkward references to both men and women. Male nouns and pronouns
should be limited to references to specific males. Parallel words should
be used when references are made to both sexes. If males are described
as "men," females should be referred to as "women" rather than "girls"
or "ladies." If men are alluded to by last name only, so should women.
If men's full names are used, so should women's. Married, divorced or
widowed women may be permitted to use the name of preference:
maiden, married, or hyphenated. At Equitable, all women are referred to
as "Ms." for business purposes. And females are never alluded to as
"gals," "girls," or "ladies," but only as "women."

A Midwest-based manufacturer annually reviews the content of personnel policies to be certain that any necessary or desirable updating is
accomplished and that no discriminatory references exist. Such a plan
can be very useful. It was not until a few years ago that a leading bank
realized that its employee handbook still stipulated that any woman

working late had to have an officer (understood to be male) stay on the floor with her!

Company publications should avoid jokes deprecating women as carefully as they do put-downs based on race, religion, or national origin. Stereotypical references should be eliminated; the marital status and parenthood of women should not be noted, for example, unless that of men is as well. Presumably, marriage and parenthood are equally important to both sexes.

The superior should make certain that women subordinates have equal access to developmental opportunities. Ideally, these would include career counseling, participation in in-house or outside training courses, access to degree-granting programs at company expense, and the proper amount of on-the-job training. The main difference in 1500 women managers' outlook on upward mobility was availability of training: 69 percent of those receiving the same training as male colleagues believed they could advance, while only 45 percent of those who felt they had had dissimilar training opportunities believed they could.[12]

## ROLE OF APPRAISAL

In some companies, women are unlikely ever to be considered "ready" for advancement unless an objective appraisal system removes subjective judgments to the greatest possible degree. Researchers have shown that stereotypical thinking impacts personnel decisions far less when specific rules are in place.[13] "One of the things companies do," opined a personnel vice president, "is want more out of a woman before she gets promoted. As a result, she doesn't move very fast up the ladder."

At least one major employer has countered possible prejudice by putting promotion decisions in each plant or division in the hands of a committee of line supervisors rather than leaving the outcomes to individual managers. "We still have our share of chauvinists, but now they only have one vote each," said the director of human resources planning for General Motors Corporation.[14]

Women need to be recognized for their contribution in the same manner as men, in accord with their performance. Happily, the old standards of seniority or untrammeled supervisory judgment have lost ground in appraising both men and women. "We have a task force studying performance appraisal right now, so we can come up with a more sophisticated approach," reported an officer of a consumer services organization. "Our appraisal covers everybody, and we've been using just two forms: a shorter one for nonexempts and the other for all levels of exempt, including the chairman of the board.''

As is true of men, women appreciate a frank and open discussion of their strengths and weaknesses, as well as insight into possible future opportunities. The superior should not provide direction but attempt to furnish information necessary in helping individuals arrive at their own conclusions regarding immediate and long-range prospects. A full knowledge of circumstances, even if these are unfavorable, will encourage women to remain. No acknowledgment or limited discussion of career track will lead females to consider outside alternatives.

Women should be given as many and varied work experiences as their talents permit to prepare them for upward mobility. Top management must be alert to stiffening resistance to the progression of women past a certain point which may seem ''acceptable'' to middle managers. A food company executive recalled that at his previous employer, ''There was a high level of concern because of the number of women coming into entry jobs, and what that might mean if they progressed into the highest levels of management.''

## WOMEN AND MONEY

One myth holds that women are not as interested in money as men and can be retained more cheaply because pay differentials have epitomized the past. Disparity in pay by sex frequently has resulted from sex segregation of the work force, although unequal pay for the same or similar work also has prevailed. Researchers have attributed from one-fourth to less than one-half of the difference in wages of men and women to work experience; labor market discrimination has played an even greater part.[15]

Some evidence does exist to substantiate the view that women might be employed more cheaply. A survey of men and women in the Stanford MBA class of 1974 showed that both sexes similarly rated the importance of many career goals: leadership, expertise, prestige, service, independence, security, self-realization, duty and pleasure. The men and women differed substantially on only one item: wealth. The mean salary men said they would like to earn was significantly more than the one cited by women, and the average expected salary of the men was also appreciably greater than that of the women.[16]

However, this outlook may have been based on realities rather than desires; a study of men and women receiving their Harvard MBAs between 1960 and 1975 showed that postgraduation salaries of women were lower than those of men.[17] Certainly, the mounting number of suits brought under the Equal Pay Act (which was extended in 1972 to cover managers and professionals) indicates that growing numbers of women are unwilling to tolerate perceived inequities in compensation.

As one example, a California woman is suing her ex-employer for $2 million. Once the secretary to the chairman and president, she was advanced to corporate secretary and later to vice president. She was the only woman and at $20,000 the lowest paid at this rank. According to press reports, she was told and believed that her low level of compensation was due to the fact that she was female and was the result of a corporate policy of illegal sex discrimination. She alleged undue harassment, saying she was criticized "for a standoffish attitude toward men in the executive department, had trouble securing their cooperation and didn't receive perquisites that other executives received."[18]

An officer of a consumer products organization noted that his company had lost "very few if any women to other companies. We've taken a look at their compensation, and they compare very, very favorably with the men. Many women have experienced accelerated salary progress because some have risen from the very lowest levels of management or even from the secretarial ranks to grow in total compensation to where the typical man at their new level is."

Research has demonstrated that, generally speaking, men are rated more on accomplishment and women more on appearance and personal attributes. "I have seen appraisals which characterize women as 'vivacious' or 'comforting,' " a key official of a leading company pointed out. "These are not valid evaluative terms for men, and they should not be used for women." Appraisal that is closely tied to measurable, job-related objectives is not only welcomed by females, but safeguards the employer from charges of discrimination.

More and more companies are turning to multiple regression analysis of compensation systems. Managements may believe they are paying for education and experience required, budget and number of people supervised only to discover that race, sex, or other factors are playing a part in determining salary.

Theoretically, males and females should be compensated equally, but this doesn't always prove to be the case. Females may be found routinely below or in the lower part of established salary ranges for their positions. If so, corrective steps must be taken to avoid illegality. In the past, bonuses have rarely been available to women since few females occupied jobs at a level deserving of incentive payment. And, of course, sex discrimination in salary might cause women to be ineligible even if men of equal rank were.

Now, men and women are found in middle and upper management, and both sexes as well as their organizations are benefitting from the trend tying incentive and salary to contribution. Even in staff functions, where women are found disproportionately and which historically have been considered too difficult to evaluate, financial incentives are being granted in relation to accomplishments rather than being formula based or purely discretionary.

Most companies have offered essentially the same benefits to men and women, except for retirement and maternity. Now, both of these areas are undergoing transformation. One of the distinctions in retirement has been sex-linked pension fund contributions, based on mortality rate differences. Since women live longer on average, pension costs are higher for females as a group. Yet, the Supreme Court ruled in 1978 that it is unlawful to require different contributions by sex for the same benefits. The Court asserted that many women "will not live as long as the average man" and that "any individual's life expectancy is based on a number of factors, of which sex is only one."

Said a consultant, "I think part of the Court's thinking was that differences between working people—whether male or female—will be minimal at some point in the future."

Another distinction has been retirement age. Some plans retire women before men, whether on a voluntary or mandatory basis. Continuation of different ages by sex, however, could lead to charges of discrimination from either men or women. "Given the Supreme Court's decision on pension contributions, it's a foregone conclusion that soon there will be no sex-based factors in retirement programs," another consultant opined.

## IMPACT OF PREGNANCY LEGISLATION

Companies have looked upon pregnancy as a condition of choice and therefore not deserving of the same benefits paid for involuntary disabilities. In addition, firms have not relished this additional expense, particularly because there is no proof that disability payments for pregnancy encourage retention of employees. A law which was effective in April, 1979, prohibits employers from discriminating in all areas of employment—including hiring, promotion, seniority rights and fringe benefits—against workers who become pregnant. Further, employers with health or disability plans must cover pregnancy, childbirth, and related medical conditions in the same manner that other conditions are covered. Employers are required to pay medical benefits for abortions only when performed to save the mother's life. But disability payments must be made in all abortion cases.

With the new law, AT&T replaced its maternity plan with an "anticipated disability" program. Now, pregnant workers can take paid leave as long as they've been certified by doctors as unable to work and unpaid leave even before that. Previously, women could take unpaid leave before giving birth, but maternity payments did not begin until childbirth. As long as a worker continues to be certified as disabled, she is eligible for as many as 52 weeks of half pay if she's been with the company for at least six months. And an employee with 25 years of service can receive 52 weeks of full pay. Formerly, maternity payments were limited to six full weeks of pay for employees with five years or more of service.[19]

In the past, organizations have determined when pregnant women should leave work without regard for their condition, and also when and if they should return. In recent years, however, companies have been encouraging managerial and professional women to continue working after marriage and to return to their jobs after pregnancy. The newly mandated pregnancy benefits should make organizations even more anxious to attract back postpartum managers and professionals.

"Atrophy varies at least by education and occupation," researchers point out. "Those with the highest levels of schooling and in highly skilled occupations find intermittent labor force participation most costly."[20]

Said a consultant, "The law may provide for a leave of absence for new mothers or other kinds of things. But the fact is, these women are going to lose time. You know what's happening in American industry right now: The technology curve is awesome—not just in terms of product but in terms of management processes. When the women get behind two, three, or four years, they have a hard time coming back."

Both women and their employers are aware of how much an extended period away from a middle or upper echelon position can cost in executive obsolescence. Already, some companies are arranging for new mothers to work part-time at home until they feel they can return to work full-time. Among these is Prudential Insurance Company, which once told any woman professional going on maternity leave that the company would grant her an interview if she wished to return to work. "The understanding was that she'd start at ground zero again," a personnel executive recalled. Now, however, the company feels its program of at-home assignments for those on maternity leave benefits both women and employer.[21]

The impact of disability payments or even seniority rights upon career orientation of new mothers is uncertain. According to The Conference Board, "There is no evidence that paying income benefits in maternity cases induces women to return to work after they leave. About 57 percent return from maternity leave, whether that leave is paid or unpaid."[22]

"We are beginning to lose some of our professional women in the 30 to 35 age bracket," explained an officer of a West Coast company. "They've had a career that's run ten or twelve years, and suddenly they realize if they're going to have a family, they'd better do it now. Over the last several years a number of these women have become pregnant. They take a leave of absence with every intention of coming back. And then they find that little person is far more captivating than they ever thought possible, and the leave of absence becomes a resignation. In our future planning, we may have to face losing a certain number of people in this age bracket."

Said a personnel executive on the opposite seaboard, "Our male/female loss rates are moving closer together. Women are returning after childbearing. In my view, job placement is more critical to the retention of new mothers than is the question of medical payments."

Perhaps a sharing of parental responsibilities would serve the careers of executive women even better than liberalized maternity benefits. Sweden has offered paternity leave since 1974, in the belief that a mother has as much right to a career as a father. About 10 to 12 percent of eligible fathers take leaves, up from 2 percent when the program started. Paternity leave also is gaining ground in Britain: a study of 400 companies showed 3 percent granted paid and 5 percent unpaid leave.[23] The concept appears to have equal application to other industrial nations with highly educated female populations, including the United States.

"Why not paternity leave?" asked a consultant. "If you're going to say that sex is no longer an issue, and then grant a leave to someone who's about to be a parent, why limit the privilege to women? Right now, some companies have programs where new adoptive parents, either male or female, can take paid leave."

Since 1979, AT&T has permitted new fathers to take up to six months of unpaid leave to care for a newborn child and still get their old jobs back. Workers of either sex adopting infants are eligible for similar unpaid leave.[24]

Today, nearly half of all mothers with children under 18 work. About 40 percent of preschoolers' mothers are employed. Five million youngsters under the age of 13 now spend 30 hours or more weekly in the care of individuals other than parents or teachers.[25] However, day-care centers are either unavailable or too costly for most mothers. Only a small proportion use them; far more rely upon relatives, neighbors, or baby-sitters.

By and large, companies do not find it feasible to furnish child-care facilities. Very few have actually undertaken to do so after studying the possibility. AT&T gave up two experimental operations when the company-sponsored day-care facilities for offspring of both male and female employees neither attracted nor retained workers of either sex. And a leading multibranch bank turned from the idea because of cost and an inability to decide upon an appropriate location. Nonetheless, companies can support child-care facilities serving their communities and can provide a child-care counseling service for parents of both sexes who could benefit from such help.

## DIFFERENT WORK SCHEDULES

Alternatives to traditional hours of work appear to be an avenue for retaining employees of both sexes, whether or not they have children. With many two-career families, more money is less attractive than more time to enjoy the fruits of current income. However, options regarding hours of work undoubtedly are most important to working women with home and child-care responsibilities.

"I think alternatives to the standard work week are inevitable," declared a vice president at a Midwest company. "Right now those departments that want flexible hours have them. My hunch is that eventually this will permeate the whole system. And it's not just because of women. People want more flexibility in their lives, and this trend is responsive to that."

Some alternatives to traditional work schedules are: flexitime, where individuals are given a choice in the timing of their hours during a full-time work period—day, week, or month; staggered hours, where employees may be allowed to pick from limited time alternatives; permanent part-time work, defined as less than 35 hours weekly for at least 48 weeks a year; and shared jobs, where two individuals combine their time and talents to perform one job and receive one salary and one set of benefits in return. While these innovations appear less appropriate for higher level positions, there undoubtedly are situations where one or more of the alternatives could be applied. Professional jobs would seem to be better subjects for experimentation than managerial positions. According to the American Management Associations, 13 percent of all private employers with more than 50 workers offer flexitime. Those firms with higher proportions of female employees are more likely to utilize it.[26]

A Chicago bank lost a fast-track woman employee a few years ago when she couldn't schedule child care to jibe with her work schedule. Refusing part-time work, she joined another company. However, in 1979 the bank won her back with a promotional opportunity and flexible full-time hours.[27]

"We have gone to complete flexitime in a number of locations so managers and professionals are included," reported an officer of an oil company. Personal business can be conducted more easily without intruding on work; thus, job satisfaction is enhanced without damaging productivity.

Indeed, flexitime may actually enhance productivity along with improving employee morale. Reviewing 8 surveys of companies using flexitime, a researcher discovered the median proportion that subjectively reported increased productivity was 48 percent. In addition, in 14 case studies, the median proportion of employees who claimed that their productivity had improved was 45 percent.[28]

The Department of Labor reports that businesses are hiring more permanent part-time workers. A study, prepared for DOL by the Georgetown University School of Business Administration, estimates that roughly one out of every 12 American workers is a permanent part-time employee. Three decades ago, only about one of twenty workers fell into this classification.[29] Currently 17 percent of all professionals and 7 percent of all managers are part-timers.[30] However, there are undoubtedly many more part-timers of this rank outside the business sector than in it. Part-time workers have been found to produce proportionately more output than full-time employees, and the quality of part-time work has been found to be as good as or better than that of full-time.[31]

Fewer than half of all working women hold year-round, full-time jobs. "Part-time employment remains the young mother's prime tool in combining work and child care," points out The Conference Board. "Many companies maintain regular part-time work forces, and 67 percent at least extend paid vacations and holidays to part-timers."[32]

A bank representative noted that officers are allowed to work part-time "whenever we can accommodate them by movement into a staff-oriented, project-oriented job. Women want to do it as new mothers, but both sexes sometimes seek part-time status for educational purposes."

Shared jobs are found in academe now, but apparently have yet to gain a toehold in business. "That's enough of a departure that I don't think companies will go to shared jobs unless people with exceptional qualifications are available only on that basis," said a personnel vice president. "Like others, I am very reluctant to do something just because it's good for some special segment of the population."

A bank officer declared, "Shared jobs intimidate us. The mechanics of keeping track of who's doing what! We're just not comfortable with that concept yet."

## CAFETERIA BENEFITS ATTRACTIVE

As The Conference Board points out, "Women enter a labor force in which employee benefits packages are largely designed for a traditional family economy with one breadwinner, working full-time, solely responsible for the family's well-being."[33]

Cafeteria-style benefits are offered by only a few companies since administrative costs are an important negative. But the concept seems well suited to a more diversified employee mix which includes greater numbers of older workers and unmarried individuals as well as numerous two-career families. Under the usual cafeteria plan, a core of benefits is provided for all employees, with supplemental benefits available for selection by the individual in accordance with age, sex, family circumstances or other relevant considerations. Thus, given a choice, household heads could carry more insurance, single parents could take more vacation days for personal business, and older individuals could increase their pension payments. This would appear advantageous not only to employees but to organizations which face ever-mounting costs for benefits that may be excessive for some recipients and deficient for others. Perhaps lack of choice makes employees insufficiently appreciative of corporate benefit outlays, which currently approximate 40 percent or more of cash compensation.

At one time, nepotism was more of a perceived problem for companies than is true today. When the nuclear family with its single breadwinner was pervasive, a "no spouse" rule was not only logical but simplified transfers and vacation scheduling and avoided any suspicion of familial favoritism. Then, if a man and woman working for the same employer chose to marry, it was typically the woman who was expected to leave.

"Of course, it wasn't stated that way," commented a banker. "The rules simply said that no two officers could be married."

The number of families with two wage earners has increased by about 25 percent in the last decade. With women far more prevalent in the work force, organizations appear to have become more lenient with regard to nepotism. Indeed, many employers encourage staff members to seek out friends and relatives as prospective employees and reward them for referrals who are hired.

Many companies now have no restrictions on spouses or other family members as employees, specifying only that one should not be in a management line or auditing the work of another. Thus, organizations are able to attract and retain managerial and professional women who would otherwise be lost to them. "We have a substantial number of husband and wife teams in the bank," reported a vice president at a major institution. "We also have many parent-child combinations."

Only about 8 percent of the employees transferred by American corporations are women, says Merrill Lynch Relocation Management.[34] However, this total is 20 times greater than five years earlier. The small proportion may be due to the paucity of women in middle and upper echelon positions, which normally involve the greatest mobility. But it also may result from a still widespread opinion that the male wage-earner's job comes first. A 1977 poll conducted by the *New York Times* and CBS News showed that "60 percent of those interviewed still balked at the idea of uprooting a family in which both spouses worked in order to allow the woman to accept a promotion in another part of the country, with 11 percent in favor of the move and 14 percent holding that it would depend upon their respective posts."[35]

"I can readily think of half a dozen cases where we've asked women if they'd like to be considered for a particular job, and they've said no," an oil company executive recalled. "They weren't geographically mobile due to their husband's careers. That's a limiting factor, since the woman restricts herself to promotional opportunities within the same area."

Some organizations assume that women will not relocate, and as a consequence, deny individuals a choice which could influence their career progress. Refusal to relocate or even the assumption of refusal can retard an individual's career. At one time, companies offered a transfer just once; if it was refused, no other offers were made. The individual could remain with the company but was off the fast track. Today, there is more mobility in middle and upper echelon positions since career paths which send people to various parts of the business are more extensive and formally charted by major organizations. However, if an individual refuses a transfer, he or she will probably be asked again when personal circumstances could be more favorable to a move.

While both men and women are demonstrating a growing reluctance to relocate, it should never be assumed that certain individuals cannot or will not do so. The women most likely to transfer are single, divorced, or widowed. But many two-career couples accommodate to transfer by commuting or by taking turns in deciding whose career has precedence. Usually commuting spouses hold well-paying jobs and are either childless or lack offspring below high school age. "The solutions to the dual career problem vary widely, but they are easier when there's a clear leader," pointed out a personnel executive in New York.

Commuting is easiest when at least one member of the couple is employed by an airline, thus sharply reducing travel costs. Even in these instances the additional time, energy, and psychological and financial cost of living apart remain burdens. Nevertheless, couples can be found today commuting between points several hundred miles, more than a thousand miles, and even a continent apart. An airline employee transferred to California while his wife, an attorney, remained in New York.

Companies should be helpful not only to married women but to married men in solving the problems of relocation. The organizations as well as the employees and their families will benefit. When a married woman accepts a transfer at a Midwest bank, officials meet with her and her husband to discuss possible problems arising from the move. However, the institution apparently does not meet with wives of transferred men, whether or not the females are employed. This could be a mistake, as any executive recruiter would be quick to testify.

All too often, husbands and/or their employers assume that wives will relocate willingly if not enthusiastically. Subsequent events may prove that even the nonworking wife will refuse to join her husband or will not remain if she has already moved. In some instances the marriage dissolves; in other cases the husband's career with the company suffers, or he elects to leave his employer.

Both two-career and one-career families take relocation considerably less lightly than even a few years ago. As a result, companies should do everything possible to smooth the transition. "Relocation is a problem with both sexes," pointed out an oil company official. "However, it is more of a problem for younger employees because more two-career families are represented there. And, to this point at least, it is more of a problem with women than with men because even younger couples perceive the male as the primary wage earner in the family unit."

"You'd be surprised at the number of couples employed by our company," commented a technical organization's representative. "If one is asked to move, we'll make every effort to accommodate the spouse with an assignment. That's easy in a major location, but if it's a small installation, it's unlikely there would be anything appropriate."

If a married couple is employed by the company, most firms will endeavor to relocate both husband and wife if one is being offered a transfer. If this is impossible due to a lack of appropriate opportunities, the company will then bend every effort to obtain suitable employment for the spouse with another organization. Many companies perform similar services even when the spouse is not an employee. Corporate personnel executives maintain a job-finding network with counterparts in all areas of the country. According to Merrill Lynch Relocation Management, 16 percent of 686 major corporations surveyed recently indicated they endeavor to help find new employment for spouses when men or women are transferred.[36]

"We stop short of saying we *will* find the spouse a new opportunity," said a personnel executive at a Manhattan-headquartered company. "But we *do* do it, when we can."

A bank vice president reported, "We moved a woman to Brazil and helped her husband find a job there. I don't think you can do much better than that! We have our contacts. It's nothing formal. Just a 'Who do you know?' arrangement."

A Midwest company's representative noted that two high-level women had experienced transfers of their spouses. "In one case the husband was sent overseas. We had nothing to offer our employee in that particular location. She elected to leave the company, but she knows we'd welcome her back if she wants to return. The other couple separated. My view is, there were problems with that marriage before the transfer came along. And the woman's making good bucks; she doesn't need to trot all over the countryside following her husband."

But a food company officer declared, "We have had a lot of men with working wives who over the years have wanted to impose our finding the spouse a job as a condition of their moving—even impose the wife's salary level! 'I'll go if you can get her another job at $20,000.' We've shied away from that because you get into hiring the world."

However, at least one major company on occasion pays a placement firm to help an employee's spouse find work in the couple's new location. In any event, it seems certain that tomorrow's family is destined to change patterns of work. "In future years, it may become a more frequent occurrence for both spouses to work only part of the year, or for more of the husbands to devote themselves to child rearing in the home, or for both to work at part-time jobs," opined a government study.[37]

In the meantime, two major companies have funded a major study by Catalyst, a New York-based organization dedicated to helping women in their careers. Catalyst intends to interview several hundred employees at 50 to 70 companies in an effort to find out where two-career couples are, how they manage their lives and what companies are doing to help.

When it appears that an organization can no longer offer a woman employment suitable to her abilities and interests, the company would be well advised to lose her rather than attempt to retain her with promises that may not be fulfilled. "There's a limit to what an employer can do," a consumer products executive noted. "We can't create jobs to accommodate the expectation of all employees. There comes a time when you have to be candid with both sexes. The employee has to come to grips with the situation and make a decision. It may be well for him or her to leave the company. The best we can do is make the individual aware of where he or she stands, what we can do and can't do. Then the man or woman has to assume responsibility for the future."

In letting a woman go, the company will be keeping a friend, particularly if an effort is made to be helpful in the employee's relocation. In keeping her, the company would risk an unproductive, dissatisfied employee who ultimately might discover a reason to file a discrimination complaint. The loyal ex-employee will not only speak in the company's behalf and refer others there but will consider returning should changed circumstances make such a move mutually advantageous.

"We had a very fine performer, a young woman who was hired away by another company," recalled a personnel executive at a diversified East Coast company. "She had been gone only two and a half years when we realized that at that point she was absolutely necessary to our organization. We rehired her at the vice presidential level, and the comparison between her compensation then and now is ridiculous!"

In sum, retaining women calls for the same consideration of individuals' needs as does retaining men. A notable difference is the greater need of women for flexible hours of work. Even this may not prove distinctive in the future, should males continue in succeeding generations to show less dedication to the work ethic and greater desire for a more balanced life. Men may seek greater fulfillment *off* the job, even as women seek greater fulfillment *on* the job.

In years to come, two-career families will give both men and women greater freedom to pursue their own goals, reduce the power of employers, and necessitate corporate adjustments to employee preferences similar to those that have already been wrought on transfer and employment of family members. At the same time, the two-income household will lessen the trauma when organizations discharge poor performers. "How to retain women executives?" asked a woman officer, then answered, "Treat them as competent, qualified individuals, and help them just as you would men."

## REFERENCES

1. Kronholz, June, "Management Practices Change to Reflect Role of Women Employees," *Wall Street Journal* 13 September 1978.
2. Lyle, Jerolyn R., *Affirmative Action Programs for Women: A Survey of Innovative Programs,* Report submitted to the Office of Research, Equal Employment Opportunity Commission, under Contract 71-45, 1973, p. 70.
3. Baron, Alma Spann, "Women in Management: A New Look," *Personnel Administrator* No. 23, p. 53 (December 1978).
4. "The Corporate Woman—How to Get Along—and Ahead—in the Office," *Business Week,* 22 March 1976, p. 107.
5. Terborg, James R., "Women in Management: A Research Review," *Journal of Applied Psychology* **62**(6):651 (1977).
6. Baron, Alma Spann, "Women in Management: A New Look," *Personnel Administrator* No. 23, p. 53 (December 1978).
7. "What's It Like for Women Executives?" *Dun's Review,* December 1975, p. 60.
8. Terborg, James, R., "Women in Management: A Research Review," *Journal of Applied Psychology* **62**(6):656-7 (1977).
9. "What's It Like for Women Executives?" *Dun's Review,* December 1975, p. 59.
10. Butterfield, L. H., ed., *The Book of Abigail and John: Selected Letters of the Adams Family, 1762–1784,* Cambridge, MA: Harvard University Press, 1975, pp. 121 and 123.
11. *Bradwell vs. Illinois,* 83 U.S. (16 Wall) 130 (1872).
12. Baron, Alma Spann, "Women in Management: A New Look," *Personnel Administrator* No. 23, p. 53 (December 1978).
13. Rosen, B. and T. H. Jerdee, "Sex Stereotyping in the Executive Suite," *Harvard Business Review* **52**(2):56 (March–April 1974).
14. Gallese, Liz R., "Women Managers Say Job Transfers Present a Growing Dilemma," *Wall Street Journal,* 4 May 1978.
15. Sandell, Steven H. and David Shapiro, "An Exchange: The Theory of Human Capital and The Earnings of Women—A Reexamination of the Evidence," *Journal of Human Resources* **17**(4):114 (Winter 1978).
16. Gordon, Francine E. and Myra H. Strober, "Initial Observations on a Pioneer Cohort: 1974 Women MBAs," *Sloan Management Review* **19**(2):19 (Winter 1978).
17. Harlan, A., *Career Differences Among Male and Female Managers,* Paper presented at the National Academy of Management, Kansas City, MO, 1976.
18. "California Life Sued on Sex-Bias Charges by Ex-Vice President," *Wall Street Journal,* 24 March 1977.
19. "AT&T Replacing Maternity Program for Its Employees," *Wall Street Journal,* 23 April 1979.
20. Mincer, Jacob and Solomon Polachek, "An Exchange: The Theory of Human Capital

and the Earnings of Women Reexamined," *Journal of Human Resources,* **17**(4):131 (Winter 1978).

21. Kronholz, June, "Management Practices Change to Reflect Role of Women Employees," *Wall Street Journal,* 13 September 1978.

22. Meyer, Mitchell, *Women and Employee Benefits,* New York: The Conference Board, 1978, p. ii.

23. Morgenthaler, Eric, "Sweden Offers Fathers Paid Paternity Leaves; About 10 Percent Take Them," *Wall Street Journal,* 29 January 1979.

24. "AT&T Replacing Maternity Program for its Employees," *Wall Street Journal,* 23 April 1979.

25. Gottschalk, Earl C., Jr., "Day Care is Booming, But Experts Are Split Over its Effect on Kids," *Wall Street Journal,* 15 September 1978.

26. Nollen, Stanley D. and Virginia H. Martin, *Alternative Work Schedules, Part 1: Flexitime,* New York: American Management Associations, 1978, p. 5.

27. Lublin, Joann S., "Two-Career Couples," *Wall Street Journal,* 9 April 1979.

28. Nollen, Stanley D., "Does Flexitime Improve Productivity?" *Harvard Business Review* **57**(5):12 (September–October 1979).

29. *Chicago Tribune,* 13 April 1978.

30. Lublin, Joann S., "Firms and Job Seekers Discover More Benefits of Part-time Positions," *Wall Street Journal,* 4 October 1978.

31. Nollen, Stanley D. et al., *Permanent Part-Time Employment: An Interpretive Review,* Washington, DC: U.S. Department of Labor, Employment and Training Administration, No. 21-11-75-16, 1976, p. 21.

32. Meyer, Mitchell, *Women and Employee Benefits,* New York: The Conference Board, 1978, p. iii.

33. Meyer, Mitchell, *Women and Employee Benefits,* New York: The Conference Board, 1978, p. ii.

34. Labor Letter, *Wall Street Journal,* 27 February 1979.

35. Meislin, Richard J., "Poll Finds More Liberal Beliefs on Marriage and Sex Roles, Especially Among the Young," *New York Times,* 27 November 1977.

36. Robins, James, "Firms Give Employees All Kinds of Assistance to Get Them to Move," *Wall Street Journal,* 2 May 1979.

37. Rawlings, Stephen, *Perspective on American Husbands and Wives,* U.S. Department of Commerce, Bureau of the Census, Special Studies Series P23, No. 77, 1978, p. 25.

# 11

# Listening to Women Executives

## ON THE ROLE OF WOMEN TODAY

Senior executive "A," consumer industry:

"The current fashion is to provide status only to women who are working full time. You meet young men who evaluate potential wives very much the way women have always evaluated potential husbands — in terms of their jobs. 'I really want to meet this gal that Fred told me about. She's a doctor and has published twice.'

"There is a tremendous pressure on my generation. I know a woman who went to Smith and married well, to a man from Yale who then went to Harvard to get his MBA and is now senior vice president of a large corporation. She's 42, and he's saying, 'Why are you sitting around doing nothing?' She has no skills; what kind of work is she going to do? He says, 'Look at Jack's wife; she's earning $35,000 a year; you should go out and do that. Go back to school and get yourself an education.'

"You meet these poor dears who believe all the stuff universities are saying about get yourself an MBA at 35 and then get a wonderful job. Of course it's not true. No large corporation would conceivably take them at that age; it's a hoax and a lie. All competition in institutionalized organizations is at peer group levels; it's age structured. It's very unrealistic to tell women they can bring up their kids to a certain age and then 'go back to work.' Yet it's very hard for these women to find anybody who will say, 'You are quite right; you are doing the proper thing by staying home now that your kids have grown up a bit; you deserve it.'

"I personally didn't choose that route, but I think women who did are understandably resentful. All the work you do should pay off with something, and in effect they're being told that it's worthless. That's a very hard thing to take. I think it's one of the reasons you're seeing anti-ERA. There is a whole segment of the population that secretly resents all this pressure."

Senior executive "A," capital goods industry:

"How any women did we have ten years ago? They were nowhere in large corporations. I see enormous progress in the fact that now we have women at least like an occasional raisin in the pudding, when we had none—absolutely none."

Senior executive "A," consumer industry:

"There are certain companies that simply wouldn't accept me, even today. And there are certain geographies where I couldn't be effective, either. That's just reality. Sure there are barriers to women. But men have barriers, too; men have to 'fit' organizations. And there are enough opportunities now that it doesn't really bother me. Besides, it will change. Companies are being pressured, and eventually they will be different."

Senior executive "B," consumer industry:

"I think significant change has occurred in the last five years or so. Not in the percentages of women in management but in terms of the attitude of men. Partly this is because there are women who are exhibiting equal or better competence than their male counterparts and partly because the managers' daughters are telling dad that he's a chauvinist, and he's starting to think about that."

Management consultant "A":

"If you'd like a summary, I think women are discriminated against, period. That's a fact. Some companies are trying very hard, but as far as I'm concerned, they're not trying hard enough. But it's inevitable. It's just a matter of time. It's not going to happen in my generation. I'm not going to be totally accepted; I'm always going to be termed a 'woman in business.' But another generation, and it'll be 'a business person'—

nothing else. Even now it's becoming much, much easier for a woman to get to the management level. Of course, it's not as easy as it is for males. Women have to be much smarter, work harder, and perform better. But they're getting there—slowly.''

## ON THE EXECUTIVE WOMAN'S SELF-IMAGE

Management consultant "B":

"In my generation, women grew up in the suburbs where the mother's role was becoming less and less meaningful as an adult life. She was segregated into all-woman communities during the day, basically chauffeuring children around, out of the mainstream. I think that model was unacceptable to a number of women in my generation, and they saw pursuing the father's model as the way to not being dependent. I think that's why women want in. It's not because it's a man's world, and they want part of it; it's because they want to be independent people!''

Middle manager, conglomerate:

"We've been telling ourselves for the last five years or so that in order to succeed at the game, you had to learn the rules and be able to play them as well if not better than the men. But now I think we may change the rules a little bit; we may have to. And I think this is a concern of a lot of men; it's not articulated, but it's there someplace.''

Management consultant "B":

"Women who are very committed to their careers are more integrated people. They take great pleasure in performing traditional female roles. They don't find these roles threatening to their career, but reinforcing. They're women who wish to be accepted as women. The women who can survive long-term are not he/shes.''

Senior executive "A," consumer industry:

"I've never presented myself as a cute, sexy thing. Successful women are supposed to be neuter, and if a woman is clearly female, that presents a problem.''

Senior executive "B," capital goods industry:

"I guess one of the qualities you really need is a certain arrogance about your own capabilities and an ability to manage your own work. I think women have not taken too much responsibility for their own functioning. They seem to feel that someone should tell them what to do, and that's really not the way it is. It takes endurance to be isolated, and it takes an ability to understand what's going on from the nonverbal rather than from conversations. It takes intuition, and then knowledge of people's motivations, and insight into how things work. Some have talent in that line, and some don't; and when you choose a woman to move ahead, you ought to be sure that she does.''

## ON COMBINING CAREER AND MARRIAGE

Senior executive ''A,'' consumer industry:

''Almost universally, the CEOs I know will say, 'I really didn't do right by my kids. When I think back on it, I probably didn't do right by my wife either. I was terribly involved in my career, and it was really impossible to do that and still maintain any kind of personal relationship with my wife and treat her as a real person.'

''I have concluded that probably nobody, male or female, can have a truly marvelous, nurturing, sustaining relationship with spouse, lover, children, or whatever *and* a full-time career. A full-time career does really occupy you virtually totally. Building your career is a very stimulating but emotionally involving experience. That's really where your life is being lived; the rest is support systems.

''I think that women are going to have to realize that the same trade-offs have to be made. 'What's really important? How ambitious am I? How much attention shall I pay to the spouse and to the kids?' Women should stop feeling guilty about making choices; the men don't feel guilty. They simply acknowledge it. I guess I think that women also have to recognize that nobody can have it all, do it all. You have to make choices. That's reality.''

Management consultant ''B'':

''I think a lot of executive women are afraid of having children because they think it will disrupt their careers. This is not so. I have a child, and I worked during my pregnancy and immediately after my pregnancy and found no hostility; it changed the quality of my relationships for the better. But a lot of women delay having children to the point where it's no longer an option. They keep putting it off until they get to X point or to Y point. I personally think that's a tragic way to make those kinds of life choices. And yet, I see that around me; I am the only woman professional I know who has a child.''

Senior executive ''B,'' capital goods industry:

''The advantage to a married woman manager is that she gains from the experience of her husband's career as well as her own, and it takes away some of the isolation that she would otherwise have. Also, when she's fired or when she leaves, she's not going to starve, and this gives an independence which is one of the compensations for having a two-career family.''

## ON THEIR VIEW OF OTHER WOMEN

Management consultant ''B'':

''When I had my child, my social peers who didn't work considered me a monster; they were vocal about it. 'What do you mean by working; you understand, don't you, that you will damage your child's life!' On and on and on. Of course these same women are saying to me now, 'How do you think I can get back into the job market?' The answer is it's too late: 40-year-old women cannot start a career that will ever amount to anything. Running the Junior League is not valid experience.''

Senior executive ''C,'' capital goods industry:

''The least flexible individuals that I've had to work with are women who have been secretaries for a very long period of time. They're doing the whole job for the boss, but really don't have to take the risk of decision making. The boss does that, and the woman is behind the scenes. That's a very different thing from being on your own, and I find that many of these women simply can't make the transition to management. I'm not hopeful about that group, and that's not a popular thing to say.''

Senior executive ''B,'' capital goods industry:

''There are lots of problems in trying to move nonexempt women into management. It's very hard to take someone who has worked for a company as a secretary for 25 years and move her into management. Even though she thinks she's doing a management job, she's not. So the best you can do is take some of the younger girls and try to move them along. I know there is resentment in this group against women in management. I have experienced it myself. There is an attitude that all women are alike, regardless of what their capabilities are.''

Management consultant ''B'':

''Many of the obstacles to their advancement are within women; it's not the men saying you can't get in; that is very exaggerated. There are very few women conditioned to succeed in a male environment, who are willing to take it on, to really take on what men take on, to really play the game. And the game is not a male game; the game is what's required in the way of behavior to manage an enterprise. There are many tough decisions to be made; there are heavy burdens to be borne.''

## ON RESISTANCE TO EXECUTIVE WOMEN

Management consultant ''C'':

''I think the older men, particularly those in senior management, are much more resistant than others. They're thinking, 'A woman's place is in the home, and there isn't a woman who could possibly have the background I need.' Their attitude is reinforced if they ever try to bounce the issue off their wives who are terribly jealous of any woman doing something they are unable to do. Men are used to dealing with women in a certain way, and they're used to women dealing with them in a certain way, and the whole psychology of women in management is just different.''

Middle manager, conglomerate:

''I have found a much different attitude among older men whose wives or daughters are professionals than older men whose wives are at home, a different perspective and a different orientation to me. An awful lot of men would like to feel as comfortable with women as with men, but they just don't. And when you get to the higher levels of management, you're talking about people who need to have a certain comfort level in order to share risk taking.''

Management consultant ''D'':

''The greatest resistance comes from white male middle management, because they're most threatened. I guess that's because they haven't quite made it, and they're most insecure about their maleness. It's hard when they're trying to prove themselves, and here come those women, getting in their way. I hope a lot of that will change when there are more dual career families. I notice a difference here now that there are more young men who have wives who work. They believe in what their wives are doing, so they don't question why other women are doing the same thing.''

Middle manager, consumer industry:

''I think there is a possibility of a greater clash between white women and black men. The minority movement cooled down a bit with the economic crunch, when the blacks were making progress and were so hopeful. There is a great deal of frustration on the part of black males who thought they were going to go like a rocket, and then the women's movement came along and got more attention. Fortunately for me, unfortunately for the black male, a woman can make the movement into management easier.''

Management consultant ''D'':

''The greatest resistance to women in management is from women, the Phyllis Schaflys of this world. The dependent role is one they like. They don't have to take any risks in their lives. It's very nice to be married to someone who does all the work and brings home all the money. You have quasi-childlike responsibilities; you don't have to be economically viable. There are a lot of people who prefer to remain children, and I think that's where the anti-ERA sentiment comes from. I have never encountered a male chauvinist pig, and I've been working for 20 years and in four different organizations. The resistance comes from the wives: 'What do you mean, you *traveled* with her?' ''

Management consultant ''E'':

''I think there are two sources of resistance to women in management. One is older white males, the people who up to now have lived in a world in which they've never had a relationship with a woman as an equal. They come from traditional marriages, and many of them have come out of all-male schools; they've never even sat in a classroom with a woman. They don't have to look at women as competition because they've already made it. But their perceptions don't allow them to see women as anything but wives and mothers and sex objects. So that's very solid resistance.

''There's another kind at the middle management level. These are men up to age 40 or so who are still very much on the make. They see women as competition. They are the ones with the most to lose. Some younger men are more accepting but not all; there are hard-core chauvinists in their twenties. They come from a background where it's been bred into them. And probably by their mothers —we are our own worst enemies.''

## ON PREPARING THE ENVIRONMENT

Senior executive "A," consumer industry:

"I know that a lot of people say that the men need training. I think that if the management says it is simply unacceptable here to say that somebody's not doing well because she has female traits, then no training is needed. There was a time when Catholics didn't get promoted. But you didn't have to run training programs for WASPs to teach them how to work with Catholics. You simply hired the Catholics, and you didn't allow anybody to say, 'I won't promote Joe because he's Catholic.' Everybody learned quickly enough. If they disliked Catholics, they kept it to themselves or talked to their wives about it.

"To me, running training programs is tantamount to acknowledging that women are different and difficult. Women are not different and difficult; women are different from each other just as men are different from each other. But women as a group are not different from men as a group in a business relevant sense. So I am very uncomfortable with training programs for men."

Senior executive "C," capital goods industry:

"Something was done for me that was extraordinarily helpful. The individual to whom I was to report sat down with each of my peers to tell him of my selection and why I was picked. That was great, because when I came into the job, people were gracious and accepting, and all the questions were behind them."

Management consultant "B":

The preparation for men who are going to be working with women executives should be in the institutions which are preparing people for management. The view of business school graduates today is totally different from what it was ten years ago. The young men in this organization are very receptive to working with women—they don't have to be convinced that women can be competent because they've experienced it throughout their education.

"I don't think a whole lot can be done about older male managers. Trust and confidence are built through personal interaction, and they have no women peers sharing a high-risk environment, making tough decisions, doing all the things those men perceive to be their burden. They don't know they can entrust responsibilities to females. They have to learn that the dependent behavior of a wife does not necessarily translate into the behavior of a woman executive."

## ON INTERVIEWING WOMEN

Management consultant "D":

"Why do men have trouble interviewing women? I suspect a lot of the problem is that many of the women now on the job market do not have the same kind of experience men do. Once you get below that group of women who have succeeded in spite of everything and therefore are demonstrably better, you get a lot of women who've had all kinds of strange jobs on their way from secretary to vice president. That's very hard for anybody to appraise. You don't have the comfort of knowing that if they were at XYZ company as product manager, they've been exposed to certain skills. I suspect this problem is diminishing because women are coming out of MBA programs and have never had that secretarial job."

## ON BRINGING WOMEN IN FROM OUTSIDE

Senior executive "B," capital goods industry:

"The corporation is a very strange animal. It took me several years to understand to learn to use its strengths, to organize its resources. I think that if you were to come in at too high a level, and you hadn't had experience with another corporation, you really would have to have a strong mentor. You would probably be observed too closely. You couldn't make all the mistakes you'd need to make. You would be judged too harshly. Of course, that's why women are brought into communications and personnel. These functions are not so dependent on utilizing the resources of the corporation. They're interfacing more with the outside world—consumers, the media, regulators."

Senior executive "C," capital goods industry:

"I was very fortunate when I assumed this post because I'd been in the organization for a long time. I knew most of the people; I knew where the bodies were buried. Coming into a whole new culture is hard. If there were some way you could bring a woman in from the outside, for instance on a consulting basis for a short period of time, so she'd get some knowledge and some acceptance before she had to take on the responsibility, that would be ideal. If that isn't possible, then perhaps bringing her in on what might be called an orientation kind of assignment would be helpful, maybe to do a particular study or to evaluate the organization, or anything that would allow her to obtain the necessary information.''

Management consultant ''C'':

''If the first women brought into the firm at higher levels are in the traditional women functions, I don't think it's going to have any effect. Get them into the key areas! That makes it much easier for the women, because in itself the positioning shows a commitment on the part of top management.''

Senior executive ''B,'' consumer industry:

''Organizations ought to bring women in at the skill level—assistant product managers in marketing, salespeople. I think as these people move through the organization a lot of biases just fall away.''

Management consultant ''E'':

''People are always saying that women are hesitant to accept line responsibility. Of course they are! It's plain common sense to be hesitant when you've got so much going against you. If I were a man, I'd have my support system; I'd have my boss rooting for me; I'd be reasonably well known, and everybody would say, 'Of course he can do it.' With a woman, it's a very different situation. The woman is always held in doubt until she proves herself. In addition, she's always holding up the sex and a man's just representing himself; he will get another chance if he fails, and she may not.''

Senior executive ''B,'' capital goods industry:

''One of our officers called me one day and said, 'I've found two very well-qualified women engineers, but I'll have to raise 30 or 40 salaries to bring those women in. What should I do?' And I said, 'Offer what is reasonable; and if they can get more from another company, let them go there. Treat them as you would a man.' You don't bring a man in way out of line unless he has some special aptitude.''

Senior executive "C," capital goods industry:

"I think you have to lower your standards, especially in respect to experience, in hiring women. The mistake comes if you expect less of the person once she is in place. That's the worst kind of discrimination; you'll never show the person the fun of working if you do that. After a reasonable introductory period, the standards for the job should be exactly the same."

Senior executive "A," consumer industry:

"I wouldn't change standards in bringing women in; I don't believe in that. That does an organization no good, and it reinforces every negative impression anybody ever had. People can say, 'We had to lower our standards and take in people who cry a lot!' It seems to me that an organization should say, 'We are going to keep our standards absolutely intact; what we're going to do is go out and look harder for women.'

"Management has got to recognize they're going to get virtually no help from what I call the headhunter community. Management cannot assume that everybody who's qualified will be turned up in a job search; only the males will be, unless the company specifically says it wants women. But it's doable. The women are there. I get furious when I hear management people say, 'But there are no qualified women!' I respond, 'Isn't it funny, but every department I've ever run was almost 50 percent female when I left.' I've never changed my standards. The difference is that I'm open to the possibility of recruiting women, so remarkably enough, we do it. And they work out fine."

Management consultant "E":

"I think it's sensible to look for wonder women when an organization is identifying its first women managers. They have to be incredibly strong just to survive. Of course, if the organization can't find wonder women, the question is, how do you insure that perfectly adequate, normal middle-range women can be effective? One of the most important things is to look at the organization and ask what's wrong with the organization rather than always looking at women and asking what's wrong with them."

## ON ATTRACTING WOMEN TO OPPORTUNITIES

Senior executive "A," consumer industry:

"Women are less likely to respond to job opportunities in remote locations than are men. Some men may want to go to Minnesota and go deer hunting on Saturdays and Sundays. They can take the wife and kiddies, and they'll be fine. I know of no woman whose dream of fulfillment is to accept a job in northern Minnesota 50 miles from the nearest town with only a factory for company. That's probably not a comment on women but a comment on social mores. The point is, a man can take his support system with him. But a woman can hardly move her husband up there unless he's a writer, and even then he might find it less than totally appealing.''

Senior executive "B," capital goods industry:

"I don't think technical companies have a harder time attracting women. If they're offered a fair job, a fair salary, and a chance for advancement, the type of company doesn't make any difference at all. And being in a company with few females is a mark of distinction. You know you are going to be observed.''

Senior executive "C," capital goods industry:

"Last year, I had a number of requests from managers saying that prospective women employees would like to meet me and talk with me. I suspect these women didn't see a great many other females and were curious as to whether there was something extraordinary about me. They wanted to learn from looking at me whether success in our organization would be possible or impossible for them.''

## ON ASSIMILATING WOMEN INTO MANAGEMENT

Management consultant "B":

"We have to invent a style of interacting. Many companies are all-male cultures, and the people who exist there are unaware of how all-male the organizations are. They view their organizations as neuter. So when women enter these environments, there's a great learning experience on both sides, and it has to be approached with a great deal of generosity by both men and women. A lot of women feel that all-male environments are hostile to them because they don't just open their arms and accept these new female executives into their fold. I think that's ungenerous. I think it's important, in introducing women into management, to do so at various levels. Ideally, the more senior ones will have had experience adapting to other organizations.''

Senior executive "A," consumer industry:

"There must be a bunch of us, age about 40 now, who had a unique one-time experience that will never happen again, I hope. If it comes to be that in any bunch of management trainees, anywhere from a third to 50 percent of the intake are female, you won't be able to talk any more about how management should deal with 'females.' Women won't be special anymore. Obviously, I would like to see women not be special. And people would no more talk about how to develop women for senior management than they would talk about how to develop blue-eyed people. It just would not be a meaningful cut. That evolution is on its way. It's happening—it's happening now. The lower ranks of management that I have exposure to are well represented with women."

Senior executive "A," capital goods industry:

"If senior management has made the decision to bring women in at the middle and upper echelons, then obviously nothing more is needed than to get on with it and treat the new women managers like any other managers. That is, if they have *really* made the decision. If they have not made the decision and are just running an experiment and in their hearts want it to fail, it won't work; and I don't know what else you can say about it."

Senior executive "A," consumer industry:

"Don't bring in just one woman. She'll have all the burdens of womanhood on her. We certainly don't look at the guy who runs the financial department and say, 'You represent manhood!' He doesn't represent manhood; he represents himself, if he's lucky. But if there's just one woman, she's going to be asked, 'As a woman, what do you think of this new tool die?' "

Management consultant "C":

"There has to be a commitment at the top level to doing it right, as opposed to just doing it—a commitment to recruiting the right women and then doing the things that are necessary to be supportive. I'm a little leery of linking the compensation of managers to their efforts to recruit women. That's resulted in an awful lot of tokenism. Tokenism doesn't work. The commitment has to be to developing the women. And when you ask how to develop women, it's difficult for me to explain. I've never been in an environment where it was done."

Management consultant "E":

"If the man at the top doesn't have any particular commitment to bringing women in, then the idea isn't going to get anywhere. The commitment must be expressed not as his idiosyncrasy, but in terms of external pressures and of corporate need. And the very best thing he can do is be a model—place a woman on his own staff. And he should make it clear that he expects to spend money recruiting women and training them. And he'll monitor what happens. Otherwise, you'll have a lot of goals, and nothing will happen.

"Where women come from depends on the culture of the organization. If it's one that has traditionally upgraded people, then it's essential not to suddenly block off top channels by bringing women in from outside. That would create an enormous amount of resentment. You can only do what the organization is comfortable with. The key is not to take any steps that create backlash."

Senior executive "B," consumer industry:

"What causes male backlash is superficial appointments, where a man sees a woman getting promoted, and he has just as good or better an appraisal."

Senior executive "B," capital goods industry:

"I think there is, among young women managers, the idea that women are going to get special treatment, and they can get along just being women. If there is no sort of policy stated, then that's the way it looks."

Management consultant "A":

"Women may need special treatment at a lower level to bring them along. But once they are at the managerial level, they shouldn't be treated any differently than males; I don't think they need to be."

Management consultant "B":

"To succeed, women have to be wonder women. They have to have extraordinary energy, incredible patience, fortitude. They have to be able to withstand isolation, have to outperform, to be constantly in a position of creating credibility for themselves. They are inventing life! There are no models for anybody; it's not just women who lack models; men have no models for their behavior, either. And people don't—

can't—transform their behavior overnight. I just don't buy the 'male chauvinist pig wants to keep us out' attitude. It takes very strong people to break new ground and find new ways of doing things."

Management consultant "E":

"The way to get results is to put it in the pay packet. The performance evaluation of male managers should include the hiring, developing, and promoting of women. If they don't do it, they suffer monetarily. That's the only way to make it meaningful to management."

## ON DEVELOPING WOMEN

Senior executive "A," consumer industry:

"I have a mentor. I have had more than one, and I certainly don't think I could have risen without strong support from the people to whom I was reporting. They took an interest in my career development and sold me to other people in the organization. You need that. I don't think there was any kind of a sexual connotation to it. I don't know exactly what I did that avoided that. Whether it was my mentors' credibility or my own, I don't know. Certainly, my mentoring was never an out-of-the-office situation."

Senior executive "C," capital goods industry:

"Give women a lot of feedback. People think of appraisal as being 'end of the year' or 'end of six months' or something like that. I do think people, especially when they are new to a culture, need both favorable and unfavorable feedback as they go along. Of course, managers—male or female—don't like to do that. In fact, with engineers, as long as you don't hear anything, you can assume everything's fine."

Management consultant "E":

"I think there's not nearly enough attention paid to sending women to major executive development programs. Senior executives look at women and think, 'Maybe she'll get married or maybe she'll have a baby.' They forget that she's been with the company for a number of years, probably longer than most of the men. What's more, if they were to offer her something like that, it would create such a bond of loyalty, she'd probably never leave."

Middle manager, financial services:

"The thing to avoid most of all is being overprotective of women. We hear so often, 'I don't want to put so-and-so in a position where she might fail.' But you must allow women to take risks; you must allow them the opportunity to fail. Otherwise, they won't learn as much as they should, and you won't get the best use out of them. I'd say forget they're women and do whatever you would do for men. You don't need to give women any special treatment. Treat them as adults, not as children."

Senior executive "A," capital goods industry:

"I don't really feel that there are too many problems that are just women problems; I think there are lots of management problems, and I think sometimes these are emphasized when a manager has women working for him for the first time. It's because he doesn't know how to manage, not because he doesn't know how to manage women."

Senior executive "A," consumer industry:

"As a younger person coming up, I would have resented any attempt by management to make allowances, because then I would have felt that I hadn't made it based on the same standards. I would have been bitterly resentful at any implication that I somehow made it because I was female. I obviously would have been resentful if I had felt that I made it despite being female; I really wanted femaleness to go away. I tended to judge my career, my growth, and my track record based entirely on how I was doing with respect to my colleagues whom I paced myself against, and personally never made allowances for being female. I think that's fairly commonly felt."

## ON RETAINING WOMEN

Management consultant "D":

"Promote women as rapidly as they deserve, and pay them market value. Then if someone is willing to pay a premium, you probably can't do anything about it. But if you've got a critical mass, so that women start being really comfortable about being valued for their abilities and not being tokens, if they have real jobs and you pay them the same as their peers, you won't get any more women leaving than you get men leaving.

"Here in our organization, all of the women have had offers for lots of money and haven't left because we have a real job to do, much more real than the outside jobs being offered. Once you have had the experience of working for a company where being a woman is almost a nonissue, you are much less likely to take the risk of being the first women somewhere else. Having been a first women once, I wouldn't do it again, ever; even if I were paid a half million dollars. . . ."

Management consultant "C":

"I have a friend who's the only woman at a professional level in her entire corporation, which is in heavy industry. She is isolated and lonely and miserable. She wants that industry, and she wants that function, but I asked her once why she was doing it; she doesn't need to be there. She said, 'I have made a commitment to the company, and it's a challenge. I've gone this far as the only woman, and I'm not going to give up now.' But how many women will do that?"

## ON DISTINCTIONS BETWEEN MALE AND FEMALE EXECUTIVES

Senior executive "A," capital goods industry:

"Women make a bell-shaped curve, just like men. Maybe the one for women is skewed in one direction or another because of our society's pressures. If you ask, 'Do women do this?' the answer is yes, and the answer is no, because of different women. For some reason men are looked upon as individuals, and women are still looked upon as women. But I think that's going to change very rapidly."

Middle manager, consumer industry:

"The people who work for me consider the department a fun place to work because I don't have that macho need as much as some of the men. I have my secretaries come to staff meetings, for example. I see absolutely no reason why they shouldn't be involved. Think of Milton's daughters who copied Latin every day and didn't know what they were copying! My peers come in and tell me I'm causing them problems— now their secretaries want to be part of staff meetings. I get all sorts of flack. I'm sure if I were 20 years younger or a bit less confident, I would fold up and cry a lot."

Middle manager, financial:

"I'm a firm believer that if you're a woman or a minority, you have to be twice as good. Organizations try to find blacks and women who are comparable to their best, rather than their average or acceptable. I tell people all the time that you only have to take four steps in this company to find a white male who's an absolute turkey! But you never see the female counterpart of that person."

Middle manager, consumer industry:

"A lot of women don't want to report to women, as you well know. Women have been taught to be so competitive for men's attention and favors that we don't work as well together as we should. When I talk to ambitious women about joining my staff, they say, 'Don't take this personally because I like you, but I just wonder if you have as much clout in this company as the men. . . .' "

Middle manager, financial:

"Women bring new thinking into an organization. Young men who come in learn very quickly the way it's always been done, and they have a great deal of difficulty thinking beyond that. But women are generally more positive in their management style than men. If somebody says, 'Hey, let's . . . !' women immediately begin thinking about how to accomplish what's needed rather than saying, 'Oh, we tried that once, and it didn't work.' I really think women could be an asset in furthering innovation within any kind of business if only they were listened to a little more seriously."

Senior executive "C," capital goods industry:

"I find myself asking a lot more questions than most of the men around here seem to do. I don't know whether that's a personal difference or whether that's characteristic of women. I know I don't find it as necessary to tell people what to do. I don't need that quite as much. All the recent management theories—Theory X and Theory Y, the Blake-Muton grids—emphasize more participation from employees, less autocracy, more listening, less telling. I think these are all characteristics that are more representative of women than of men. It's the way we've been brought up. So I think we have a plus. It's very interesting that women are beginning to go into management just when these traits are favored."

Middle manager, financial:

"A woman has to think on two planes all the time. She's trying to do her job, and she's also asking herself, 'How am I coming across to this person I'm dealing with?' A woman is always trying to interpret the data sent to her— 'What did he mean by that?' I don't think a man goes through that. He assumes he'll be accepted; he expects to be given the benefit of the doubt."

Senior executive "C," capital goods industry:

"There have been a lot of articles written about the personal attributes of women and what that would contribute to jobs, and I don't really see that. Individual differences really surmount all of the 'male' and 'female' attributes when it comes down to a given person and a given job."

## ON THE ROLE OF WOMEN TOMORROW

Management consultant "D":

"I don't see the movement of women into management as a cycle because of what I see in the younger generation. If you look at the population, there are so many now coming through the 'B' schools who are well trained that I think there's not any way to stop it. The women coming in don't have a chip on their shoulder any more. They just go about their jobs in the normal course of events, and it's so natural."

Middle manager, conglomerate:

"The younger women coming into business are more career oriented than we were. They start off thinking that they're going to be working for the next 30 years. That will impact how they behave and how far they can go. Even 10 or 15 years ago, we just did not do that; we thought about jobs as isolated blocks of activity, without building step 1, step 2, step 3, as men did."

Management consultant "B":

"It's an irreversible trend. My child emulates what you would think of as reasonable female behavior, but it does not enter her mind that she will not have a career. It is not if she will or she won't; it is what shall I be? Certainly by the time she's an adult (she's nine now), women will be regarded as individuals as men are by both men and women in business organizations. One third of her class have working mothers; that's a very large population of young females who are growing up with the notion that men and women are equal.''

Senior executive ''B,'' capital goods industry:

''I think the movement of women into the work force is an economic necessity. There are those who are capable and ambitious to go into management, and they will. The transition stage will last around 25 years. It's a generation thing. In science when there's a new theory, the people of the current generation aren't going to be able to use it because they'd have to change their way of thinking. A great many things will have happened in another generation, insofar as acceptance of women is concerned.''

Senior executive ''A,'' capital goods industry:

''Women are going to enter the work force; they're going to enter it at all levels because there is an inexorable requirement. Nobody is doing this because it's right; if we were doing it for that reason, it would take another 2000 years. You simply cannot take 50 percent of the brains and not use them. There is no way for society to do this. So it isn't because you and I think it's a good thing. It isn't because the government passes a law. No, women are in the work force to stay at every level, not just the bottom, because brains are in limited supply. That's the reason. There's nothing else.''

Management consultant ''E'':

''I'm not fighting for all women to be managers; I am fighting for all women to have that choice. I would like our society to be one where women could choose from a range of roles. If one wanted to put all her effort into becoming president of General Motors, then she would be entitled to do so. Or another would be respected if she said, 'That's not for me. I want to have a good life raising my kids.' And I would like the same freedom for men, too. Men could spend more time at home and be more involved with their children. There are many men who feel deprived and shut out of that side of their lives.''

## ON THE CONSEQUENCES OF SEXUALLY INTEGRATED MANAGEMENT

Management consultant ''B'':

''To me, the more an organization reflects real life, the more successful it is likely to be as an institution of people and as an enterprise. It's more pleasant, more fun. One's work life is more complete if you can share it with men and women. I do think men and women are different, and I think the relationship between men and women is different than the relationship between men or the relationship between women. I think the presence of both sexes in management is enriching."

Senior executive "A," consumer industry:

"I don't think it's management's business to worry about what a woman's family life is going to be like. That's her problem. It's the manager's privilege if he wants to ponder the bigger issues of society, but his real concern should be this: Half the population is female, and the genetic pool for talent is equally distributed across both sexes. You double your chances of having better business by opening up your management cadre to females as well as males. We have been excluding half the population and therefore half the talent pool. Business is very difficult, and you have to surround yourself with the best people you can get, for the good of the company."

Middle manager, consumer industry:

"I think women have been denied in the way they have been raised and the options that were offered to them; I think men have, too. I hope my grandchildren will be working in a much more androgynous situation. We're all too self-conscious about it at this point. But I think the work environment will change, and it will get better—better for both sexes."

Middle manager, conglomerate:

"I think the economy probably cannot absorb everybody who wants to work. What's going to happen is that different kinds of people are going to end up not working. I personally see absolutely nothing wrong with men staying home and cooking and cleaning and whatever. If the best person for a particular job happened to be a woman, and that freed up a man to go write a book or do something else, that could only benefit society. There are those who think that that much flexibility is really not good because most people can't deal with it. But I think we're headed along that path. And if I had the ability to either stop it or to encourage it, I would encourage it."

# 12

# The Effects of Equal Opportunity

"When you look at the highest paid females in the country today, most are relatives of business owners," emphasized a vice president of a technical company. "It's discouraging to see how little progress American industry has made in advancing women."

In the past decade, however, women have gained positions of prominence on their own merits, and the number of trained and motivated females continues to grow. What will be the effects on organizations of the continuing movement of women into the middle and upper echelons of management? Among the positive results is availability of a bigger talent pool; selections can be made from both male and female candidates. The resulting higher level of performance should enhance profitability. This advantage is considered the most important benefit to organizations, in the view of women officers at major companies.[1]

"I feel having a larger percentage of the population available for positions is a tremendous advantage," declared an East coast executive. "We're no longer saying that it's just white male Protestants who are available for senior management positions—it's everybody."

A West Coast officer pointed out that "it's incumbent upon management to staff all jobs with the best qualified people. Sex is an irrelevant issue. Women who are trained and have the capabilities ought to be given the opportunity."

Substantiating this view, a personnel executive in banking remarked, "Outstanding intellects are not limited to any one group. The introduction of women expands the percent of the management population that is superior."

A transportation company official emphasized, "We've looked at performance appraisals; we've looked at assessment center results, and essentially there is no difference between men and women. That is so simple you would think it could have been spotted long ago."

"If you're selecting the right people, sex does not have a bearing on performance," concluded a personnel executive in the Midwest.

Said an oil company official, "We have not noticed any significant difference between the performance of men and women. We get the same range in both sexes. Some are excellent; others are average, and still others are below average. Women have as much to offer as any category of individuals, minorities, or white males. I think we've been underutilizing a valuable resource for a long time. There are an awful lot of bright women around, and we as a society have not in the past fully used their talents. I think women have every right to be in the work force; they have every right to be at all levels of the work force, and they have every possibility of contributing at all levels of the work force. There is no reason not to use them if they desire to participate."

However, an East Coast executive noted that in his organization "the prevailing thinking holds that if we let women in, they won't be as good, they won't be as motivated, they won't work as hard, and they'll quit to have babies."

An official in the Midwest reported, "We're expecting a high level of backlash from our younger white males. It will come from the older ones as the women move up. Male employees complain to their bosses, 'How come I can't get promoted? I'm not a woman or a black so it looks as if I might as well forget about a career here.' "

And a senior executive in financial services pointed out, "Critics would imply that all we're doing is catering to the whims of women and minorities while building a staff of incompetent people at higher levels. That's talk that can be damaging, but it is irresponsible and inaccurate."

Certainly, American business has done well with limited participation by women in responsible positions. And there are those today who say, "Why bother? Who needs women?"

## EVIDENCE OF MERIT

In addition to the better level of talent from a larger pool, selection of the most suitable candidate for a position—without exclusion by sex or other extraneous factors—will demonstrate that merit is the determinant of recognition and reward within an organization. Knowing they will be judged by contribution rather than seniority or friendship, both men and women in management will be motivated to greater accomplishment. A meritocratic environment should stimulate retention of the better performing individuals while encouraging those not as able to seek less objective surroundings.

"One of the most positive results of the pressures for equal opportunity and affirmative action has been a trend within organizations toward more effective human resource systems and practices," emphasized Dr. Douglas W. Bray, director of management selection and development research at American Telephone and Telegraph Company. "Organizations would always have been much better managed had management ability been accurately evaluated and systematic attention given to the advancement of that talent to its proper level in the organization."[2]

Without question, equal employment opportunity (EEO) has accorded the personnel function a higher priority. Changes in personnel policies and practices resulting from legislation serve to make recruiting, hiring, placement, development and promotion less subjective, to the advantage of both employees and organizations. The impact of individual managers' nonjob related preferences is minimized, while reserving for the superior the final selection decision.

"There's nothing really wrong with the EEOC regulations if they are applied with common sense," emphasized a consultant. "The rules really say to managers, 'Hey, don't be stupid and put some requirements on jobs that have nothing to do with performance.' And that's simply good management."

What's more, "All of the programs installed under affirmative action are deterrents to union infiltration," noted a financial services executive.

"If you have the opportunity to introduce processes that employees like, that are motivational without penalty, why shouldn't you do it?" asked a personnel executive at a major company in the East. "It's wrong from a business standpoint not to, aside from questions of law and ethics. I cannot prove to you how it hurt us, but I am certain it was injurious to our corporate performance to have a substantial number of managers feel they were discriminated against."

The Conference Board reported that four-fifths of 265 companies surveyed "volunteered that they have gained some important benefits from their efforts to improve the job opportunities they provide to women." Most frequently mentioned were "more appropriate human resource utilization and changed employee attitudes," followed by "improved personnel policies and practices, changed management perceptions, and improved community relations."[3]

A bank officer told me, "Roughly four years ago we held a miniconference of about a dozen of our most senior women. We solicited their thoughts on what the bank should be doing differently to improve use of the female resource. Most of their suggestions have been put into place. And the concepts weren't simply benefits for women, but for everyone: career management, job posting, better evaluation of performance, and identification of role models."

On occasion, executives contend that the demands of affirmative action prevent selection of the "best qualified" to the detriment of the organization. (The head of one of America's largest companies argued this recently, although earnings were at an all-time high.) But a personnel executive in the East pointed out, "The claim that in the past the 'best qualified' people were promoted is largely a myth." He emphasized that the title was automatically applied to those who had been selected for promotion.

Organizations moving more rapidly to take advantage of the still largely untapped female resource will not only gain greater public recognition but possess an edge in attracting the very best female talent. While the competitive advantage should be significant domestically, it could prove even more important internationally. Other nations lag the United States in placing women in leadership positions.

A multinational executive opined, "Using able women should improve the productivity of the United States. The average brain power will be higher; the average motivation level will be higher; the overall talent level will be higher. We'll be better off—significantly better off."

However, the movement of women into the middle and upper echelons of management must be accomplished in the proper manner, with regard to the culture and condition of the organization. "Otherwise you're going to create resentment and even end up with a less effective organization," an oil company executive declared.

## RESISTANCE APPEARS CERTAIN

Even under the most thoughtfully conceived and executed program, there will be resistance from certain male and female employees. The men most likely to oppose the upward mobility of women are average performers who feel threatened by added competition. Their female counterparts are those unwilling or unable to vie for more demanding jobs themselves who feel that it is equally inappropriate for other women to do so.

"We assign number values to performance categories," explained a chief personnel officer, "with category #1 being high. Our category 1 and 2 males can count on being promoted. It's the category 3 males who feel the impact. If we are considering an average white male along with a woman and/or a minority, the edge will go to one of the latter two if all other things are equal. Category 3 is the group where we're probably going to see the greatest problem in years to come. I don't think we'll ever get to the point where we're depriving our category 1 or 2 performers of opportunities.''

A Midwest EEO executive said, ''I think the attitude of managers depends on the individual's ability to compete. Most people know whether they've been getting by simply because there was no one better around to threaten them. Males who feel they're not as qualified as others are voicing the loudest complaints. The abler ones know they're going to make it no matter what the competition is. So they're less likely to complain.''

Said a key official in retailing, ''We say only semifacetiously that a guy who used to go home and explain that he failed to get the promotion because his boss didn't like him now has a much better excuse: affirmative action! In truth, women and minorities are still a long way from taking over—a long way. Although the makeup of our management group has changed, the numbers aren't dramatically different. But I see a lot of guys whose sons won't be making the money the older generation did if they're the same talent level. The women and minorities are simply better than they are.''

A personnel executive on the East Coast reported, ''I've had conversations with men in our organization, and the ones who are honest will tell you they are really scared. Not only is there more competition today, but the quality of the competition is higher. There is a better educated, more qualified group of people in the labor force now than some of these guys have ever had to deal with. The younger men are fearful of women their own age and justifiably so. They know it's a different game, and they don't know all the rules yet, so they're less comfortable than men have ever been. I think this is a problem which is still growing; the competition will continue to get more keen.''

The Conference Board found that companies cited far fewer disadvantages than advantages relative to their efforts to improve job opportunities for women. Among drawbacks mentioned were a negative reaction from some male employees, increased recruiting and training costs, and higher turnover on some nontraditional jobs.[4]

Certainly, short-term disruptions of organizations will occur. Men and women at every level are destined to experience feelings of unease as traditionally sex-segregated hierarchies are displaced. Yet, sooner or later, many may not only accept but welcome the change. "I prefer a more sexually mixed work setting to the traditional male-dominated one. Many other men and women do also," declared a male personnel executive. "Pluralism is more enjoyable, and it's a benefit without cost."

And a vice president-personnel noted, "Men try to be sharper when there are women around. I think the mixed-sex work place brings out the best in both sexes."

But an EEO head on the East Coast remarked, "I have no trouble with the premise that merit alone should be our selection criterion. But my problem is in explaining to managers why this is true. The manager may say, 'Why should I hire a woman? Then I have to take awareness training, and she has to take awareness training, and we have problems with the law, and all this takes time from my job. Why don't I just go ahead and hire a guy with equal ability since I know what to expect from him, and we'll get a better return?' I say it's to our advantage to bring in people with varied backgrounds, but I don't know whether that's true or not. You know the Harvard law firms—they don't want anybody from Stanford because it takes too long to assimilate them."

The Conference Board, however, found that some companies "have been especially surprised by the remarkably competent performance of women on some nontraditional jobs and also by the rapid acceleration in the number of women expressing interest in career opportunities—and willing to put the time and effort into enhancing their qualifications to advance—once there were a few successful role models."[5]

## IMPACT OF GOVERNMENT

Said a retailing executive, "With affirmative action, we're overcoming stereotyping. People become involved with individuals and gradually learn that their generalizations aren't right. The first woman in a department creates trauma for both the woman and her male peers. With the second woman, it's much easier. Later the problem disappears."

Some executives believe that the regulatory thrust could prove inimical to equal opportunity, however. "The manner in which the government has made its demands and organized its programs has seemingly decreased rather than increased management support for female equal opportunity," reported two business consultants in the *Harvard Business Review*. "High level executives, even those with EEO responsibilities, feel the government's demands are at times both unreasonable and oblivious to practical business considerations."[6]

And a *Fortune* writer noted that "the effort to promote equal opportunity in the labor market has made the business of hiring and firing crushingly time consuming, complex, and frustrating."[7]

"Think of the time a typical personnel officer has to spend in the EEO area," complained an East Coast executive. "There are affirmative action plans to prepare and compliance reviews which require mountains of data which we are convinced nobody is ever going to examine."

Recently, Sears Roebuck filed a class action suit against ten federal agencies, charging that veterans' programs and raising of the mandatory retirement age jeopardize efforts to recruit and promote women and minorities. The suit, which has been dismissed, alleged that federal agencies themselves have violated antidiscrimination laws.[8] The latter point was substantiated by a Justice Department task force, which reported after reviewing personnel policies and employment statistics of federal agencies that it "generally found the familiar pattern of men in top-level, policy-making positions and women in low-level jobs." In addition, the task force said that government agencies are lax in enforcing sex-discrimination laws affecting the public.[9]

Now, after a six-year investigation, the Equal Employment Opportunity Commission has filed a series of suits against Sears, charging discriminatory employment practices.

A manufacturing company's EEO head declared, "When companies get to the point of feeling that an onerous burden has been placed on them by federal bureaucrats, they've got the power to roll back progress. We've seen it in the recession experienced in environmental matters."

But a vice president-personnel declared, "Government pressure has not hurt; pressure establishes priority."

Organizations are destined to experience disruptions due to two-career family-company conflicts. "Rigid policies are giving way to case-by-case exceptions, which are bound to give way in time to major shifts in policies as more couples enter the work force," noted two specialists in dual careers.[10] They pointed out that two-career couples may refuse to relocate, are less eager for promotions, and are less willing or able to travel.

"The biggest negative of women in management has been the inability to move them as easily as men. But that's not as important as it has been, because now men have wives who refuse to move," remarked a Midwest vice president-personnel.

Organizations increasingly will be compelled to adjust to the younger generation's demands for a more balanced life style. Both men and women will be more self-centered; pursuit of individual pleasure and interests is rising. Fewer than one-quarter of a nationwide sample queried annually by Yankelovich, Skelly and White now looks to work as a source of fulfillment, compared with nearly half in 1970.[11] Changes in management are more likely to be generational, rather than sex linked.

"We've done assessments of everybody in the company," explained a personnel officer at a billion dollar corporation. "Among the top 200 people in management we found a lack of empathy, an inability to deal with people on a human level. A lot of women bring strong interpersonal skills to jobs. What we're examining is how to take advantage of that since we now have quite a large population of women at a fairly senior level."

But a consultant opined, "If women are more human, does that mean men are more inhuman? No, it's an individual characteristic. But sensitivity is important and something you should be looking for in selecting management."

"We looked at our women and minority store managers," explained a retailing executive. "We discovered these people are really no different from their white male counterparts, either in their personal attitudes or in the way they're perceived by employees."

"Women are going to be like men in management," declared another consultant. "Management is management; it's really not going to change. Woman play different roles in different locations just as men do. The mother at home and the mother in management are two different people."

There may be some differences between men managers as a group and women managers as a group for some time due to societal conditioning. But the distinctions are not likely to be long lasting.

## INFLUENCE ON ECONOMY

Some individuals contend that the economy cannot support all those who wish to work and bemoan the continuing entrance of women into the labor force. Yet, both our society and our economy would gain from the widest possible merit-based competition for however many employment opportunities there may be. Further, working women with their $250 billion or more in annual earnings are proving to be "one of the more lucrative, if often difficult, marketing challenges to come along in decades."[12] The impact is substantial, from big ticket items which become affordable to the two-paycheck family, to personal-service businesses which help the employed woman with her home chores.

"If we had a major recession, a shortage of opportunities and large unemployment, you'd see an awful lot of resistance to working women on the part of male breadwinners," pointed out a chief personnel officer at a technical company. "There are still a lot of men who believe women are working until they get married or afterward only for a supplemental income. You find a lot less resentment in a period of labor shortage.''

An East Coast personnel executive suggested, ''It would be helpful if our society were more accepting of a man staying home and taking care of the family. I know couples where it would work out much better that way.''

''I think the greatest problem is the pressure of young people on older ones,'' declared a retailing executive. ''In this inflationary era, older people want to keep on working. The pipeline will be plugged for both men and women on the way up. Alongside this one, the male-female contest is nothing.''

''Those born during the fifties baby boom are entering the job market now,'' pointed out a consultant. ''A substantial proportion of college graduates are going to have to take jobs that require no college training at all. Large numbers of people who are management potential are not going to find opportunities there. The women and the blacks who have not been contenders before are going to increase that problem. Add to that the higher retirement age which came about not for social reasons but economic ones (we couldn't fund Social Security), and what's going to happen? The competent, highly paid executives will be going out on schedule. But the less capable middle managers are going to stay rather than suffer from inflation.''

As Peter Drucker pointed out recently, ''The class of 1979 isn't the last class of the 'baby boom' years to reach adulthood. Five more such classes are still ahead of us. But the class of '79 may be the first one to find that the bases ahead of them are loaded.''[13]

Despite a majority of employers freezing benefits at 65, employees apparently prefer to continue working rather than suffer a loss of income. Sears Roebuck, for example, forecast that one-third of its employees would choose to work beyond the previous mandatory retirement age. The company estimated that the age 70 amendment would reduce job openings by more than 5,000 over a six-year period and would eliminate about four times as many promotions and job changes. That prediction has been exceeded, with more than three of four salaried employees remaining beyond the former retirement date.[14]

''Even though the Labor Department told Congress that only 200,000 people a year would exercise their legal option to maintain their job past 65, it is now conceding that estimate was too low,'' reported a Washington-based journalist. ''By 1990, said Malcolm Morrison, a Labor Department expert, the nation may see a large increase in the number of over-65 people holding down jobs, although he isn't prepared now to predict how many.''[15]

It was John Stuart Mill who declared more than a century ago, "In all things of any difficulty and importance, those who can do them well are fewer than the need, even with the most unrestricted latitude of choice; and any limitation of the field of selection deprives society of some chance of being served by the competent, without ever saving it from the incompetent."[16] Executive recruiters and their client organizations can attest to the chronic paucity of talent for the middle and upper echelons of management.

"There's a critical shortage of good management, and we're not looking to fill that void based on sex," declared a personnel executive in the Midwest. "We're going to take the best performers wherever they might come from."

The EEO head of a New York corporation declared, "You may be looking at a generation rather than a decade before women are assimilated into the work force on the basis of merit and without particular notice."

Said an EEO head in the Midwest, "It may take 100 years before we're out of the transition period. Remember, affirmative action is still a very new concept, no more than a decade old."

And The Conference Board reported, "Knowledgeable observers point out that it is likely to be several decades before women (and minorities, too) come anywhere near parity of representation in many skilled craft jobs and in jobs at the very top echelons of business, especially in highly technical industries. Some doubt that it will ever happen for women. Yet a change process leading in that direction is now clearly under way, and it has already had an important effect in at least some very large U.S. corporations."[17]

A vice president-personnel on the West Coast declared, "Women won't be going back to full-time homemaking, not in our society. Today's young woman manager is going to bring her kids up with a wholly different set of attitudes. The business of raising girls to get married and have a family—period—is part of the past. The higher aspirations of women are not going to go away, just as the government is not going to go away."

If present trends hold, the proportion of working-age women who are either employed or looking for jobs will rise to 57 percent in the next ten years. And studies have shown that women who choose nontraditional careers were raised in families where the mother worked full-time.[18]

In a speech delivered at the National YWCA Tribute to Women in International Industry, James D. Robinson III, chairman of American Express Company, declared, "Women are a vital ingredient in our corporate mix. While we recognize that the advancement of women in business is rooted in fairness and equity, the truth is, it is equally rooted in self-interest. Ultimately, in today's competitive market, success—survival perhaps—demands that the corporation develop *all* its human resources. . . . Now corporations cannot single-handedly wipe out decades of discrimination. But they can radically alter the way in which women are recruited, trained, motivated, evaluated, and promoted. Needless to say, it is my firm conviction that business should be proactive rather than reactive. It should vigorously commit itself to the advancement of women in the corporate world. . . . Personally, I look forward to the day when we do not think of good jobs for women, but good careers for people. When affirmative action goals are no longer necessary, and EEO withers away.''

## REFERENCES

1. Heidrick and Struggles, Inc., *Profile of a Woman Officer*, Chicago, 1979, p. 6.
2. Bray, Douglas W., "Identifying Managerial Talent in Women," *Atlanta Economic Review* 26(2):43 (March–April 1976).
3. Schaeffer, Ruth G. and Edith F. Lynton, *Corporate Experiences in Improving Women's Job Opportunities*, New York: The Conference Board, 1979, pp. 27–8.
4. Ibid., p. 29.
5. Ibid., p. 27.
6. Fretz, C. F. and Joanne Hayman, "Progress for Women—Men Are Still More Equal," *Harvard Business Review* 51(5):135 (September–October 1973).
7. Smith, Lee, "Equal Opportunity Rules Are Getting Tougher," *Fortune*, 19 June 1978. p. 152.
8. "Sears Roebuck Charges U.S. Actions Hurt Firms' Efforts to Hire Women, Minorities," *Wall Street Journal*, 25 January 1979.
9. "Sex Discrimination By U.S. Agencies Is Claimed in Report," *Wall Street Journal*, 4 October 1978.
10. Hall, Francine S. and Douglas T. Hall, "Dual Careers—How Do Couples and Companies Cope with the Problems?" *Organizational Dynamics* 6(4):72 (Spring 1978).
11. Ricklefs, Roger, "Monitoring America," *Wall Street Journal*, 2 October 1978.
12. Yaeger, Deborah S., "Many Companies Find Employed Women Are a High-Profit Market," *Wall Street Journal*, 31 October 1978.
13. Drucker, Peter F., "Baby Boom Problems," *Wall Street Journal*, 5 February 1979.
14. "Sears Roebuck Charges U.S. Actions Hurt Firms' Efforts to Hire Women, Minorities," *Wall Street Journal*, 25 January 1979.
15. Neikirk, Bill, "Retirement at 70 Gives Birth to a Revolution," *Chicago Tribune*, 30 September 1979.
16. Mill, John Stuart, *The Subjection of Women*, Cambridge, MA: MIT Press, 1970, p. 20.
17. Shaeffer, Ruth G. and Edith F. Lynton, *Corporate Experiences in Improving Women's Job Opportunities*, New York: The Conference Board, 1979, p. 15.
18. Terborg, James R., "Women in Management: A Research Review," *Journal of Applied Psychology* 62(6):647 (1977).

# Appendix I

## FEDERAL LEGISLATION DEALING WITH SEX DISCRIMINATION IN EMPLOYMENT*

*The Equal Pay Act of 1963* with amendments prohibits discrimination on the basis of sex in the payment of wages for substantially equal work requiring equal skill, effort and responsibility and performed under similar working conditions.

*Title VII of the Civil Rights Act of 1964* with amendments prohibits discrimination by employers of 15 or more persons on the basis of sex, as well as color, race, religion, or national origin.

*Executive Order 11246* with amendments prohibits discrimination by federal contractors and subcontractors with contracts exceeding $10,000 and requires companies bidding on federal contracts to establish affirmative action programs.

---

* In addition, 40 states prohibit sex discrimination in employment, and 37 states ban sex discrimination in pay.

# Appendix II

## PROFESSIONAL ORGANIZATIONS OFFERING ASSISTANCE TO EMPLOYERS

The following organizations offer a variety of services without charge or on a fee basis to employers seeking women for middle and upper echelon positions and/or corporate directorships. However, inclusion of organizations does not automatically constitute endorsement of them.

### ACCOUNTANTS

American Society of Women Accountants
35 East Wacker Drive
Chicago, IL 60601
312/341-9078

Contact:  Eileen Mueller, executive director
Membership:  6000 women nationwide, organized in more than 100 chapters
Services available:  Prospective employers are invited to furnish brief job descriptions for the Talent Bank. They may also advertise in *The Woman CPA*, a quarterly.

American Woman's Society of Certified Public Accountants
Box 389
Marysville, OH 43040
513/644-5416

Contact:  Barbara I. Rausch, CPA, administrative director
Membership:  Approximately 3600 women CPAs
Service available:  Prospective employers may run classified ads in the bimonthly newsletter.

### CHEMISTS AND CHEMICAL ENGINEERS

American Chemical Society
1155 16 Street, NW
Washington, DC 20036
202/872-4528

Contact:  Audra B. Rafter, manager Employment Aids Office

Membership:    116,000 of whom 10 percent are women
Service available:    Prospective employers are invited to register positions with
the Employment Clearing House.

## COMMUNICATIONS SPECIALISTS

Advertising Women of New York
153 East 57 Street
New York, NY 10022
212/593-1950

Contact:    Headquarters
Membership:    More than 500 women in advertising, marketing, merchandising,
research, promotion, public relations, the media.
Services Available:    Headquarters will contact individual members who might
be suitable for a specific job opening. Also, advertising space in the organization's publication is available.

Women in Communications
PO Box 9561
Austin, TX 78766
512/345-8922

Contact:    Mary Utting, executive director
Membership:    9000 of whom 20 percent are students enrolled in college communications courses.
Services available:    Prospective employers may list job openings free in semi-
monthly job bulletin or they may advertise in the monthly newsletter or the
quarterly *Matrix*. A directory of members may be purchased.

## DIRECTOR CANDIDATES

Catalyst
16 East 60 Street
New York, NY 10022
212/759-9700

Contact:    Betsy Jaffe, director, Programs for Employers
Membership:    Catalyst is not a membership organization. It is a national,
nonprofit organization that helps women choose, launch, and advance their
careers through a national network of 190 career counseling centers, 60 career
publications, a library, and information center.
Services available:    Catalyst's Corporate Board Resource assists corporations
in locating outstanding women to serve as directors.

## ECONOMISTS

Committee on the Status of Women in Economic Professions

Contact:    A. F. Friedlaender
            Department of Economics

Massachusetts Institute of Technology
Cambridge, MA 02139
617/253-1476

Membership: More than 2500 women
Services available: Prospective employers may obtain a roster of women economists listing highest degree, field of specialization, and work experience.

## EDUCATORS

National Association for Women Deans, Administrators, and Counselors
1028 Connecticut Avenue, NW
Washington, DC 20036
202/659-9330

Contact: Anna Rankin Harris, interim executive director
Membership: 2500 women
Services available: Prospective employers may contact Dr. Dorothy M. Carrington, director-Job Matching Service at 207 Hovey Hall, Illinois State University, Normal, IL 61761, regarding the listing of positions.

## MATHEMATICIANS

Association for Women in Mathematics
Wellesley College Women's Research Center
828 Washington Street
Wellesley, MA 02181
617/235-0320 X430

Contact: Margaret Munroe, office manager
Membership: 1100 of whom 80 percent are women
Services available: Prospective employers may advertise in the newsletter, which is published five times a year.

## PERSONNEL SPECIALISTS

American Personnel and Guidance Association
2 Skyline Place, Suite 400
5203 Leesburg Pike
Falls Church, VA 22041

Contact: Dr. Jane Howard-Jasper
Membership: 40,000; approximately 24,000 are women.
Services available: Prospective employers may advertise in the quarterly newsletter, *Guidepost*. Placement services are also available.

## International Association for Personnel Women

PO Box 3057-Grand Central Station
New York, NY 10017
212/734-8160

Contact:    Connie Sternberg, executive director
Membership:    1200
Services available:    Prospective employers may advertise in the quarterly Journal. A membership roster may be purchased.

## PHYSICISTS

Committee on the Status of Women in Physics
American Physical Society
335 East 45 Street
New York, NY 10017
212/682-7341

Contact:    Dr. Judith R. Franz, chairman, Steering Committee
Department of Physics, Indiana University
Bloomington, IN 47401
812/337-4359
Membership:    30,000; approximately 8000 are women.
Services available:    Prospective employers may obtain a directory of women graduate students and postdoctoral fellows in Physics.

## SCIENTISTS AND ENGINEERS

Association for Women in Science
1346 Connecticut Avenue, NW - Room 1122
Washington, DC 20036
202/823-1998

Contact:    Mary Lee Schneiders, registrar
Membership:    3000 women
Services available:    Prospective employers may advertise in the bimonthly newsletter. A National Registry of Women in Science and Engineering is also available.

## STATISTICIANS

Caucus for Women in Statistics
American Statistical Association
806 15 Street, NW
Washington, DC 20005
301/763-7028

Contact:    Dr. Irene C. Montie, president
U.S. Department of Energy, Room BG-014
Forrestal Building, 1000 Independence Avenue, SW
Washington, DC 20585
Membership:    175; 95 percent are women.
Services available:    Prospective employers may advertise in the quarterly newsletter which also lists job applicants.

# Appendix III

## SEMINARS FOR AND ABOUT WOMEN IN MANAGEMENT

(All fees subject to change)

This list of representative seminars is presented as an aid to selection but does not signify endorsement.

### IN-HOUSE SEMINARS

*Management Skills for Women* - $3100 per day - no limit on number of attendees

Conducted by: AMR International
1370 Avenue of the Americas
New York, NY 10019
212/765-6400

*Management Development Series for Women* - $1250 per day - three days - no limit on number of attendees
Conducted by: Batten, Batten, Hudson & Swab, Inc.
820 Keo Way
Des Moines, IA 50309
515/244-3176

*His and Hers Personal Development Seminar* - $1000 per day - no limit on number of attendees
Conducted by: Lee Boyan & Associates
11813 Crawford Road West
Minnetonka, MN 55343
612/938-5904

*Men and Women Working Together* - $110 per person per day - minimum of 24
Conducted by: Effective Resource Group, Inc.
6709 Topaz Drive, SW
Tacoma, WA 98498
206/584-0232

*Management Skill Development for Women Through Assessment Centers* - $200 per person plus expenses - two days - minimum of 10
Conducted by:  Garson & Associates
2127 Powers Ferry Road, Suite D
Marietta, GA 30067
404/952-0246

*Women in Business* - $255 per person - two days
Conducted by:  Interpersonal Growth Systems, Inc.
640 East Grant Street
Minneapolis, MN 55404
612/338-7770

*Especially for Men: Working More Effectively with Women* - $500 a consultant day
*Especially for Women: Effective Women Executives* - $500 a consultant day
Conducted by:  Organization Renewal, Inc.
755 Lincoln Avenue
Winnetka, IL 60093
312/446-8027

*Women and Management* - $1,200 per day - two days - no limit on number of attendees
Conducted by:  Personal Development, Inc.
835 Sterling Avenue, Suite 225
Palatine, IL 60067
312/359-3309

*Today's Woman in Management* - $70 per person - per day
Conducted by:  Supervisory Development Training Associates
Route #3, Box 696
Conover, NC 28613
704/464-3313

*Women in Management* - $250 - one day - maximum of 30 attendees
Conducted by:  Timshell Enterprises Associates
Route #1, Box 176 A
Prairie du Sac, WI 53578
608/544-3242

*Life Planning and Time Management for Today's Woman* - $1350 - one day - no limit on number of attendees
Conducted by:  Time Management Center
3952 30 Street, SW
PO Box 5
Grandville, MI 49418
616/531-1870

## OUTSIDE SEMINARS

Frequently arrangements can be made to have these presented in-house also, if desired.

*Equal Employment Opportunity Seminar*
One day - Atlanta and Chicago - $120/members - $145/nonmembers
Sponsored by: American Compensation Association
PO Box 1176
Scottsdale, AZ 85252
602/994-1112


*Development Seminar for the Woman Manager in a Changing Environment*
Three days - Atlanta, Boston, Chicago, New York, San Francisco - $425/members - $490/nonmembers
*Equal Employment and Affirmative Action: Positive Management Approaches to Compliance—A Basic Orientation*
Two days - Atlanta, Boston, Chicago, Houston, Newport Beach, New York, San Francisco, Washington - $305/members - $350/nonmembers
*Equal Employment and Affirmative Action: Positive Management Approaches to Compliance—An In-Depth Program*
Three days - Atlanta, Boston, Chicago, Houston, Newport Beach, New York, San Francisco, Washington - $425/members - $490/nonmembers
*Management Development For Women Financial Managers*
Three days - Atlanta, Chicago, New York - $450/members - $520/nonmembers
*Women in Management: Building Job and Life Management Skills*
Three days - Chicago and New York - $425/members - $490/nonmembers
Sponsored by: American Management Associations
135 West 50 Street
New York, NY 10020
212/586-8100
*Executive Development for the Woman Manager*
Three days - New York and Washington - $495/$425 for two or more

*Management Skills for Women Managers*
Three days - Ten cities throughout the U. S. - $495/$395 for two or more
Sponsored by: AMR International
1370 Avenue of the Americas
New York, NY 10019
212/765-6400


*How to Conduct a Lawful Employment Interview*
One day -Thirty-eight U. S. cities - $95 for 1, $90 for 2 to 4, $85 for 5 or more

*Management Development Series for Women*
Ten U. S. cities - $325 for three days, $255 for two days, $125 for one day
Sponsored by: Batten, Batten, Hudson & Swab
820 Keo Way
Des Moines, IA 50309
515/244-3176

*Leadership and Managerial Effectiveness for Women Managers*
Three days - Cincinnati - $425
Sponsored by: Professional Development Program
College of Business Administration
University of Cincinnati
Cincinnati, OH 45221
513/475-2043

*Affirmative Action Programs, Design and Implementation*
One day - New York - $125

*Nondiscriminatory Selection*
One day - New York - $125

*The Law of Equal Employment Opportunity*
Two days - New York - $245
Sponsored by: Cornell University
New York State School of Industrial and Labor Relations
3 East 43 Street
New York, NY 10017
212/697-2247

*The Woman Manager in a Rapidly Changing Environment: Developing Executive Skills*
Two days - Chicago - $350/$315 for three or more
Sponsored by: Elmhurst College
190 South Prospect
Elmhurst, IL 60126
312/834-3606 or 279-4100

*Presentation Skills for Women Managers*
Two days - Atlanta, Chicago, New York - $750
Sponsored by: ExecuSpond
Division of Corporate Response, Inc.
675 Third Avenue
New York, NY 10017
212/986-6543

*Advanced Management Training for Women*
Four days - Washington - $360

*Basic Management Training for Women*
Two days - Washington - $160
Sponsored by: Continuing Management Education
Georgetown University
36 and N Streets, NW
Washington, DC 20057
202/625-3001

*Effective Management Skills for Woman Managers*
Three days - Atlanta - $395
Sponsored by: Center for Professional Education
College of Business Administration
Georgia State University
Atlanta, Georgia 30303
404/658-2745

*Time Management*
Two days - Washington, New York, Albany - $245 (each additional person from same firm $195)

*Professional Growth*
Two days - New York, Washington, Philadelphia - $245 (each additional person from same firm $195)

*The Professional Manager*
Two days - Westchester County, Washington, Philadelphia, Hartford, New York - $245 (each additional person from same firm $195)

*Unlocking Creativity*
Two days - Philadelphia, Westchester County, Boston, Albany, New York - $245 (each additional person from same firm $195)
Sponsored by: Hunter College
Center for Lifelong Learning
101 Park Avenue
New York, NY 10017
212/889-5488

*The Professional Woman Manager*
Three days - Atlanta, Chicago, Cleveland, Minneapolis - $395/$350 for three or more
Sponsored by: Learning Dynamics, Inc.
PO Box 323, 161 Highland Avenue
Needham, MA 02194
617/449-4057

*Women in Management*
Three days - San Francisco - $495
Sponsored by: Learning Resources Corporation
7594 Eads Avenue
La Jolla, CA 92037
714/454-3193

*Communication Skills for the Woman in Management*
Three days - Madison, WI - $195

*Women in Middle Management*
Three days - Madison, WI - $210

Sponsored by:  Management Institute of the University of Wisconsin
432 North Lake Street
Madison, WI 57306
608/262-2155

*Affirmative Action and Equal Employment Opportunity Workshop*
One day - Atlanta, Chicago, New Oreleans, San Francisco, Washington - $95
Sponsored by:  National Graduate University
1101 North Highland Street
Arlington, Virginia 22201
703/527-4800

*Interpersonal Skills for Women Supervisors and Managers*
Three days - Boston, Chicago, San Francisco, Washington - $495
Sponsored by:  New York University
School of Continuing Education
Division of Career and Professional Development
326 Skimkin Hall
New York, NY 10003
212/953-7266

*Male-Female Awareness Programs: Concepts and Designs*
Three days - Washington - $375

*Men and Women in Organizations: Personal Exploration*
Five days - Washington - $750

*Professional and Personal Skills for Women Managers*
Five days - Cincinnati and New York - $300
Sponsored by:  NTL Institute
PO Box 9155
Rosslyn Station, VA 22209
703/527-1500

*Women at Work*
One day - Chicago and Cincinnati - $95
Sponsored by:  Fred Pryor Seminars
5909 Martway - Suite 100
Mission, Kansas 66202
913/384-6400

*For Career Women*
Three days - Calgary, Montreal, Ottawa, Quebec - $400

*Games Organizations Play*
One day - Calgary, Toronto - $150
Sponsored by:  Richardson Management Associates

2162 Sherbrooke Street
West Montreal, Quebec H3H 1G7 Canada
514/935-2593

*The Woman Manager in a Rapidly Changing Environment: Developing Executive Skills*
Two days - San Diego - $330
Sponsored by: Center for Continuing Education in Business
School of Business Administration
San Diego State University
San Diego, CA 92182
714/286-5881

*Middle Management Program for Women*
Ten weeks - Boston - $5500 total cost
Sponsored by: Simmons College
Graduate Program in Management
409 Commonwealth Avenue
Boston, MA 02215
617/738-3133

*Executive Images for Success*
One day - Dallas - $25 for business persons
Sponsored by: Women in Business
Cox School of Business
Southern Methodist University
Dallas, TX 75275
214/692-2776

*The Challenge of Leadership: An Advanced Development Program for Women in Management*
Three days - Ann Arbor, MI - $345

*Managerial and Administrative Skills for the Professional Woman*
Three days - Ann Arbor, MI - $345
Sponsored by: Division of Management Education
Graduate School of Business
The University of Michigan
1735 Washtenaw Avenue
Ann Arbor, MI 48109
313/763-1000

*Assertiveness Training for Women in Business*
One day - Bloomington, MN - $100 per person with multiple attendance from one firm - 30-person limit
*Management Development for Women*
Three days - Hudson, WI - $350/double - $385/single; with multiple attendance from one firm: $330/double - $350/single - 24-person limit

*Managing Conflict*
One day - Minneapolis, MN - $120 - $100/multiple attendance - 30-person limit
*Women in Organizations: Exerting Positive Influence*
One day - St. Paul, MN - $120 - $100 multiple attendance - 30-person limit
Sponsored by: Department of Conferences
　　　　　　　Continuing Management Education
　　　　　　　The University of Minnesota
　　　　　　　Minneapolis, MN 55414
　　　　　　　612/373-3499

# *Bibliography*

## BOOKS

Allport, Gordon W. *The Nature of Prejudice*. Reading, MA: Addison Wesley Publishing Co., 1954.

Atkinson, John and Raynor, Joel. *Personality, Motivation and Achievement*. New York: John Wiley and Sons, Halsted Press, 1978.

Atlantic Richfield Co., Public Affairs Division. *Getting the Job Done: Women at Arco*. Los Angeles, 1978.

Barnett, Rosalind C. and Baruch, Grace K., *The Competent Woman*. New York: Irvington Publishers, Inc., 1978.

Basil, Douglas C. *Women in Management: Performance, Prejudice, Promotion*. New York: Dunellen Publishing, 1972.

Bennett, James and Loewe, Pierre. *Women in Business*. Toronto: Maclean-Hunter, 1975.

Bird, Caroline. *The Two-Paycheck Marriage*. New York: Rawson Associates Publishers, 1979.

Bird, Caroline. *Women: Opportunity for Management*. New York: The President's Association, Special Studies No. 53, 1973.

Bisconti, Ann Stouffer. *Women: Marriage, Career and Job Satisfaction*. Bethlehem, PA: College Placement Council Foundation, 1978.

Black, James M. *How to Get Results from Interviewing*. New York: McGraw-Hill Book Co., 1970.

Blaxall, Martha and Reagan, Barbara, eds. *Women and the Workplace: Implications of Occupational Segregation*. Chicago: University of Chicago Press, 1973.

Burrow, Martha G. *Developing Women Managers: What Needs to be Done?* New York: American Management Associations, AMACOM Division, 1978.

Butz, William P. and Ward, Michael P. *The Emergence of Countercyclical U.S. Fertility*. Santa Monica: The Rand Corporation, 1977.

Curtis, Jean. *Working Mothers*. Garden City, NY: Doubleday, 1976.

Epstein, Cynthia F. *Woman's Place: Options and Limits in Professional Careers*. Berkeley: University of California Press, 1971.

Equal Employment Opportunity Commission. *Affirmative Action and Equal Employment: A Guidebook for Employers*. Vol. 2. Washington, DC, 1974.

Farley, Jennie. *Affirmative Action and the Woman Worker.* New York: American Management Associations, AMACOM Division, 1979.

Fear, Richard A. *The Evaluation Interview.* 2d ed. New York: McGraw-Hill Book Co., 1978.

Fitzpatrick, Robert and Cole, Mary E. *Some Characteristics of Female and Male Managers.* Pittsburgh, PA: Psychological Service of Pittsburgh, 1977.

Foxley, Cecelia H. *Locating, Recruiting and Employing Women: An Equal Opportunity Approach.* Garrett Park, MD: Garrett Park Press, 1976.

Frank, Harold H. *Women in the Organization.* Philadelphia: University of Pennsylvania Press, 1977.

Friedan, Betty. *The Feminine Mystique.* New York: W. W. Norton, 1963; Dell, 1974.

General Electric Co. *Women and Business: Agenda for the Seventies.* Business Environment Report No. 5, 1972.

Ginzberg, Eli. *The Manpower Connection: Education and Work.* Cambridge, MA: Harvard University Press, 1975.

Ginzberg, Eli and Yohalem, Alice M., eds. *Corporate Lib.* Baltimore: Johns Hopkins University Press, 1973.

Gordon, Francine E. and Strober, Myra H., eds. *Bringing Women into Management.* New York: McGraw-Hill Book Co., 1975.

Graham, Ellen, ed. *What Do Women Really Want?* New York: Dow Jones Books, 1974.

Hall, Francine and Douglas T. *The Two-Career Couple.* Reading, MA: Addison Wesley Publishing Co., 1979.

Hayghe, Howard. *Families and the Rise of Working Wives—An Overview.* U.S. Department of Labor, Bureau of Labor Statistics' Special Labor Force Report 189, 1976.

Heidrick and Struggles, Inc. *Profile of a Chief Executive Officer.* Chicago, 1977.

Heidrick and Struggles, Inc. *Profile of a Chief Personnel Officer.* Chicago, 1977.

Heidrick and Struggles, Inc. *Profile of a Woman Officer,* Chicago, 1979.

Heidrick and Struggles, Inc. *Profile of a Woman Officer.* Chicago, 1978.

Heidrick and Struggles, Inc. *Profile of a Woman Officer.* Chicago, 1977.

Hennig, Margaret and Jardim, Anne. *The Managerial Woman.* Garden City, NY: Anchor Press/Doubleday, 1977; Pocket Book, 1978.

Higginson, Margaret V. and Quick, Thomas L. *The Ambitious Woman's Guide to a Successful Career.* New York: American Management Associations, AMACOM Division, 1975.

Huber, Joan, ed. *Changing Women in a Changing Society.* Chicago: University of Chicago Press, 1973.

Jackson, Tom. *Interviewing Women: Avoiding Charges of Discrimination.* New York: Executive Enterprises Publications, 1976.

Janger, Allen R. *The Personnel Function: Changing Objectives and Organization.* New York: The Conference Board, 1977.

Jewell, Donald O., ed. *Women and Management: An Expanding Role.* Atlanta: Georgia State University, 1977.

Jongeward, Dorothy and Scott, Dru. *Affirmative Action for Women: A Practical Guide for Women and Management*. Reading, MA: Addison Wesley Publishing Co., 1973.

Kanter, Rosabeth M. *Men and Women of the Corporation*. New York: Basic Books, 1977.

Killian, Ray A. *The Working Woman: A Male Manager's View*. New York: American Management Associations, 1971.

Kreps, Juanita. *Sex in the Marketplace: American Women at Work*. Baltimore: Johns Hopkins University Press, 1971.

Kreps, Juanita, ed. *Women and the American Economy: A Look to the 1980s*. Englewood Cliffs, NJ: Prentice-Hall, 1976.

Kreps, Juanita and Clark, Robert. *Sex, Age and Work: The Changing Composition of the Labor Force*. Baltimore: Johns Hopkins University Press, 1975.

Kundsin, Ruth B., ed. *Women and Success: The Anatomy of Achievement*. New York: William Morrow, 1974.

Larwood, Laurie and Wood, Marion M. *Women in Management*. Lexington, MA: D.C. Heath, 1977.

Lazer, Robert I. and Wikstrom, Walter S. *Appraising Managerial Performance: Current Practices and Future Directions*. New York: The Conference Board, 1977.

Lloyd, Cynthia B., ed. *Sex Discrimination and the Division of Labor*. New York: Columbia University Press, 1975.

Loring, Rosalind and Wells, Theodora. *Breakthrough: Women into Management*. New York: Van Nostrand Reinhold, 1972.

Lyle, Jerolyn R. *Affirmative Action Programs for Women: A Survey of Innovative Programs*. Report submitted to the Office of Research, Equal Employment Opportunity Commission, under Contract 71-45, 1973.

Lynch, Edith M. *The Executive Suite—Feminine Style*. New York: American Management Associations, AMACOM Division, 1973.

Maccoby, Eleanor Emmons and Jacklin, Carol Nagy. *The Psychology of Sex Differences*. Stanford, CA: Stanford University Press, 1974.

Mednick, Martha T.; Tangri, Sandra S.; and Hoffman, Lois W., eds. *Women and Achievement*. Washington, DC: Hemisphere Publishing, 1975.

Meyer, Mitchell. *Women and Employee Benefits*. New York: The Conference Board, 1978.

Mill, John Stuart, *The Subjection of Women*. Cambridge, MA: MIT Press, 1970.

Nollen, Stanley D. and Martin, Virginia H. *Alternate Work Schedules, Part I: Flexitime*. New York: American Management Associations, AMACOM Division, 1978.

Nollen, Stanley D. et al. *Permanent Part-Time Employment: An Interpretive Review*. Washington, DC: U.S. Department of Labor, Employment and Training Administration, No. 21-11-75-16, 1976.

Peres, Richard. *Dealing with Employment Discrimination*. New York: McGraw-Hill Book Co., 1978.

Phillips, Linda. *UCLA Career Development Research Project—Executive Summary.* Los Angeles, 1977.

Pickens, Judy E.; Rao, Patricia W.; and Roberts, Linda C., eds. *Without Bias: A Guidebook for Nondiscriminatory Communication.* San Francisco: International Association of Business Communicators, 1977.

Rawlings, Stephen. *Perspective on American Husbands and Wives.* U.S. Department of Commerce, Bureau of the Census, Special Studies Series P23, No. 77, 1978.

Rothman, Sheila M. *Woman's Proper Place.* New York: Basic Books, 1978.

Shaeffer, Ruth G. *Monitoring the Human Resource System.* New York: The Conference Board, 1977.

Shaeffer, Ruth G. *Staffing Systems: Managerial and Professional Jobs.* New York: The Conference Board, 1972.

Shaeffer, Ruth G. and Lynton, Edith F. *Corporate Experiences in Improving Women's Job Opportunities.* New York: The Conference Board, 1979.

Shaeffer, Ruth G. and Axel, Helen. *Improving Job Opportunities for Women: A Chartbook Focusing on the Progress in Business.* New York: The Conference Board, 1978.

Smith, Ralph E., ed. *The Subtle Revolution: Women at Work.* Washington, DC: Urban Institute, 1979.

Smith, Ralph E. *Women in the Labor Force in 1990.* Washington, DC: Urban Institute, 1979.

Stead, Bette A., ed. *Women in Management.* Englewood Cliffs, NJ: Prentice-Hall, 1978.

Stellman, Jeanne M. *Women's Work, Women's Health.* New York: Pantheon, 1977.

Stewart, Nathaniel. *The Effective Woman Manager.* New York: John Wiley, 1978.

Tsuchigane, Robert and Dodge, Norton. *Economic Discrimination Against Women in the United States.* Lexington, MA: D.C. Heath, 1974.

United States Department of Commerce, Bureau of the Census. *A Statistical Portrait of Women in the U.S.* Special Studies Series P23, No. 58, 1976.

United States Department of Health, Education and Welfare, Office of Education, Bureau of Occupational and Adult Education. *Women in Non-Traditional Occupations—A Bibliography.* Item 455-D, 1976.

United States Department of Labor, Bureau of Labor Statistics. *Employment in Perspective: Working Women.* Report 547, Third Quarter, 1978.

United States Department of Labor, Bureau of Labor Statistics. *U.S. Working Women: A Databook.* Bulletin 1977.

United States Department of Labor, Employment and Training Administration. *Women and Work.* R&D Monograph No. 46, 1977.

United States Department of Labor, Women's Bureau, Employment Standards Administration. *Working Mothers and Their Children.* Report 720-065/6711 3·1, 1977.

Williams, Juanita H. *Psychology of Women.* New York: W. W. Norton, 1974.

## PERIODICALS

Acker, Joan and Van Houten, Donald R. "Differential Recruitment and Control: The Sex Structuring of Organizations." *Administrative Science Quarterly* 19(2):152 (June 1974).

Ackerman, Robert W. "How Companies Respond to Social Demands." *Harvard Business Review* 51(4):88 (July–August 1973).

"Acting Affirmatively to End Job Bias." *Business Week,* 27 January 1975, p. 94.

Albrecht, Maryann. "Women, Resistance to Promotion and Self-Directed Growth." *Human Resource Management* No. 17, p. 12 (Spring 1978).

Anderson, Harry B. "Formal Job Appraisals Grow More Prevalent But Get More Criticism." *Wall Street Journal,* 23 May 1978.

Anthony, William P. and Bowen, Marshall. "Affirmative Action: Problems and Promises." *Personnel Journal* 56(12):616 (December 1977).

"As Employers Hunt for Skilled Women, Blacks." *U.S. News and World Report,* 17 July 1978, p. 75.

"AT&T Has Complied with Antibias Degree, U.S. Attorneys Say." *Wall Street Journal,* 18 January 1979.

"AT&T Replacing Maternity Program for Its Employees." *Wall Street Journal,* 23 April 1979.

Badawy, M. K. "How Women Managers View Their Role in the Organization." *Personnel Administrator* No. 23, p. 60 (February 1978).

Barkhaus, Robert and Bolyard, Charles. "Career Development: Whose Responsibility?" *S.A.M. Advanced Management Journal,* Society for the Advancement of Management, 43(3):51 (Summer 1978).

Baron, Alma Spann. "Women in Management: A New Look." *Personnel Administrator* No. 23, p. 52 (December 1978).

Bartol, Kathryn M. "The Sex Structuring of Organizations: A Search for Possible Causes." *Academy of Management Review* No. 3, p. 805 (October 1978).

Bartos, Rena. "What Every Marketer Should Know About Women." *Harvard Business Review* 56(3):73 (May–June, 1978).

Battaile, Janet. "Debate on Nepotism Rules Grows With a Rise in Working Couples." *New York Times,* 9 May 1978.

Bayes, Marjorie and Newton, Peter M. "Women in Authority: A Sociopsychological Analysis." *Journal of Applied Behavioral Science* 14(1):7 (1978).

Bender Marylin. "When the Boss is a Woman." *Esquire,* 28 March 1978, p. 35.

Berlew, David E. and Hall, Douglas T. "The Socialization of Managers: Effects of Expectations on Performance." *Administrative Science Quarterly* 21(3):207 (September 1966).

"The Big Business of Teaching Managers." *Business Week,* 25 July 1977, p. 106.

Bigoness, William J. "Effect of Applicants' Sex, Race and Performance on Employers' Performance Ratings: Some Additional Findings." *Journal of Applied Psychology* 61(1):80 (1976).

Biles, George E. and Pryatel, Holly A. "Myths, Management and Women." *Personnel Journal* 57(10):572 (October 1978).

Blackman, Ann. "Women Lead in Quantity, Not (E) Quality." *Chicago Tribune,* 27 August 1976.

Blitz, Rudolph C. "Women in the Professions, 1870–1970." *Monthly Labor Review,* U.S. Dept. of Labor, **97**(5): (May 1974).

Blundell, William E. "Chat with 11 Women Finds Anger at Sexism, Hope for Better Jobs." *Wall Street Journal,* 5 September 1978.

Bolton, Elizabeth B. and Humphreys, Luther Wade. "A Training Model for Women—An Androgynous Approach." *Personnel Journal* **56**(5):230 (May 1977).

Bowman, G. W.; Worthy, N. B.; and Greyser, S. A. "Are Women Executives People?" *Harvard Business Review* **43**(4):16 (July–August 1965).

Bralove, Mary. "Now and Then: The Feminists After 10 Years." *Wall Street Journal,* 1 April 1977.

Bray, Douglas W. "Identifying Managerial Talent in Women." *Atlanta Economic Review* **26**(2):38 (March–April 1976).

Bree, Marlin. "Women Welcome." *Corporate Report* **9**(11):20 (November 1978).

Brennan, Frank. "Why Women Work." *Chicago Daily News,* 27 February 1978.

Brenner, Elizabeth. "Women at the Top: Ladder is Slippery." *Chicago Tribune,* 17 May, 1978.

Brief, Arthur P.; Rose, Gerald L.; and Aldag, Ramon J. "Sex Differences in Preferences for Job Attributes Revisited." *Journal of Applied Psychology* **62**:645 (1977).

Briggs, Jean A. "How You Going to Get 'em Back in the Kitchen? (You Aren't.)" *Forbes,* 15 November 1977, p. 177.

Brookmire, David A. and Burton, Amy A. "A Format for Packaging Your Affirmative Action Program." *Personnel Journal* **57**(6):294 (June 1978).

Brooks, Patricia and Lester. "Meet the Industrial Woman." *Exxon, U.S.A.,* 2d Quarter 1978, p. 8.

Cappo, Joe. "Un-Suite Picture for Women Execs." *Chicago Sun-Times,* 20 March 1978.

Carmichael, Carole A. "The Working Woman: Her Income Becomes a 'Must'." *Chicago Tribune,* 5 September 1977.

"Chase Bank Reaches Job Bias Settlement with Female Workers, U.S. for $2 Million." *Wall Street Journal,* 3 November 1978.

Chase, Marilyn. "Kaiser Aluminum Case May Help in Clarifying Reverse Job Bias Issue." *Wall Street Journal,* 21 September 1978.

Chayes, Antonia Handler. "Make Your Equal Opportunity Program Court-Proof." *Harvard Business Review* **52**(5):81 (September–October 1974).

" 'Commuter Marriages'—Latest Product of Women's Changing Status." *U.S. News & World Report,* 24 October 1977, p. 109.

"Companies Offer Benefits Cafeteria-Style." *Business Week,* 13 November 1978, p. 116.

"Company Courses Go Collegiate." *Business Week,* 26 February 1979, p. 90.

Cook, Mary F. "Is the Mentor Relationship Primarily a Male Experience?" *Personnel Administrator* **24**(11):82 (November 1979).

"The Corporate Woman: Commuting, A Solution For Two-Career Couples." *Business Week,* 3 April 1978, p. 66.

"The Corporate Woman: 'Company Couples' Flourish." *Business Week,* 2 August 1976, p. 54.

"The Corporate Woman: How to Get Along—and Ahead—in the Office." *Business Week,* 22 March 1976, p. 107.

Cox, Meg, "Courses For Women," *Wall Street Journal,* 1 October 1979.

De Pasquale, John A. and Lange, Richard A. "Job-hopping and the MBA." *Harvard Business Review* **49**(6):4 (November–December 1971).

Dipboye, Robert L.; Arvey, Richard D.; and Terpstra, David E. "Equal Employment and the Interview." *Personnel Journal* **55**(10):520 (October 1976).

Driscoll, Jeanne Baker and Hess, H. Richard. "The Recruiter: Woman's Friend or Foe?" *Journal of College Placement* **34**(4):48 (Summer 1974).

Dullea, Georgia. "Vast Changes in Society Traced to the Rise of Working Women." *New York Times,* 29 November 1977.

Dunn, Rita and Kenneth. "How to Raise an Independent Woman." *Chicago Sun-Times,* 16 October 1977.

Duval, Betty Ann and Courtney, Roslyn S. "Upward Mobility: The GF Way of Opening Employee Advancement Opportunities." *Personnel* No. 55, p. 43 (May–June 1978).

"EEOC Issues Guidelines for Identifying Patterns of Job Bias in Personnel Policies." *Wall Street Journal,* 20 March 1978.

"EEOC Reports 'Substantial' Rise in Minority and Female Employment Since 1966." *Fair Employment Report* **13**(2):195 (6 October 1975).

Ekberg-Jordan, Sandra. "Preparing for the Future: Commitment and Action." *Atlanta Economic Review* **26**(2):47 (March–April 1976).

Evan, William M. "Peer Group Interaction and Organizational Socialization: A Study of Employee Turnover." *American Sociological Review* **28**:436 (1963).

"Exploding a Myth of Executive Job-hopping," *Business Week,* 11 June 1979, p. 127.

Fahey, Patrick E. and Pati, Gopal C. "Trying to be Equable About Equal Employment." *Conference Board Record* **12**(9):37 (September 1975).

Falk, Carol H. "A lid on Reverse Bias Suits?" *Wall Street Journal,* 1 October 1979.

Falk, Carol H. "The 'Benign Discrimination' Issue." *Wall Street Journal,* 1 April 1977.

"Federal EEOC Proposes Rules to Shield Employers From White Males' Claims." *Wall Street Journal,* 22 December 1977.

"Female Airline Pilots Flying High." *Chicago Tribune,* 4 February 1979.

Ferber, Marianne A. and McMahon, Walter W. "Women's Expected Earnings and their Investment in Higher Education." *Journal of Human Resources,* **14**:405 (1979).

"Firm to Pay Off on Sex Bias," *Chicago Tribune,* 17 August 1979.

"41% of U.S. Workers in '77 Were Women." *Chicago Tribune,* 14 May 1978.

Fowler, Elizabeth M. "Sex Differences in Retirement Age," *New York Times,* 14 April 1978.

Fox, Harold W. and Renas, Stanley R. "Stereotypes of Women in the Media and Their Impact on Women's Careers." *Human Resource Management* 16(1):28 (Spring 1977).

Fretz, C. F. and Hayman, Joanne. "Progress for Women—Men Are Still More Equal." *Harvard Business Review* 51(5):133 (September–October 1973).

Fuchs, Victor R. "Women's Earnings: Recent Trends and Long-Run Prospects." *Monthly Labor Review,* U.S. Dept. of Labor, 97(5):23 (May 1974).

Gallese, Liz Roman. "Some Companies Fight Tougher Federal Drive on Job Discrimination." *Wall Street Journal,* 17 February 1978.

Gallese, Liz Roman. "Dual Career Professionals." *Wall Street Journal.* 23 July 1979.

Gallese, Liz Roman. "Women Managers Say Job Transfers Present a Growing Dilemma." *Wall Street Journal,* 4 May 1978.

Gallup Opinion Index, American Institute of Public Opinion, No. 128:45 (March 1976).

Garland, Howard and Price, Kenneth H. "Attitudes Toward Women in Management and Attributions for Their Success and Failure in a Managerial Position." *Journal of Applied Psychology* 62:29 (1977).

"GE to Pay $32 Million in Bias Pact." *New York Times,* 6 June 1978.

"GM's Challenge: The Search for the Unconventional Woman." *Chicago Sun-Times,* 10 March 1978.

Gordon, Francine E. and Strober, Myra H. "Initial Observations on a Pioneer Cohort: 1974 Women MBAs." *Sloan Management Review* 19(2):15 (Winter 1978).

Gottschalk, Earl C., Jr. "Day Care Is Booming, But Experts are Split Over Its Effect on Kids." *Wall Street Journal,* 15 September 1978.

Haefner, James E. "Sources of Discrimination Among Employees: A Survey Investigation." *Journal of Applied Psychology* 62:265 (1977).

Hall, Douglas T. and Francine S. "What's New in Career Management." *Organizational Dynamics* 5(1):17 (Summer 1976).

Hall, Francine S. "Gaining EEO Compliance with a Stable Work Force." *Personnel Journal* 56(9):454 (September 1977).

Hall, Francine S. and Douglas T. "Dual Careers—How Do Couples and Companies Cope with the Problems?" *Organizational Dynamics* 6(4):57 (Spring 1978).

Heiner, J. Stephen; McGlauchlin, Dorothy; Legeros, Constance; and Freeman, Jean. "Developing the Woman Manager." *Personnel Journal* 54(5):282 (May 1975).

Herbert, Theodore T. and Yost, Edward B. "Women as Effective Managers—A Strategic Model for Overcoming the Barriers." *Human Resource Management* 17(1):18 (Spring 1978).

Herman, Deborah D. "More Career Opportunities for Women: Whose Responsibility?" *Personnel Journal* 53(6):414 (June 1974).

Hershman, Arlene, "The Big Clout of Two Incomes," *Dun's Review,* April 1979, p. 43.

Hodgetts, Richard M. et al., "A Profile of the Successful Female." *Academy of Management Proceedings,* 38th annual meeting, San Francisco, August 1978, p. 373.

Houston, Jack. "Researchers Find Pay Gap Widens for Men, Women." *Chicago Tribune,* 30 November 1975.

"How Men Adjust to a Female Boss." *Business Week,* 5 September 1977, p. 90.

"How Population Shifts Are Changing America." *U.S. News and World Report,* 5 March 1978, p. 76.

"How to Spot the Hotshots." *Business Week,* 8 October 1979, p. 62.

Hymowitz, Carol. "Business Is Booming For Those Who Help Women in Business." *Wall Street Journal,* 31 August 1979.

Ignatius, David. "The Rich Get Richer as Well-to-do Wives Enter the Labor Force." *Wall Street Journal,* 8 September 1978.

"The Industrial Salesman Becomes a Salesperson." *Business Week,* 19 February 1979, p. 104.

"Ineligibility of Uniroyal for U.S. Jobs Is Upheld." *Wall Street Journal,* 23 July 1979.

Ingrassia, Lawrence. "Sears Suit Challenging U.S. Enforcement of Antibias Laws Raises Some Key Issues." *Wall Street Journal,* 7 March 1979.

Jasen, Georgette. "Ma Bell's Daughters." *Wall Street Journal,* 28 February 1978.

Kanter, Rosabeth Moss. "Tokenism: Opportunity or Trap?" *MBA,* January 1978, p. 15.

Keaveny, Timothy; Jackson, John H.; and Fossum, John A. "Are There Sex Differences in Job Satisfaction?" *Personnel Administrator* No. 23, p. 55 (March 1978).

"Kids in Kindergarten Declined This Year by Record Number." *Wall Street Journal,* 31 March 1978.

Koten, John "Psychologists Play Bigger Corporate Role in Placing of Personnel." *Wall Street Journal,* 11 July 1978.

Kotulak, Ronald. "Working Women Are Happier." *Chicago Tribune,* 9 January 1979.

Kronholz, June. "Stagnant Birth Rate is Expected to Climb Within a Few Years." *Wall Street Journal,* 29 July 1977.

Kronholz, June. "Management Practices Change to Reflect Role of Women Employees." *Wall Street Journal,* 13 September 1978.

"Labor Market Still Segregated by Sex." *Fair Employment Report* 13(2):14 (23 January 1975).

Lecht, Leonard A. "Women at Work." *Conference Board Record* 13(9):16 (September 1976).

Ledvinka, James. "Technical Implications of Equal Employment Law for Manpower Planning." *Personnel Psychology* 28(3):299 (Autumn 1975).

Lehner, Urban C. and Falk, Carol H. "High Court Approves Affirmative Action in Hiring, Promotion." *Wall Street Journal,* 28 June 1979.

"Lengthy Shake-up in Family Statistics is Expected to Abate." *Wall Street Journal,* 15 February 1979.

Linden, Fabian. "Woman, Worker." *Across the Board* 14(3):25 (March 1977).

Lodge, George C. "Equality of Result, not Equality of Opportunity." *Across the Board* 15(3):56 (March 1978).

Loomis, Carol J. "AT&T in the Throes of Equal Employment." *Fortune,* 15 January 1979, p. 45.

Lovenheim, Barbara. "A Test to Uncover Managerial Skills." *New York Times,* 21 January 1979.

Lublin, Joann S. "Firms and Job Seekers Discover More Benefits of Part-Time Positions." *Wall Street Journal,* 4 October 1978.

Lublin, Joann S. "Two-Career Couples." *Wall Street Journal,* 9 April 1979.

Lublin, Joann S. "Life in Morton Grove Hasn't Been the Same Since Wives Took Jobs." *Wall Street Journal,* 22 September 1978.

Malabre, Alfred L., Jr. "As Their Ranks Swell, Women Holding Jobs Reshape U.S. Society." *Wall Street Journal,* 28 August 1978.

Matteson, Michael T. "Attitudes Toward Women as Managers: Sex or Role Differences?" *Psychological Reports* 39:166 (1976).

Maynard, Cathleen E. and Zawacki, Robert A. "Mobility and the Dual-Career Couple." *Personnel Journal* 58(7):468 (July 1979).

McCord, Bird. "Identifying and Developing Women for Management Positions." *Training and Development Journal* 25(11):2 (November 1971).

Meislin, Richard J. "Poll Finds More Liberal Beliefs on Marriage and Sex Roles, Especially Among the Young." *New York Times,* 27 November 1977.

Mincer, Jacob and Polachek, Solomon. "An Exchange: Women's Earnings Reexamined." *Journal of Human Resources* 17(4):118 (Winter 1978).

Miner, John B. "Motivational Potential for Upgrading Among Minority and Female Managers." *Journal of Applied Psychology* 62(6):691 (1977).

Missirian, Agnes K. "The Female Manager As a Shelf-Sitter." *Human Resource Management* 17(4):29 (Winter 1978).

Mitnick, Margery Manesberg. "Equal Employment Opportunity and Affirmative Action: A Managerial Training Guide." *Personnel Journal* 56(10):492 (October 1977).

"More Americans Delay Tying Marriage Knots," *Wall Street Journal,* 27 June 1979.

Morganthaler, Eric. "Sweden Offers Fathers Paid Paternity Leaves: About 10% Take Them." *Wall Street Journal,* 28 January 1979.

Morrison, Robert F. and Sebald, Maria-Luise. "Personal Characteristics Differentiating Female Executive from Female Non-executive Personnel." *Journal of Applied Psychology* 59(5):656 (1974).

Moses, Joseph L. and Boehm, Virginia R. "Relationship of Assessment-Center Performance to Management Progress of Women." *Journal of Applied Psychology* 60(4):527 (1975).

Mossholder, Kevin W.; Gordon, Michael E.; Nurick, Aaron J.; and Pryor, Norman N. "An EPA Exceptions Model—Cracking the Sex-Based Wage Differential." *Compensation Review,* 1st quarter 1979, p. 42.

"Moving Employees More and More Means Helping their Spouses Find New Jobs." *Wall Street Journal,* 20 November 1979.

"Moving Up by Managing the Production Line." *Business Week,* 13 June 1977, p. 92F.

Neal, Patricia. "Special Women." A letter to the *Wall Street Journal,* 17 April 1978.

Neikirk, Bill. "Retirement at 70 Gives Birth to a Revolution." *Chicago Tribune,* 30 September 1979.

"The New Corporate Wife Goes to Work." *Business Week,* 8 April 1979, p. 88.

"New Life for Flexible Compensation." *Dun's Review,* September 1978, p. 66.

"The New York Times Agrees to 4 Year Plan Settling Sex-Bias Suit." *Wall Street Journal,* 9 October 1978.

Nollen, Stanley P. "Does Flexitime Improve Productivity?" *Harvard Business Review,* **57**(5):12 (September–October 1979).

Nordheimer, Jon. "The Family in Transition: A Challenge From Within." *New York Times,* 27 November 1977.

Ornati, Oscar A. and Giblin, Edward. "The High Cost of Discrimination." *Business Horizons* **18**(1):35 (February 1975).

Parrish, John B. "Women in Professional Training." *Monthly Labor Review,* U.S. Dept. of Labor, **97**(5):40 (May 1974).

"A Path Up for Women Bankers." *Business Week,* 13 June 1977, p. 105.

Pati, Gopal C. "Reverse Discrimination: What Can Managers Do?" *Personnel Journal* **56**(7):334 (July 1977).

Patten, Thomas H., Jr. "Pay Discrimination Lawsuits: The Problems of Expert Witnesses and the Effects of the Discovery Process." *Personnel* **55**(6):27 (November–December 1978).

Patton, Arch. "The Coming Wave of Young Executives." *Bell Telephone Magazine,* July–August 1977, p. 8.

Perham, John. "New Life for Flexible Compensation." *Dun's Review,* September 1978, p. 66.

Pifer, Alan. "Women Working: Toward a New Society." *Annual Report of Carnegie Corporation,* 1976, p. 3.

Powell, Gary N. and Butterfield, D. Anthony. "The 'Good Manager': Masculine or Androgynous?" *Academy of Management Journal* **22**(2):395 (1979).

"President Calls EEO Plan Single Most Important Civil Rights Action in Decade." *Fair Employment Report* **16**(5):35 (6 March 1978).

"A Productive Way to Vent Employee Gripes." *Business Week,* 16 October 1978, p. 168.

"Profile of an Aging America." *U.S. News and World Report,* 8 August 1977, p. 54.

"Prudential Settlement of Job-Bias Suit Gets Initial Court Clearance." *Wall Street Journal,* 8 March 1979.

Purcell, Theodore V. "How GE Measures Managers in Fair Employment." *Harvard Business Review,* **52**(6):99 (November–December 1974).

Putnam, Linda and Heinen, J. Stephen. "Women in Management: The Fallacy of the Trait Approach." *Michican State University Business Topics,* Summer 1976, p. 46.

Rankin, Deborah. "Business of Women is Business." *New York Times,* 30 April, 1978.
"Reader's Digest Sets $1.6 Million Payment to End Sex-Bias Suit." *Wall Street Journal,* 7 November 1977.
Reha, Rose K. "Preparing Women for Management Roles." *Business Horizons* 22(2):68 (April 1979).
Reinhold, Robert. "U.S. to Monitor Hiring Practices of Big Concerns." *New York Times,* 5 January 1978.
Renwick, Patricia Ann and Tosi, Henry. "The Effects of Sex, Marital Status and Educational Background on Selection Decisions." *Academy of Management Journal* 21(1):93 (March 1978).
Ricklefs, Roger. "Small Firms Specialize in Helping Companies Find Blacks, Women." *Wall Street Journal,* 20 September 1977.
Robertson, David E. "Update on Testing and Equal Opportunity." *Personnel Journal* 56(3):144 (March 1977).
Roche, Gerard R. "Much Ado About Mentors." *Harvard Business Review* 57(1):14 (January–February 1979).
Rose, Gerald L. and Andiappin, P. "Sex Effects on Managerial Hiring Decisions." *Academy of Management Journal* 21(1):104 (March 1978).
Rosen, Benson and Jerdee, Thomas H. "Coping with Affirmative Action Backlash." *Business Horizons* 22(4):15 (August 1979).
Rosen, Benson and Jerdee, Thomas H. "Effects of Applicant's Sex and Difficulty of Job on Evaluation of Candidates for Managerial Positions." *Journal of Applied Psychology* 59(4):511 (1974).
Rosen, Benson and Jerdee, Thomas H. "Influence of Sex Role Stereotypes on Personnel Decisions." *Journal of Applied Psychology* 59(1):9 (1974).
Rosen, Benson and Jerdee, Thomas H. "On-the-job Sex Bias: Increasing Managerial Awareness." *Personnel Administrator* 22(1):15 (January 1977).
Rosen, Benson and Jerdee, Thomas H. "Sex Stereotyping in the Executive Suite." *Harvard Business Review* 52(2):45 (March–April 1974).
Sandell, Steven H. and Shapiro, David. "An Exchange: The Theory of Human Capital and the Earnings of Women—A Reexamination of the Evidence." *Journal of Human Resources* 17(4):103 (Winter 1978).
Sargent, Alice G. "The Androgynous Blend: Best of Both Worlds?" *Management Review* 67(10):60 (October 1978).
Schein, Virginia E. "Sex Role Stereotyping, Ability and Performance: Prior Research and New Directions." *Personnel Psychology* 31(2):259 (Summer 1978).
Schein, Virginia E. "The Relationship Between Sex Role Stereotypes and Requisite Management Characteristics." *Journal of Applied Psychology* 57(2):95 (1973).
Schein, Virginia E. "Relationships Between Sex Role Stereotypes and Requisite Management Characteristics Among Female Managers." *Journal of Applied Psychology* 60(3):340 (1975).
Schein, Virginia E. "Think Manager—Think Male." *Atlanta Economic Review* 26(2):21 (March–April 1976).

Schneier, Dena B. "The Impact of EEO Legislation on Performance Appraisals." *Personnel* 55(4):24 (July–August 1978).

Schuler, Randall S. "Male and Female Routes to Managerial Success." *Personnel Administrator* 24(2):35 (February 1979).

Schwartz, Eleanor Brantley and Waetjen, Walter B. "Improving the Self-concept of Women Managers." *Business Quarterly,* School of Business Administration, University of Western Ontario, 41(4):20 (Winter 1976).

Scott, Charlotte, H. "Managers As Teachers." *Wall Street Journal,* 9 October 1978.

"Sears Enters Appeal In Job-Bias Lawsuit Against Government." *Wall Street Journal,* 16 July 1979.

"Sears Is Charged in Series of EEOC Suits with Discrimination in Hiring Practices." *Wall Street Journal,* 23 October 1979.

"Sears Roebuck Charges U.S. Actions Hurt Firm's Efforts to Hire Women, Minorities." *Wall Street Journal,* 25 January 1979.

"Sex Discrimination by U.S. Agencies is Claimed in Report." *Wall Street Journal,* 4 October 1978.

"The 60's Kids as Managers." *Time,* 6 March 1978, p. 62.

Smith, Lee. "The EEOC's Bold Foray into Job Evaluation." *Fortune,* 11 September 1978, p. 58.

Smith, Lee. "Equal Opportunity Rules Are Getting Tougher." *Fortune,* 19 June 1978, p. 152.

Smith, Lee. "What's It Like For Women Executives?" *Dun's Review,* December 1975, p. 58.

Snider, Arthur J. "Oh, Baby! U.S. May Pay to Ensure Birthrate." *Chicago Sun-Times,* 5 April 1978.

Stead, Bette Ann. "Real Equal Opportunity for Women Executives." *Business Horizons* 17(4):87 (August 1974).

Stegmann, Claire. "Women Engineers: Brainy, Yes. But Don't Label Them Fragile." *Think* 44(1):15 (January–February 1978).

Student, Kurt R. "Back to Basics for Improved Human Resource Management." *Management Review* 67(8):51 (August 1978).

"Suddenly, a New Shortage of Secretaries." *Business Week,* 8 August 1977, p. 84.

Terborg, James R. "Women in Management: A Research Review." *Journal of Applied Psychology* 62(6):647 (1977).

Treiman, Donald J. and Terrell, Kermit. "Sex and the Process of Status Attainment: A Comparison of Working Women and Men." *American Sociological Review* 40(2):174 (April 1975).

Ulbrich, Holley H. "Women and Wages." *Atlanta Economic Review* 26(2):44 (March–April 1976).

"Uniroyal Agrees to Pay Workers $5.2 Million to Settle Job-Bias Suit." *Wall Street Journal,* 24 October 1979.

"U.S. Adopts New Rules to Protect Women, Minorities in Hiring and Promotion Tests." *Wall Street Journal,* 23 August 1978.

Wagel, William H. "Roundup." *Personnel* 54(6):42 (November–December 1977).

Wagner, Warren N. "Programming Failure: Another Look at Affirmative Action." *Personnel Journal* 56(6):278 (June 1977).

Waldman, E. and McEaddy, B. J. "Where Women Work—An Analysis by Industry and Occupation." *Monthly Labor Review,* U.S. Dept. of Labor, 97(5):50 (May 1974).

Weaver, Charles N. "What Women Want in a Job." *Personnel Administrator* No. 22, p. 66 (June 1977).

Weaver, Warren, Jr. "Affirmative Action Given New Support by Supreme Court." *New York Times,* 4 July 1978.

Weber, Arnold R. "Spousal Nepotism." *Wall Street Journal,* 17 September 1979.

Weir, Tamara and Burke, Ronald J. "Two People, Two Careers, and One Relationship! Making It Work." *Business Quarterly,* School of Business Administration, University of Western Ontario, 44(1):47 (Spring 1979).

"Why So Few Women Have Made It to the Top." *Business Week,* 5 June 1978, p. 99.

Wilson, John E. and Tatge, Walter Aston. "Assessment Centers—Further Assessment Needed?" *Personnel Journal* 52(3):172 (March 1973).

"Women Finally Get Mentors of Their Own." *Business Week,* 23 October 1978, p. 74.

"Women, Minorities Still Out of Focus on TV, Agency Says." *Wall Street Journal,* 16 January 1979.

"Women Outnumber Men in Two-Year Colleges." *New York Times,* 7 April 1978.

Wood, Marion M. "Women in Management: How is It Working Out?" *S.A.M. Advanced Management Journal,* Society for the Advancement of Management, 41(1):22 (Winter 1976).

"Working Women—Joys and Sorrows." *U.S. News and World Report,* 15 January 1979, p. 64.

Yaeger, Deborah S. "Many Companies Find Employed Women Are a High-Profit Market." *Wall Street Journal,* 31 August 1978.

## SPEECHES

"Managing Public Issues by Objectives." Presented by Donald P. Brennan, executive vice president-human resources and external affairs, International Paper Co., on February 10, 1977 to The Conference Board in New York City.

"New American Revolution." Presented by David J. Mahoney, chairman of the board and president, Norton Simon, Inc., on June 2, 1972 to the Equal Opportunity for Women Conference in New York City.

"Tribute to Women in International Industry." Presented by James D. Robinson III, chairman, American Express Co., on June 6, 1978 to the National YWCA in New York City.

# Index